THE MUSIC AND ART OF RADIO

For Emma

The Music and Art of Radiohead

Edited by

JOSEPH TATE
Oregon State University, USA

ASHGATE

Published by
Ashgate Publishing Limited
Gower House
Croft Road
Aldershot
Hants GU11 3HR
England

Ashgate Publishing Company
Suite 420
101 Cherry Street
Burlington, VT 05401-4405
USA

Ashgate website: http://www.ashgate.com

British Library Cataloguing in Publication Data
The music and art of Radiohead. – (Ashgate popular and folk
   music series)
   1. Radiohead (Group) 2. Rock music – History and criticism
   I. Tate, Joseph
   782.4'2166'0922

Library of Congress Cataloging-in-Publication Data
The music and art of Radiohead / edited by Joseph Tate.
         p. cm.—(Ashgate popular and folk music series)
      Includes bibliographical references (p.) and index.
         ISBN 0-7546-3979-7 (hardcover: alk. paper) ISBN 0-7546-3980-0 (paperback:
alk. paper)
   1. Radiohead (Musical group) I. Tate, Joseph, 1973– II. Series.

   ML421.R25M87 2004
   782.42166'092'2—dc22

                                                                    2004004820

ISBN 0 7546 3979 7 (HBK)
ISBN 0 7546 3980 0 (PBK)

Typeset by Express Typesetters Ltd, Farnham, Surrey
Printed and bound in Great Britain by T.J. International, Padstow, Cornwall

Contents

List of Figures

Notes on Contributors

Kevin J.H. Dettmar is Professor and Chair of the Department of English at Southern Illinois University in Carbondale, Illinois. He is co-editor of *Reading Rock and Roll: Authenticity, Appropriation, Aesthetics*, and has authored books on modernism and postmodernism.

Dai Griffiths heads the Music Department at Oxford Brookes University in Oxford, England. Born in South Wales with English as his second language, he read Music at Cambridge before going on to postgraduate degrees at King's College London, where his doctoral dissertation was on the songs of Anton Webern. His teaching focuses on pop music and contemporary musical culture and he was a founding member of the Critical Musicology group in Britain. His publications cover aspects of music analysis and critical musicology, historical and theoretical topics in popular music, and several studies of single songwriters and songs; he also composes and occasionally performs his own music.

Greg Hainge attended New College School, Oxford, until the age of 13. His best school friend from this period taught Thom Yorke how to play guitar a few years later. He received his PhD in French Literature and Critical Theory from the University of Nottingham and is currently Professor in French at the University of Adelaide, Australia. He is the author of *Capitalism and Schizophrenia in the Later Novels of Louis-Ferdinand Céline: D'un ... l'autre* (Peter Lang, 2001), and has published numerous articles and chapters on French literature, theory, film, noise and other unrelated subjects.

Mark B.N. Hansen is an Assistant Professor in the Department of English at Princeton University. He is the author of *Embodying Technesis: Technology Beyond Writing* and co-editor of the forthcoming *Cambridge Companion to Merleau-Ponty*. He has published articles on topics including Deleuze and Guattari's biophilosophy, William Burroughs' virology, Mary Shelley's *Frankenstein*, the digital image, virtual-reality art, and Pynchon's *Gravity's Rainbow*. He is currently writing *Becoming-Human, an Ethics of the Posthuman*, and *Cinema 3: the Digital-Image, a Study of Digital Art and Architecture*.

Erin Harde is completing a graduate degree in journalism at the University of Western Ontario. She has an article forthcoming in *Catching a Wave*, has written for several periodicals and has lectured at numerous academic conferences. Erin looks forward to working as a music journalist and author.

Anwar Ibrahim gained a BMus degree at Cardiff University and an MA in Advanced Musical Studies at Bristol University. His MA thesis was concerned with listener perceptions of the Radiohead track 'Kid A' (2000). He is currently undertaking doctoral research with Professor Allan Moore at Surrey University, exploring analytical approaches to Radiohead from a listening perspective.

Carys Wyn Jones is a doctoral research student at Cardiff currently doing research into canon formations in popular music. She has previously completed a Master's in Music, Culture and Politics, also at Cardiff.

Paul Lansky, composer, is Professor of Music at Princeton University. Most of his work for the past 30 years has involved computer synthesis. *Alphabet Book*, his latest project, was published by Bridge Records in 2002. More information and sounds can be found at his web page: http://www.paullansky.org/.

Lisa Leblanc is presently Senior Interpretive Planner at the Canadian War Museum in Ottawa, Canada. She has studied both Theatre and Art History, and is interested in the role of the audience in the exhibition space, and in contemporary art practice.

Allan F. Moore is Head of the Department of Music and Sound Recording at the University of Surrey. His books include *Rock: The Primary Text* (Ashgate), the collection *Analyzing Popular Music* (Cambridge) and a forthcoming study of Jethro Tull's *Aqualung* album. He is on the editorial board of both *Popular Music* and *Twentieth-century Music*, and has published widely on the musicology of popular music. He is also a regular broadcaster on BBC Radio 4.

Davis Schneiderman is an Assistant Professor of English at Lake Forest College. His essays have appeared in *Revista Canaria de Estudios Ingleses*, *The Iowa Review*, *Studies in the Novel*, and *Radical Teacher*. His fiction has been nominated for a 2001 Pushcart Prize and has been accepted by *Exquisite Corpse*, *Quarter After Eight*, *The Little Magazine*, *Neotrope: Progressive Fiction*, *Happy*, *Gargoyle*, *EnterText* and *The Café Irreal*. He is also co-founder and editor of the media and cultural studies journal *to the QUICK*, and is currently developing an anthology on William S. Burroughs and globalization.

Joseph Tate is finishing a PhD in English at the University of Washington while teaching at Oregon State University. He has lectured nationally and internationally on Shakespeare, meter, reader-response theory, and the music videos of Radiohead. He has also published essays in the journals *Postmodern Culture*, *Early Modern Literary Studies*, and *Shakespeare and the Classroom*.

Curtis White is a Professor in the Department of English at Illinois State University and the author of *Requiem* and *Memories of My Father Watching TV*, as well as other books. He is also the editor of *Context: A Forum for Literary Arts and Culture*.

General Editor's Preface

The upheaval that occurred in musicology during the last two decades of the twentieth century has created a new urgency for the study of popular music alongside the development of new critical and theoretical models. A relativistic outlook has replaced the universal perspective of modernism (the international ambitions of the 12-note style); the grand narrative of the evolution and dissolution of tonality has been challenged; and emphasis has shifted to cultural context, reception and subject position. Together, these have conspired to eat away at the status of canonical composers and categories of high and low in music. A need has arisen, also, to recognize and address the emergence of crossovers, mixed and new genres, to engage in debates concerning the vexed problem of what constitutes authenticity in music and to offer a critique of musical practice as the product of free, individual expression.

Popular musicology is now a vital and exciting area of scholarship, and the *Ashgate Popular and Folk Music Series* aims to present the best research in the field. Authors will be concerned with locating musical practices, values and meanings in cultural context, and may draw upon methodologies and theories developed in cultural studies, semiotics, poststructuralism, psychology and sociology. The series will focus on popular musics of the twentieth and twenty-first centuries. It is designed to embrace the world's popular musics from Acid Jazz to Zydeco, whether high tech or low tech, commercial or non-commercial, contemporary or traditional.

Professor Derek B. Scott
Chair of Music
University of Salford

Foreword

Kevin J.H. Dettmar

And the wise man say I don't want to hear your voice ...

'Stop Whispering'

It is the unique privilege of the foreword writer (forewordista?) to weigh in at the last minute: a foreword is always, after all, a very last-minute word, really a kind of afterword with 20/20 hindsight – last written, first printed. I write having devoured the two most recent additions to the Radiohead canon, *Hail to the Thief* and Christopher O'Riley's *True Love Waits* (piano transcriptions of songs from the first five studio albums). I'll use this teleological cheat – I have to 'go first,' but get to write last, reading the stock ticker after the market has closed to the collection's other contributors – in order to think through what these two most recent records tell us about the trajectory and energy of the Radiohead project. The foreword, then, is always a kind of insider trading. Call me Martha Stewart.

There are many things to admire about the body of work Radiohead has created to date, and many of them are addressed thoughtfully and imaginatively in the essays for this volume. Joseph Tate, in his Introduction, has done a wonderful job of suggesting the synergies and crosscurrents uniting these essays; for this foreword I'd like to take a somewhat different tack, and think a little bit about one of the many stories the evolving Radiohead *œuvre* itself has to tell.

Thus sitting down to listen through the six studio albums, along with *I Might Be Wrong: Live Recordings* and O'Riley's *True Love Waits* – and with the memory of a recent live show fresh in my mind, bolstered by a two-CD bootleg of the show I found on eBay – one story in particular seems to me to tell itself across the body of work Radiohead has made. It is, on one level, a quintessential (and very nearly clichéd) story of modern anomie, the struggle of the isolated and deracinated individual resisting the large, impersonal forces of the modern world. It's a story that has often been told in modern and postmodern literature: Ezra Pound's 'apparition of these faces in the crowd,' from 'In a Station of the Metro'; T.S. Eliot's 'A crowd flowed over London Bridge, so many / I had not thought death had undone so many,' in *The Waste Land*; Septimus Smith's unsuccessful attempt to reintegrate himself into modern London after the horrors of the Great War, in Virginia Woolf's *Mrs. Dalloway* (as well as Richard's suicide in Michael Cunningham's 1999 rewriting of Woolf, *The Hours*); Oedipa Maas's heroic (if ultimately unsuccessful) struggle against the Tristero in Thomas Pynchon's *The Crying of Lot 49*.

Such social and psychic displacement has long been a topic in popular music as well, but the music of Radiohead doesn't just take alienation as a theme: this isn't, in other words, merely the 'teenage wasteland' of The Who's 'Baba O'Riley,' seemingly overcome through overdriven guitars and macho shouting (and, in the event, a Lowrey Berkshire Deluxe TBO-1 organ with 'marimba repeat' and 'wow-wow' settings engaged). Rather the songs of Radiohead stage this alienation, dramatically, as an almost epic battle between Thom Yorke's frail voice and the music which alternatively undergirds and overwhelms that voice. It's hardly a fair fight – Yorke plays David to Jonny and Colin Greenwood, Ed O'Brien, and Phil Selway's collective Goliath. And yet, as the biblical metaphor suggests, it's the little guy who ultimately wins. In the small victories won by that small voice, Radiohead's fans find just about as much affirmation as anyone can stomach in these irony-laden times.

Fender vs tenor: it's a showdown that's there in Radiohead's music from the very beginning, of course. 'Prove Yourself,' the band's first single, was described by *NME* (May 16 1992) as opening 'with some deceptive winsome vocals, before exploding into a monster headache.' The next single and Radiohead's first Big Song, 'Creep,' makes dramatic use of the battle between ax-wielding Greenwood and an unarmed and wholly overmatched Yorke: as Thom plaintively sings 'I wish I was special / You're so fucking special,' Jonny's wholly unsentimental guitar attacks him with a visceral punch. In an early interview, O'Brien explained that the unearthly guitar noise 'is the sound of Jonny trying to fuck the song up. He really didn't like it the first time we played it, so he tried spoiling it.' As Sharon O'Connell described the collision of voice and noise, hope and despair, in *Melody Maker* (September 19 1992): '"Creep" ... is a perfect monster of a malevolent pop song that kicks in with a minimal, dismal shuffle and laconic whisper ... before two huge, coruscating clips of ten ton guitar come crunching awesomely down all over the possibility of romance.'

The album that later collected these two tracks, *Pablo Honey*, itself closes with another high-stakes battle between human and guitar voices: on 'Blow Out,' the instrumental that begins as a nightclubby rhythm background track slowly builds in volume and intensity, adding layers of rhythm, guitars, and bass as it progresses, until a crescendo of dissonant guitars overwhelms the song and upends the melody during the bridge. Yorke attempts to come back in after the bridge, but can't quite regain the upper hand: singing at the top of his range, at the top of his lungs, he strains to be heard above the instrumental din that just won't die down. It's a dynamic not unlike the wrestling match between Brian Eno (vocals) and Robert Fripp (guitar) on Eno's classic track, 'Baby's On Fire': launching into an anarchic, pyrotechnic guitar solo that lasts three full minutes (longer than the rest of the song proper) and moves hyperkinetically all over the sonic map, Fripp refuses to yield the right of way when Eno attempts to come back in for the final verse. Eno having failed utterly to restore order, the song comes to a metallic screeching halt, with a thud that sounds like nothing so much as a prison door slamming. So too on the closing track of *Pablo Honey*: Yorke is quite simply 'blown out,' blown away, as the guitars have the final say. When voice tangles with the guitars in these early tracks, there's never any real question who will win; those familiar with D.A. Pennebaker's concert film *Ziggy Stardust and the Spiders from Mars* might remember the cheesy showdown during David Bowie's singing of 'Time,' where guitarist Mick Ronson 'slaughters' Bowie/Ziggy on stage and exults over his prostrate body.

On Radiohead's second album, *The Bends*, the same mythic battle plays out in songs like the first single, 'Fake Plastic Trees,' but with somewhat more complex results. The song starts simply, Yorke singing softly over a strummed acoustic guitar. The musical texture builds with each verse, adding by degrees bass, cello, electric rhythm guitar, keyboards, and drums; and Yorke's voice builds in tandem as he tries to sing over it, tries to keep ahead of it. Then suddenly the sonic rug is pulled out from under him: Greenwood's electric guitar unceremoniously buries Yorke's acoustic at the two-and-a-half-minute mark, and the instruments overtake the vocals in the mix. The bass has been building slowly from the second verse, and glistening layers of keyboards have been accumulating; but it's the electric guitar onslaught that seems to change everything. As a weary Yorke sings just before the guitars reach maximum volume, 'It wears me out, it wears me out.'

Having played out its sound and fury, the big-band sound gradually fades down, and 'Fake Plastic Trees' comes to a close on the stripped-down instrumentation with which it had opened; but Yorke's voice audibly quivers now, seemingly exhausted, spent, as he delivers the song's last lines: 'And if I could be who you wanted / If I could be who you wanted / All the time, all the time.' The Green Plastic Radiohead website (www.greenplastic.com) records that 'Thom recorded the vocals in two takes and broke down in tears'; those tears are there for all to hear in those closing lines, the repeated '*beeeeee*' requiring a high B flat that Yorke's ravaged voice can't quite achieve. The thick instrumental arrangement from the song's middle section reappears and takes us out after Yorke has finished his swansong; but rather than triumphing over his fragile confession of inadequacy and self-doubt, the rich orchestration seems instead to imbue it with a kind of tragic dignity. The overall shape of the song is quite literally tragic as well, assuming the structure of Freytag's Pyramid: *rising action*, made up of *exposition* (first verse, 'fake plastic earth') and *complication* (second verse, with increasingly complex instrumentation), leads to the *climax* (electric lead guitar usurping acoustic); thereupon follows the *falling action* with its *reversal* ('She looks like the real thing') and *catastrophe* ('If I could be who you wanted'). But having replaced hubris with vulnerability – and substituted indie (dare we say, proto-emo?) honesty for cock-rock posturing – Radiohead seems to have figured out a way to emerge victorious while singing of defeat. Nowhere is Radiohead's debt to Nirvana more obvious.

The little voice of Thom Yorke locked in mortal combat with Jonny

Greenwood's Telecaster: this dynamic receives its richest treatment on the triptych which is not quite a trilogy: *OK Computer / Kid A / Amnesiac*. Through the course of these three albums, alternative rock moves from the twentieth into the twenty-first century, as something of a closet drama is played out between the voice and the noise. We might think, to begin, of the big distorted guitar sounds that open 'Airbag' and *OK Computer* – and if those weren't big enough, the thoroughly red-line bass line that comes in at 0:15, overdriving the tape beyond any possible headroom. Though Yorke sings throughout that he's 'back to save the universe,' his heroic declaration can hardly be heard above the din: musical logic trumps lyrical assertion, Yorke's mouth writing checks that his ass can't cash. And lyrically, of course, the song is precisely about the prosthetic logic of the late twentieth century, the mechanical propping up of the human: in an earlier incarnation the song was called 'An Airbag Saved My Life,' with sly reference to Indeep's 'Last Night a DJ Saved My Life.' Life support, the lyrics suggest, is a chronic rather than an acute state of affairs: rage as one might against the machine, there's no wishing it away, no forcing that genie back in its bottle – and, more worrying, no way to know (to paraphrase a song from *Hail to the Thief*) where it ends and I begin. Influenced as this track is by the work of DJ Shadow, with its drum loop built of a three-second sample of Selway's drumming, an affected technological naiveté seems not to be an option.

Four quick time-cue beeps sweep us into 'Paranoid Android.' If the popular long-running BBC radio program has taught us to rank our music in terms of Desert Island Discs, this is my desert island track: 'Paranoid Android' is quite simply the pinnacle of Radiohead's achievement to date, the most significant and powerful work it has ever done. And not just because it's the band's longest track: more importantly, it's an emotional roller-coaster ride both for its singer and for its audience. Indeed, the emotion is so palpable, so visceral, that the song's often indecipherable – and when decipherable, often incomprehensible – lyrics hardly seem to matter; when they are most moving, the lyrics serve merely as shapes for Thom Yorke's vocalizations, along the lines of the Dadaist poetry of Hugo Ball. (In this, again, their most important forebears are Kurt Cobain and Nirvana, perhaps the first rock band to move profoundly an audience that often couldn't make out their lyrics.) In the song's opening movement, Yorke's minor-key plaint rides along a bossa nova rhythm section; and while the mood of distress is immediately recognizable in the vocal line, the precise source of Yorke's anguish is rather less accessible: 'Please could you stop the noise, I'm trying to get some rest / From all the unborn chicken voices in my head.' Word.

A bass-heavy bridge brings us 'kicking and squealing' into the song's middle section, 'Gucci little piggy'; by the end of the section Yorke is buried in a pile of frantic guitar noise as Greenwood moves into a solo and another bridge. And here, just beyond the bridge – or perhaps, as Cobain would have it, underneath the bridge – something quite magical happens. After a resonant explosion of sustained keyboard chords and shimmering cymbals, something like a choir of angels rises out of and above the song's rubble, and Yorke follows with a contemporary riff on The Who's 'Love, Reign O'er Me':

> Rain down, rain down
> Come on rain down on me
> From a great height
> From a great height ... height ...

Text and voice here coalesce in the frailest of affirmations: like Faulkner's description of the servant Dilsey on the last page of *The Sound and the Fury*, we can only say that the singer has endured – but under the circumstances, that seems like a lot. In part, this quiet affirmation is achieved through the intertextual echo; in the Who song that Radiohead invokes, Roger Daltrey had sung 'Only love can bring the rain / That falls like tears from on high.' 'Paranoid Android' ends with another manic instrumental burst which suggests that the alternating cycle of calm and fury is endless; the affirmation is not final or stable, but provisional – but none the less real for all that. Yorke's last snarled line, 'God loves his children, God loves his children, yeah!', is certainly bitter; it is, at the same time, the defiant and hard-won gesture of a man who has come through.

Beginning with *OK Computer*, and with growing urgency on the subsequent two albums, Radiohead also explores whether the human voice can retain its authority and authenticity in the reign of Walter Benjamin's 'age of mechanical reproduction,' through the inhuman processing of human utterance. On 'Paranoid Android,' the Macintosh computer-synthesized voice of 'Fred' contributes 'backing vocals' ('I may be paranoid, but I'm not an android'), but because the song's texture is especially thick at these moments, an overwhelmed listener might be excused for not picking him out of the mix. Fred goes nearly a cappella on 'Fitter Happier,' however, reading robotically through a thoroughly '90s list of self-improvement desiderata for life in the fast lane. (That the voice of Macintosh's Fred is based on the human voice of Fred Cooper only deepens this particular *mise en abyme*.) This, too, is a technique foreshadowed in the work of Brian Eno – in this case, the 'Enossification' of Peter Gabriel's voice for the track 'The Grand Parade of Lifeless Packaging' on Genesis's *The Lamb Lies Down on Broadway*. That record also, in its none-too-subtle way, explored the human cost of our increasingly mechanized and technological world; by 1997 standards, however, the technological nightmares of 1974 came to seem like kids' stuff.

Examples of this structure can be multiplied almost indefinitely; the human voice is seemingly pitted against the cold inhuman machinery of electric (and electronic) instruments in a Romantic battle for the soul of humankind. A song like 'Airbag' suggests that this dichotomy is too neat, however: not only is the human voice never unmediated in an 'age of mechanical reproduction,' but in the hands of a skilled player a guitar can be every bit as expressive and 'personal' as the voice. (In which of the following is the voice more immediately recognizable: three bars of a Neil Young guitar solo, or two verses of a Mandy Moore song?)

The battle of the voice for transcendence is nowhere more memorably staged in Radiohead's work than in the video for 'No Surprises,' included in the collection *7 Television Commercials*. In a clear homage to Stanley Kubrick's *2001: A Space Odyssey*, as the lights come up in the video Grant Gee's camera finds Thom Yorke isolated not in an astronaut's helmet, but a deep-sea diver's; and as he sings of 'a job that slowly kills you,' that helmet gradually fills with water, threatening slowly to kill him. As the water moves above mouth level, Yorke goes under, giving up any pretense at singing; and, after an unbearably long time submerged, Yorke freaks out and wrests himself free. Helmet drained, breath regained with difficulty, he again joins the glockenspiel-embroidered track, lip-synching his way to what the song calls 'silent silence,' and achieving along the way a kind of quiet dignity.

I promised at the outset to suggest how the two most recent Radiohead-branded releases, the band's own *Hail to the Thief* and Christopher O'Riley's *True Love Waits*, might round out this story. Both *Kid A* and *Amnesiac* take the processing of Thom Yorke's voice into far stranger and more disturbing territory than had *OK Computer*; the heavily processed vocal tracks on cuts like 'Everything in its Right Place,' 'Kid A,' 'The National Anthem,' 'In Limbo,' and 'Morning Bell,' from *Kid A,* and 'Packt Like Sardines in a Crushd Tin Box,' 'Pyramid Song,' 'Pulk/Pull Revolving Doors,' 'You and Whose Army,' and 'Like Spinning Plates,' from *Amnesiac,* collectively suggest that the studio has become a logical appendage of the human voice, and the voice itself a low-tech 'content provider' for digital editing and Pro Tools. For the most part, the songs on *Hail to the Thief* return to the somewhat cleaner distinction between man and machine characteristic of *The Bends.* This may owe something to the more explicit political project of the new album (which takes its title from the taunts hurled at George W. Bush after his stolen Florida election); but from the opening track, '2 + 2 = 5,' Yorke's voice is first and foremost a vehicle not for the deconstruction of the human, but for the passionate expression of human emotion (anger first and foremost). Thom Yorke's back in full voice because he's mad as hell, and isn't going to take it anymore.

O'Riley's record of piano transcriptions was warmly received in the critical press, reviewers typically expressing their surprise in discovering, in these spare arrangements, just how densely beautiful many of Radiohead's songs are. Love it or hate it, Yorke's is a distinctive and, to many ears, grating voice; stripped away, the intricate melodies of songs like 'Black Star,' 'Subterranean Homesick Alien,' even 'Airbag,' become much easier to appreciate.

But O'Riley's project can sometimes have precisely the opposite effect; this is the case with his setting of 'Exit Music (For a Film).' The song was composed as a commission for Baz Luhrmann's *Romeo + Juliet*, though it also makes its way on to *OK Computer*. Structurally, it is virtually identical to 'Fake Plastic Trees,' discussed above: it starts quietly and sparely, just Yorke and an acoustic guitar, voice mic'd very close; the arrangement builds slowly, and the vocals along with it; and the whole thing comes to a crashing climax before the final stillness sets in. For the listener without a lyric sheet very little can be discerned with any certainty, until the quiescence of the song's dénouement. Yorke's words here are shockingly clear, however, and repeated three times: 'We hope that you choke, that you choke.' They are delivered in a faltering voice that, if not choking with emotion, certainly sounds as if it has fought long and hard.

O'Riley's 'Exit Music (For a Film),' of course, strips away all this human drama in the process of underscoring the song's dynamic musical structure. His transcriptions have a remarkable ability to reproduce the wide dynamic range of much of Radiohead's work, and even to suggest the contrapuntal complexity that a five-piece band with three guitarists (not to mention a studio full of tricks) can muster; at the same time, hearing them stripped down to their melodic heart, even a listener quite familiar with Radiohead's music can gain a new appreciation for the sophistication and elegance of their songwriting. O'Riley's 'Exit Music' succeeds on all these counts; and yet – and yet. O'Riley is able, quite beautifully, to isolate the solid rock against which Thom Yorke breaks his oh-so-human voice; but finally it's the voice, and not the rock, that we need. That we crave.

This is why I – why many of us, I suspect – cherish the music of Radiohead: it is what Nietzsche might have called 'human, all too human.' It couldn't have come at a better time.

Acknowledgements

Grateful acknowledgement is made to all of the following for permission to reprint previously published work. A version of the Introduction appeared earlier as 'Response to Reader Mail,' *Postmodern Culture,* 13.1 (September 2002). Curtis White's essay originally appeared in his book *The Middle Mind: Why Americans Don't Think for Themselves* (HarperCollins Publishers Inc, 2003/Penguin, 2004). My essay 'Radiohead's Antivideos: Works of Art in the Age of Electronic Reproduction' appeared in a slightly different form under the same title in *Postmodern Culture*, 12.3 (May 2002).

I would also like to thank the editors and staff at Ashgate Publishing. Heidi May and Sarah Charters deserve especial thanks for their patience and encouragement. Jeremy Arnold initiated a productive exchange of ideas on Radiohead that became the Introduction. Rob Weller is a dear friend and co-worker who tolerated my work on the book with equal amounts of humor and compassion. I am indebted to Conseula Francis and Cody Walker, two close friends with sharp intellect and wit to spare, both of whom read my work at various stages and offered thoughtful suggestions and invaluable encouragement. Brent Carlson, Paul Drews, Tom Hogan, and Linda Sunday all deserve particular recognition for unloading the moving truck while I was finishing the final chapter.

Thanks go to all the contributors, without whose dedication and interest this book would not exist. I am grateful also that readers continue to visit my Radiohead website, *Pulk-Pull*: An On-going Investigation of the Music and Art of Radiohead*: http://pulk-pull.org/. Those readers are perhaps the foremost reason this book became a reality.

Finally, I am fortunate to have Lisa Hogan as a friend, supportive wife, indispensable colleague, and a loving mother to our newborn daughter Emma. This book would not exist without her.

Introduction

Joseph Tate

The book you have in your hand is a collection of academic essays about Radiohead, a five-member music group from Oxford, England. As an academic collection, the book brings together close readings of this English band's music, lyrics, album cover art, and music videos, as well as critical commentary on interviews, reviews, and the documentary film *Meeting People is Easy*. By emerging and established academic scholars alike, each of the essays engages concerns of broader implication to contemporary cultural studies to examine topics ranging from Radiohead's various musical and multivalent social contexts to their contested situation within a global market economy.

There are less flattering ways to describe this book's project, however. In a 2001 interview with Alex Ross, the *New Yorker*'s classical music critic, percussionist Phil Selway voiced a persistent aggravation of the band, one attested to in countless interviews: the over-intellectualization of Radiohead's music by fans and critics alike. 'Really,' Selway said, 'we don't want people twiddling their goatees over our stuff. What we do is pure escapism' (Ross 2001: 115). Immediately, Ross himself confesses to the reader that, 'The records, the videos, the official Web site, even the T-shirts all cry out for interpretation' (2001: 115), but this sort of interpretation, Ross adds casually, is the province of 'teen-agers.' This book, however, has not a single teen-ager among its authors. Instead, a group of scholars are critically engaged in what Selway might derogatorily term 'goatee-twiddling': thinking seriously about music that is historically dense in musical allusion, sonically inventive, lyrically ambiguous and ironic, and unabashedly engaged in its social context.[1]

Not only are band members unhappy about this approach; some listeners are as well. In 2001, I first published 'Radiohead's Antivideos' in the journal *Postmodern Culture*. The essay received a substantial amount of reader mail for an academic essay, and not all positive. One response in particular, from Jeremy Arnold, posed questions significant enough for the editors to request that I respond. In responding to Arnold, I began where he concluded his letter. Arnold wrote: 'I don't need Thom Yorke to tell me that we live in a technological world, nor do I need him to understand capitalism[']s dirty little remainder. What I do need Radiohead for is the aesthetic brilliance, the originality, the possibility that they provide.' The aesthetic brilliance to which Arnold alluded – presumably an objective quality of the work and/or band members – is undoubtedly linked to what he mentioned earlier in the letter, that Radiohead's music refers 'us not to a dematerialized sphere of virtuality,' but it 'sends us back to the real human emotions (or the difficulty in feeling those emotions) involved in any situation.' The songs send the listener or, put differently, they *transport* the listener back to real emotions. Though what each variant of 'real' is meant to connote ('real,' 'the Real,' and 'reality' are used interchangeably) is unclear, Arnold's 'real human emotions' in this instance are likely shorthand for what might be called phenomenological presence, a presence reachable via Radiohead's music. Thus, objective aesthetic brilliance induces a 'real' emotional state, and it is this state my essay and similar academic work on the band fails to address.

Neither my essay nor the other essays herein touch on this phenomenon, largely because Radiohead's entire project can be read, almost successfully, as an argument against this very sort of listener experience. I use Wallace Stevens' phrase 'almost successfully' because Stevens' poem, 'Man Carrying Thing,' is indeed instructive in this instance: 'The poem must resist the intelligence, / Almost successfully' (in Stevens 1997: lines 1–2, 350). The poem, or in this case the music of Radiohead, must and does resist intelligence almost successfully – that is, not quite successfully: art does indeed resist critical understanding, but never does it remain completely inarticulate or inscrutable. We can and should, I think, as Stevens says in closing his poem, 'endure our thoughts all night, until / The bright obvious stands motionless in cold' (lines 13–14, 351). The 'bright obvious' here being that Radiohead's music doesn't return us to 'a reality,' to use Arnold's phrase, or 'real human emotions' at all. Instead, with systematic clarity, Radiohead's work asks for anything but the aesthetic transport of the listener.

Reading the band's work as self-reflexive, the lyrics of the title track to *Kid A* represent aesthetic response, or musical ecstasy to be exact (similar to Selway's professed escapism), as an experience with potentially horrifying results.[2] As the song ends, Yorke's barely decipherable, computer-manipulated voice sings: 'The rats and children follow me out of town / The rats and children follow me out of their homes / Come on kids.' Via overt allusion to the Pied Piper story, Radiohead's exaggeration of its music's power to sway listeners would seem, like the Pied Piper story itself, to be a cautionary tale.[3]

If children in this song and others are read as symbols of emotional sincerity, the band's lyrics have an anxiety-ridden perspective on affective honesty. The 2001 b-side 'Fog' figures the perpetual presence of a child as a fast-growing, subterranean baby alligator familiar from urban mythology:

There's a little child
Running round this house
And he never leaves
He will never leave
And the fog comes up from the sewers
And glows in the dark

Baby alligators in the sewers grow up fast
Grow up fast

Similarly, amid the *OK Computer* song 'Fitter Happier' and its catalog-like litany of mundane self-help advice, there intervenes a chilling line meant to have a conventional cinematic visual layering effect: '(shot of baby strapped in back seat).' The speaker of the *Kid A* track 'Morning Bell' thrice intones the imperative, 'Cut the kids in half,' and two songs from *Hail to the Thief* refer to youth and children: 'We Suck Young Blood' mentions not just any blood, but 'young' blood, and taking the singer-speaker's children away is one of the most horrible acts 'A Wolf at the Door' has threatened to commit:

> I keep the wolf from the door
> But he calls me up
> Calls me on the phone
> Tells me all the ways that he's gonna mess me up
> Steal all my children
> If I don't pay the ransom
> And I'll never see 'em again
> If I squeal to the cops

Likewise, instead of sincerely asking listeners to follow them childlike out of town, the band warns in 'Dollars and Cents' from *Amnesiac* that:

> we are the DOLLARS & CENTS
> and the PoUNDS and Pence
> the MARK and the YEN
> we are going to crack your little souls
> we are going to crack your little souls

The 'we' of these lines is not literally autobiographical, but the we is metaphorically Radiohead, a product we buy with pounds and pence that is going to physically crack (open up or break down?) the listeners' supposedly diminutive souls. Again and again, the message of the music: beware.

Thus, any pleasure listeners experience with Radiohead's music is mired in the foregrounded trappings of its marketplace consumption: the 'aesthetic brilliance' cannot be arrived at without first paying for it: with dollars and cents, pounds and pence. In large part, twenty-first-century music is a physical commodity made in a factory. Radiohead's music, I argue, does not want or allow listeners to forget that the product they are listening to is just that: a product. Thinking of the experience otherwise, we fall prey to what Baudrillard described: 'We make believe that products are so differentiated and multiplied that they have become complex beings, and consequently purchasing and consumption must have the same value as any *human* relation [*sic*]' (2001: 17).

Relations in Radiohead's music, however, are severely plagued not by personal immediacy, but by perpetual delay, a static waiting for connection to happen, a connection that often never does happen. In 'The Bends' the speaker asks:

Where do we go from here
The words are coming out all weird
Where are you now, when I need you

Later in the song the speaker has a 'drip-feed on,' is talking to a 'girlfriend / waiting for something to happen' and is 'scared that there's nothing underneath.'[4] In the first lines of *Amnesiac*'s 'Packt like Sardines in a Crushd Tin Box,' the song's 'reasonable man' tells us that 'After years of waiting / Nothing came,' and 'Knives Out' on the same album narrates an ambiguous survival scenario where those left behind are told to fend for themselves:

I want you to know
He's not coming back
He's bloated and frozen
Still there's no point in letting it go to waste

So knives out
Catch da mouse
Squash his head
Put him in the pot

Pointing to the band's lyrics in the incomplete way I have above by no means establishes an authoritative reading. Nevertheless, I do think there is a strong case for the assertion that the band's project time and again calls emotional legitimacy, immediacy, aesthetic response into question.[5] To repeat the song 'Let Down' from *OK Computer*: 'Don't get sentimental / It always ends up drivel.'

Given the insistent questioning that can be found in the band's lyrics, what the band's real position is on these issues we'll never know, nor do we need to. However, we might glimpse their perspective on critical inquiry approximately 52 minutes into *Meeting People is Easy*, the 1998 documentary on the band, when Thom Yorke complains in a moment of irritated honesty to an interviewer:

If they're going to call it a concept record, and they're going to focus on the technology thing, it's like, just let them, it's fucking noise, anyway. We've done our job, you know. It just adds to the noise. It would be interesting to see …

In that ellipsis, in the radiant lacuna where Yorke's voice trails off before the scene visually and aurally fades out to a shot of an empty airport waiting area, therein reside our agreements and disagreements, our sound and fury, our addition to the noise. And the noise made by this collection's contributors is varied in pitch, pace, and volume.

Reappraising Theodor Adorno's theoretical formulations via the twenty-first century's cultural context, Curtis White argues in his essay, 'Kid Adorno,' that in an otherwise closely controlled art world, rock music entails the latent possibility for 'social explosiveness.' Admittedly a tightly administered corner of the culture industry, this contested position enables rock to have broad social consequence, The Sex Pistols, The Beatles, and Radiohead included. White then moves on to read Nick Hornby's now notorious *New Yorker* review of *Kid A* as exemplary resistance to this mode of rock's influence. Hornby's perspective restrains Radiohead's social and aesthetic possibilities by applying accustomed conventions of derision, e.g. the band's experimentation is 'self-indulgent.' Instead, White maintains that the artistic and political health of the band is evident in its refusal of the commodification Hornby's critique desires.

Davis Schneiderman's contribution, 'We got Heads on Sticks / You got Ventriloquists': Radiohead and the Improbability of Resistance,' defies easy summary. The electric movement of Davis's prose disputes the band's radicalized position as 'antirock rock stars.' Though Radiohead's lyrics may voice the economic subject's predicament, he questions whether Radiohead can escape being a tool of, and thus twisted by, marketplace pressures. Schneiderman surveys the band's commercialized resistance with special reference to its internet presence, the 'viral marketing techniques' deployed by the band's various promoters, and finally an anatomization of Grant Gee's tour-film documentary *Meeting People is Easy*. A tightly woven collage of convincing re-visionings of the band's entire project (from music to marketing), the essay thoroughly unsettles any notion of the band's aesthetic or commercial autonomy.

In 'The Aura of Authenticity: Perceptions of Honesty, Sincerity, and Truth in "Creep" and "Kid A,"' Carys Wyn Jones investigates the differing types of authenticity to which the two vastly different songs aspire. Radiohead, Jones argues, is uniquely situated in relation to authenticity insofar as the band is typically viewed as possessing artistic integrity despite its mainstream status, two positions most often considered mutually exclusive. In the end, the purpose of Jones's work is not only to use various and contested concepts of authenticity to analyze the music of Radiohead, but also to use Radiohead's music to critique claims to authenticity more generally.

Erin Harde's essay, 'Radiohead and the Negation of Gender,' observes that while the members of Radiohead do not identify themselves as androgynous, they do not overtly portray either a specific sexuality or gender identity. Traversing this problem, a genealogy of pop music androgyny is traced through 1970s glam rock and transvestism (e.g. David Bowie's Ziggy Stardust persona) to the present popular infatuation with the *über*-gendered Britney Spears, for example. Harde thus contextualizes Radiohead's success in relation to its decidedly non-sexual image, an anomalous negation of gender in a recording industry that is hyper-concerned with the clearly defined, if not hyperbolized, performance of sexuality. Ultimately, the relevance of Harde's essay resonates powerfully within the larger context of contemporary debates on the myriad of issues comprising gender and sexuality studies.

Grounded firmly in Gilles Deleuze's philosophy, Greg Hainge's essay, 'To(rt)uring the Minotaur: Radiohead, Pop, Unnatural Couplings, and Main-stream Subversion,' investigates the unusual flexibility of mainstream popular musical culture to coil seemingly unconventional forms of expression into its own comforting refrain, a repetition that summons a homely familiarity. Beginning with *Pablo Honey* and *The Bends*, Hainge analyzes how, despite its alternative labeling, Radiohead's early career collaborated with mainstream expectations. Turning to what he calls the '[t]wo antipopulist movements' embodied in the promotional artwork surrounding *Kid A* and *Amnesiac*, Hainge considers the band's latest efforts a coded and forceful disavowal of the mainstream.

Since the 1995 release of *The Bends*, visual artist Stanley Donwood has collaborated with the band to create a complex iconography that complements and even extends Radiohead's music. Interestingly and perhaps uniquely, Donwood's work develops alongside the music so that the two, sound and vision, are complicit in what Lisa Leblanc's essay, '"Ice Age Coming": The Apocalypse, the Sublime, and the Paintings of Stanley Donwood,' terms 'a multidisciplinary dialogue, supporting and completing one another.' With a careful, considered critique rooted in (but not reliant on) interviews with Donwood himself, Leblanc maps the artist's image-trajectory from sterile cityscapes with *OK Computer* to monumental landscapes in the *Kid A* paintings, from suburban life to melting polar ice caps. While thematically consistent, Donwood's execution and subject matter have mutated into a colossally scaled apocalyptic vision. Leblanc finally frames the credibility of Donwood's apocalypse by way of its elicitation of perhaps the most overwhelming aesthetic sensation: the sublime.

Joseph Tate's essay, 'Radiohead's Antivideos: Works of Art in the Age of Electronic Reproduction,' explores the appearance of 'test specimens' in computer-animated music video shorts titled 'antivideos,' 10–30-second videos released only on the internet concurrently with *Kid A*. The test specimens, wide-eyed bears with murderous grins, punctuated the art of Radiohead from CD packaging and packing slips, to website images and promotional stickers. Although directly analogous to all-too-familiar character-mascots that establish a product's brand identity, the bears are read as protagonists in a self-referential aesthetic that pastiches the band's commodification and the operation of capital at large.

In 'Deforming Rock: Radiohead's Plunge into the Sonic Continuum,' Mark Hansen considers Radiohead against several issues related to the music-sound-noise complex. Opposing the claim that *Kid A* and *Amnesiac*'s digital explorations represent radical departures for the band, Hansen foregrounds neglected continuities between the more recent studio albums and the previous three by illuminating how the band's sonic experiments form a juncture between rock and indie music, and yet differ from more radical contemporary sound experimentation in the non-commercial art world. A persuasive argument is made for Radiohead's unique ability to conjoin categories normally at odds – analog and digital, rock and techno, breath-based and machine beat – in a manner that ultimately discloses the sonic relationship between noise and music, and expands the notion of 'rock' itself.

Firmly grounded in musicology, Anwar Ibrahim and Allan Moore's essay, '"Sounds Like Teen Spirit": Identifying Radiohead's Idiolect,' makes a persuasive argument for a musical idiolect unique to Radiohead, one derived from, but not totally reliant on, The Pixies. However, while unpacking the fundamental formal structures of the band's musical strategies from album to album, the authors find that Radiohead's music problematizes any specification of idiolect: the unpredictability of Radiohead's music is its only true constant and a feature essential to the band's wide-ranging and long-lasting appeal.

Dai Griffiths' essay, 'Public Schoolboy Music: Debating Radiohead,' explores how the shared economic background of the band members shaped their approach to music. In particular, Griffiths lingers over the fact that Radiohead all attended Abingdon School in England, a representative example of the expensive, private education peculiar to the country's social landscape. Though an important bit of biography frequently passed over in critical examination of the band, this adolescent experience is a latent geological force that continues to sculpt Radiohead's musical materials. Griffiths details the near-modernist complexity and conventions of the band's compositional practices, reading both as a direct result of its members' private education.

Departing somewhat from the collection's atmosphere, musical composer Paul Lansky's 'My Radiohead Adventure' is an intimate recounting of a composer's personal interaction with the band. Contacted by Radiohead's Jonny Greenwood in 2000, Lansky consented to the band's use of a sample from his 'mild und liese' to underpin the *Kid A* track 'Idioteque.' The brief sample from Lansky's composition – a haunting piece composed from 1972–73 on a room-sized computer that needed one hour to process and then produce one minute of music – is shown to ground Radiohead's electronica-based song on a number of levels. The autobiographical account, however, subtly shifts to the critical as Lansky explores with exacting precision Radiohead's bending of harmonic languages in 'Idioteque' and other songs to achieve musical effects peculiar to the band's art.

Ending the collection is Joseph Tate's essay, '*Hail to the Thief*: A Rhizomatic Map in Fragments.' This final contribution explores and maps the vast textual terrain covered by the most recent album's occasionally obscure and often allusive lyrics. Some lines of inquiry lead into ponderous and unpaved culs-de-sac, while others trace wide spans of well-traveled roads. What emerges is not a single interpretation of the album, but a representation of the album's uncontainable and fragile heterogeneity of subject matter, a heterogeneity that points in the direction of Radiohead's past, present, and future.

Notes

1. In the preface to *The Rules of Art* (1992), Pierre Bourdieu discusses this same issue at length in the context of sociological analysis of literary works: 'countless are those

who forbid sociology any profaning contact with the work of art … I would simply ask why so many critics, so many writers, so many philosophers take such satisfaction in professing that the experience of a work of art is ineffable, that it escapes by definition all rational understanding; why they are so eager to concede without a struggle the defeat of knowledge; and where does their irrepressible need to belittle rational understanding come from, this rage to affirm the irreducibility of the work of art, or, to use a more suitable word, its transcendence' (xvi).

2.   An example of escapism, of letting oneself drift off into one's own world, is illustrated in 'Karma Police.' The black comedy of the singer's exaggeratedly totalitarian wishes is revealed, in the end, to have been only a passing daydream: 'Phew, for a minute there I lost myself.' Escaping from the moment, in this case, has resulted in an extended reverie wherein people are arrested for bad hairstyle choices and for sounding like 'a detuned radio.' The interjection 'Phew' confirms that the speaker is glad the escapist moment is over.

3.   In another instance, Radiohead critiques aesthetic rapture: the beloved in 'Creep' from *Pablo Honey* is said to 'float like a feather in a beautiful world,' but the speaker ultimately admits his inadequacy in the face of such beauty: 'I'm a creep.' Confronting something beautiful, or something perceived as beautiful, repeatedly causes problems for the protagonists in Radiohead's music. Other examples include 'No Surprises' from *OK Computer*: 'Such a pretty house / Such a pretty garden' and 'Like Spinning Plates' from *Amnesiac*: 'While you make pretty speeches / I'm being cut to shreds.' The adjective pretty works as it does in Nirvana's 'In Bloom' from *Nevermind:*

> He's the one
> Who likes all our pretty songs
> And he likes to sing along
> And he likes to shoot his gun
> But he knows not what it means

Pretty, in these instances, takes on the force of a caustically insincere compliment.

4.   The 'bends' is another name for Caisson disease, or decompression sickness. According to the *OED,* the word 'caisson' originally meant a chest for the transportation of explosives or ammunition, but around 1753 the word came to mean a large watertight case or chest used in laying the foundations of bridges in deep water. With the disease, nitrogen gas bubbles form in the body as the result of rapid transition from a high- to a low-pressure environment. When the bubbles form in a victim's joints, he or she is said to have the 'bends' because they are unable to straighten their limbs. Other problems caused by the disease include paralysis, convulsions, difficulties with muscle coordination, sensory abnormalities, numbness, nausea, speech defects, and personality changes.

Historically, the disease is relatively new. Beginning in the early 1800s, caissons were sunk to a lake or river bottom and pressurized with air to create a watertight compartment for workers excavating bridge foundations. By the mid-1800s doctors observed that the duration of exposure to the caisson's increased air pressure and the worker's speed of ascent correlated with development of joint pains. More generally, one could argue that the disease results from the conflict of human biological limitations and technological innovation.

5.   This suspicion is linked to, but not synonymous with, what Frederic Jameson calls 'the waning of affect in postmodern culture' (Jameson 1998: 10).

Chapter 1

Kid Adorno

Curtis White

Theodor Adorno's notorious Dialectic of Enlightenment consists substantially of the movement between the universal and the particular. In art, the universal is the Law of Genre, a 'collective bindingness.' On the other side, the particular (or the individual and subjective) represents the theoretically boundless world of human possibility and play (which Adorno (1997) attempts to capture through the word 'spontaneity'). Art's fundamental concept from the perspective of the particular is autonomy. Art realizes its own concept when it makes itself not through the conventions of the universal (genre: the rules for the proper construction of sonata or sonnet, etc.) but 'by virtue of its own elaborations, through its own immanent process.' To be sure, these elaborations can only deploy themselves in a context made available by the world of convention; none the less, when an artwork is successful, it is in spite of the presence of convention, not because of it. This is why, ultimately, craft has little to do with whether or not a work is a successful piece of art.

The most powerful and sinister gambit of what Adorno (1997) calls 'administered society' is to promise the freedom of individuality while simultaneously prohibiting it. For example, consumers have been promised the 'freedom of the open road' by auto-makers for the last half century, but with each passing year the realization of that freedom becomes more unlikely for all the familiar reasons (not least of which is the perverse insistence of other 'individuals' on using the same roads promised for your freedom).

By extension, the critical artistic question for Adorno is how an autonomous or free art can be produced in a context of enduring societal unfreedom. (Actually, the logic of Adorno's aesthetic might also lead to the conclusion that art can only happen in the context of unfreedom. Art is a response to repression.) The exemplary works of artistic autonomy were, for Adorno, the 'experimental' works of modernism, especially the music of Arnold Schoenberg and in literature the antinovels of Samuel Beckett. For us, however, the failure of, or, we might say, the passing of the opportunity for modernism leaves us in a situation that can still be thought through in Adorno's terms but not with his examples.

The administration of reality in the second half of the twentieth century succeeded in separating the arts into the public arts of commerce (i.e. the Culture Industry and its aesthetics of hedonism; art is for 'enjoyment' just like your Coca-Cola), and the private arts of the 'serious.' The private arts are the 'finer' pleasures of the privileged (art collectors and patrons of symphonies, ballets, and distinguished not-for-profit literary presses). Of course, nobody – especially the privileged – is obliged to take the 'serious' seriously – that is, as the suggestion of an alternative to the Ruling Order of Things. 'Serious' art remains merely a class marker.

The one area in contemporary culture in which the administered universal and the particular (with its impulse to freedom) continue a consequential and sometimes deadly engagement is in the theater provided by 'rock.' In an otherwise domesticated art world, rock still has the potential for 'social explosiveness' (Adorno 1997). This is not news that Adorno would have been happy to hear. For Adorno, the idea that the struggle for the virtue of 'spontaneity' was being waged within pop culture would have been the assurance of its failure.

I wouldn't contend otherwise. I would only contend that this profitable and well-managed sector of the Culture Industry, the Music Industry, is also the place where the question of authenticity (understood as the freedom to wander from convention) is most broadly and dramatically engaged. It is here, and not in the experimental novel or in poetry, that artists can still have broad social consequence, as The Beatles, The Sex Pistols, and now perhaps Radiohead can testify. But the fact that the dialectic of the universal and particular, the Dialectic of Enlightenment, is still forcefully and fatefully alive in popular music does not mean that it is not also doomed, and well in advance. For rock music, too, must seize its possibility in the context of its impossibility.

Consider the instance of Radiohead and its recent and controversial album *Kid A*. The music of *Kid A* and its public reception make explicit the drama implicit in the relationship between an autonomous art (or, at least, an art with the desire for autonomy) and an administered culture. Take, for example, the review of *Kid A*, written by novelist Nick Hornby ('Beyond the Pale,' *New Yorker*, October 30 2000).

Hornby's review is not an objective evaluation of an artwork. It is the reassertion of a familiar, grim and very repressive aesthetic. Hornby begins his review with the obligatory homage to Ray Charles and Elvis Presley, thus establishing his orthodoxy, his faithfulness to the one true Church of the Commodified Vernacular. Hornby can then begin to lay out the aesthetic grounds for Radiohead's heresy to what Hornby calls 'the old-fashioned dynamics of rock': '*Kid A* demands the patience of the devoted; both patience and devotion become scarcer commodities once you start picking up a paycheck.'

Could he be any plainer? Art is about exchange. We give the artist our hard-earned money and the artist … what? Doesn't try our patience?

Hornby gives more content to what it is we expect in return for that which we've given from our paycheck. Hornby argues that Radiohead's previous album, *OK Computer*, had 'some extraordinarily lovely tracks,' and in *Kid A*'s best moments 'something gorgeous floats past.' So, in the World of Art According to Nick Hornby, the first and highest principle is that it should be a fair exchange, you should 'get your money's worth' (as his mother probably told him), and aesthetic tenet #2 is that the art should be 'gorgeous' and also maybe a little bit 'lovely.' Now, beyond the obvious fact that this is an old romantic tautology and Hornby has no idea what he's talking about, it does reveal that the fundamental premise of Hornby's aesthetic insistence is pleasure. My money is well spent if I 'enjoy' the album/movie/sitcom/football game.

As Adorno put it, pithily, 'whoever concretely enjoys artworks is a philistine; he is convicted by expressions like "a feast for the ears."' Hornby's aesthetic is the aesthetic of the balance sheet: 'heard the Ninth Symphony last night, enjoyed myself so and so much.' As Adorno concludes, and Hornby substantiates, 'such feeble-mindedness has by now established itself as common sense.'

Not to cheat Hornby of the full import of his thought (feeblemindedness notwithstanding), he also suggests that it is good for art to have a message. '*Pablo Honey* [Radiohead's first album] ... contained one song, 'Creep,' that gave voice to everyone who has ever felt disconnected, alienated, or geeky ...' So, in summary, art should be a fair exchange of money for pleasure and it's nice if it can also 'give voice' to something, a message, or something that someone somewhere once 'felt.'

To be sure, there is also *ad hominem* innuendo in case the reasoning behind this hatchet job is too subtle for you, reader of the esteemed *New Yorker*. Radiohead is a 'band that has come to hate itself;' it has suffered a 'failure of courage;' and, that old kumquat served to the experimental, the band has been 'self-indulgent' in making its music.

Well, I can't defend Radiohead from these charges because, to tell you the truth, I've never met the guys and as far as I know they might hate themselves, they might indeed lack courage and they might be self-indulgent as all get-out. Hey, some folks are. But I do have an alternative hypothesis, one that strikes me as being very probable indeed: this is a band that hates you, Nick Hornby, you and your ilk, with your philistine taste and the abominable arrogance that allows you to claim you know what rock 'n' roll ought to be about. Rock 'n' roll is about 'fair exchange of money for pleasure'?! You are the very Soul Man, aren't you?

The real basis of Hornby's critique is this: Radiohead is perverse. Hornby imagines his ideal art consumer yelling at *Kid A*, 'You're supposed to be a pop group! ... You're supposed to use your gifts for songwriting, and singing, and playing.

'You're supposed to be a commodity, stupid! Just make your money and give us what we expect.'

But, of course, Radiohead has made it loudly and widely known that it did not set out to be a commodity; it set out to make art, which is to say that no band since Nirvana has made it more abundantly clear that its 'intention' (for what that's worth) is to seize freedom from the context of unfreedom. As I've argued, only the popular music scene allows for this as a possibility on such an international stage, but the crazy-making irony is that this intent cannot be realized in the only context in which it is possible to express the intent.

'Fuck Corporate Rock!'

'Can we put that on a T-shirt and sell it at the concert?'

Commodify your dissent. Ask Kurt Cobain about how it works in practice.

Fortunately, Radiohead is politically savvy in a way that Cobain rarely was. Radiohead's political *bête noire* is what Adorno called 'instrumental rationality.' A techno-totalized world. Its artistic quandary is not how to prosper within this totalized context (as well-wisher Nick Hornby encourages) but how to respond to it in a way that is adequate to what the artist wants: the feel of the authentic, the spontaneity of autonomy, even a tiny gap between itself and the universal other, the Corporate Life World.

Call it a self-indulgent refusal of its job description (why, 'there's no room for anything approaching conventional pop music,' Hornby whines), but this is the obligation or the duty, if you will, that art itself feels it owes to the social. It's as if art's primary function is simply to remind us that there is a difference between freedom and repression, that change is real and the possible is possible.

The problem, though, is that a strategy to create this gap works for a period but is then used up ('entombed in the pantheon of cultural commodities,' as Adorno (1997) put it) and a new strategy must be discovered. At times, *Kid A* seems like a catalog of devices that have been used to create this gap between the artwork and the law of the universal:

- dissonant orchestral waves ('How to Disappear Completely')
- avant-garde free jazz extrapolations à la Mingus ('The National Anthem')
- surreal lyrics and aural landscapes ('Treefingers')
- punk/grunge crudeness in bass lines and guitar crunching ('The National Anthem')
- homage to The Beatles' avant-gardism in the echoes of Ringo's drum rhythms on 'Strawberry Fields Forever'
- electronic ambience à la Brian Eno ('Motion Picture Soundtrack')
- psychedelic noodling in guitar lines ('In Limbo')
- homages to Led Zep vocal and guitar breakthroughs, what Jeff Beck called the sound of 'my guitar being sick' ('In Limbo')
- sampling and a general feel of the aesthetics of pastiche (rooting the band not only in hip-hop but also in Dada) ('Idioteque').

In the most expansive and forceful cuts on this album – 'The National Anthem' and 'Idioteque'– it seems as if nearly all of these strategies are brought to the fore. But no one of these strategies is sufficient for Radiohead's ultimate purposes. It's as if the band wanted to provide a historical reprise of oppositional strategies before coming to its own most central concerns.

In short, as its name, the titles of its last two albums, most of its lyrics and all of the graphics clearly indicate, Radiohead is centrally concerned with the following questions. What does it mean to be a human being in a context in which every relationship is mediated by technology and technical rationality? (How can we 'live and breathe' when 'everyone is broken,' it asks in *The Bends*, echoing explicitly the ethical thinking behind Adorno's concept of 'damage'.) And, Radiohead asks, what does it mean to be artists opposed to technical rationality when we are obliged not only to create our art through computers, in highly technical and utterly engineered recording studios, but also in cooperation with international mega-corporations? (These boys are not Ani DiFranco with her own publishing, recording and distribution set-up; these boys are with EMI/Capitol.) For the most prominent stylistic force on *Kid A* is techno, synthetic sound, synthetic rhythm. And what is most plaintive and appealing in Radiohead's art are the moments in which it contrives to allow its own voice, its created 'style,' its humanity in an utterly nineteenth-century sense, to transcend, to rise above the unfreedom of their context and even the conventionalized unfreedom of their own medium, pop music. In these inspired moments of Mahlerian sweetness the band rises above the mire of our shared condition. (What else does Mahler try to do, in symphony after symphony, but dramatize this one desire?) In a cut called 'Exit Music' on *OK Computer*, the angelic but synthetic background chorus makes it seem as if Radiohead wishes to inspire even the androids to claim humanity. And there is a weird pathos in the computer-processed speaking voice on 'Fitter Happier' and the lead vocal on 'Kid A,' a song that could be called 'The Robot Child's Lament.'

Radiohead's aesthetic strategy is not to avoid the enemy but to inhabit it and reorient its energies. As Buddhists would argue, there is nothing inherently evil about machines, even computers are OK, it's the mind that inhabits the machine that can be malign. What really bugs critics like Nick Hornby is that as Radiohead's albums have progressed, this strategy has been taken up less through an explicit 'message' in the lyrics while the music remains more or less standard pop-rock (even if very good pop-rock) and gets taken up more integrally in the textures of the music itself. This is what sends *Kid A* 'beyond the pale.' In fact, I would argue that Radiohead's intuition that its politics are best made not explicitly in its lyrics but integrally with the music is a very good indication of the artistic and political health of the band. By so doing, it not only eludes Hornby's commodity fetishism but also refuses the error of politically correct art that seeks to make its artistic effect dependent on the virtue of its political message. As Adorno (1997) writes, 'Artworks that want to divest themselves of fetishism by real and extremely dubious political commitment regularly enmesh themselves in false consciousness as the result of inevitable and vainly praised simplification. In the shortsighted praxis to which they blindly subscribe, their own blindness is prolonged.'

Don't misunderstand me, Radiohead's *Kid A* is 'dead' more often than it is alive. It is a pop band. Its music is finally 'acceptable.' The harmonic structure of its music is often conventional. How else could it be second, in *USA Today*'s best-of-the-year evaluation, only to U2 (that other artist-critic of the same Culture Industry that made it rich and famous)? As Thom Yorke has said, 'That's how they get ya,' and they have got Radiohead, but it's never enough, and any part that escapes the great maw of the universal is ipso facto subversive and dangerous. And so enough light escapes to allow us to imagine that perhaps it's not entirely dead, and so perhaps we're not entirely dead, and so perhaps something other than the smothering present is *possible*.

With admirable frequency, Radiohead's music realizes this enormous purpose, to achieve the human in the midst of the inhuman, the free in the midst of the unfree. In an instant. The wonderfulness of that instant is all we have any right to ask of it. As Radiohead says on 'Exit Music (For a Film)':

Breathe. Keep breathing.

Chapter 2

'We got Heads on Sticks / You got Ventriloquists': Radiohead and the Improbability of Resistance

Davis Schneiderman

Twentieth-century New York City magnetized the filaments of both American and world culture, from the iron filings of postindustrial Pop Art to the steel-reinforced architectural marvels of the financial district. The analog is nineteenth-century Paris, where in the work of French caricaturist Jean Ignace Isidore Grandville, 'Saturn's ring becomes a cast iron balcony on which the inhabitants of the planet take the air in the evening' (Benjamin 1986: 153). A century later, in that *American* metropole of replication and reduplication – moving from the once-fixed singularity of the Empire State Building to Jean Baudrillard's 'vertigo of duplication' (1983: 136) inhabiting the recently leveled Twin Towers – the city relentlessly signals to the emerging global order across both popular and ambient channels. The noise of New York City spins itself from every vertiginous side street and each interconnected corporate byway. The Loudmouth Collective Sound Orchestra plays *Everywhere USA*, a *mélange* of piano, ambient typewriters, and exploding balloons, as oblivious executives hum along to the muzak of multinational capital. If something, anything, and everything has been done before, that doesn't mean it can't be done again. Repetition has a cadence all its own, and Radiohead, frequent visitors to all channels of the city, are constantly negotiating a new rhythm.

Recent world events aside, the rock music centrifuge of cyclical production, promotion, and consumption endlessly spins those alterna-rock darlings and *Billboard* scions Radiohead – Thom Yorke, brothers Colin and Jonny Greenwood, Ed O'Brien, and Phil Selway – as somewhere between the *next* great rock messiahs and last minute's overblown demiurge. Upon the release of the 'arty, experimental' *Kid A* album, *Rolling Stone* (that perennial defender of the status quo) labeled the October 2000 debut 'soft' at 207,393 units, calling Radiohead's fourth full-length offering a 'weird, non-commercial album' (Skanse 2000). Almost a year later, Alex Ross would describe the band's bass player, Colin Greenwood, in equally 'non-commercial' terms: 'you might peg him as a cultish young neo-Marxist professor, or as the editor of a hip quarterly. But he is a rock star, with several Web pages devoted to him' (Ross 2001: 114). Scanning for that young Baudrillard beneath the close-cropped hair on Colin or, more likely, the errant tousle of his brother, guitarist and multi-instrumentalist Jonny Greenwood (on glockenspiel, transistor radio, and the obscure ondes martenot), produces the same results as resolving the 'contradictions' of Baudrillard's NYC meta-culture: 'All of this defines a digital space, a magnetic field for the code, with polarizations, diffractions, gravitations of the models and always, always, the flux of the smallest disjunctive unities …' (1983: 138).

Swirling media representations of this eternally reproducing *hyperreal* populate every point of the Manhattan grid, an exemplar for the new order of the United States, with downtown sheets of ecstasy pills changing into uptown racks of high-priced fashion, the liquid disintegration of hallucinogenic dreams channeled effortlessly into pre-programmed video clips looping forever across flat television screens. Smooth images dangle from the faux-warehouse rafters of populist boutiques and gleam like metal mirrors from the effervescent windows of MTV's Times Square digs – and everything, absolutely everything, is transmuted, in this vortex of infotainment, by the alchemy of commercialized resistance.

A music of the body – of expression once located beyond the obvious vectors of global capital – compartmentalizes itself into the post-*American Bandstand* era of chemical movement to technological masters, moving from the first cylinders of a replicating phonograph into a feedback loop consuming and collapsing all stages of production, distribution, and listener consumption/expression into an automated dance of brains dispersed into *collective* bodies. Musicians and the 'industry' people have long understood (at least on a subcutaneous, perhaps genetic, channel) that the location of the economic listener/consumer can be tricked into a facsimile of brain movement – of thinking as a simulacrum of counter-hegemonic thought – by the spectacle of their favorite musical acts undergoing all sorts of seemingly inspired physical contortions. Whenever those long-gone mop-tops shake their follicles (spurring a sneaker 'revolution'), The Who's Pete Townshend does his familiar windmill (I call that a 'bargain,' the best *I've* ever had), or neo-rapper Nelly applies those distinctive little bandages (are they Band-Aid-brand bandage strips?), the economic subject finds her hair, arms, and even the pores of her face consolidated into a ghost body of rebellion that French academic and economist Jacques Attali identifies as 'a refuge from the great uncontrollable machines, a confirmation of the individual's sameness and the collectivity's powerlessness to change the world. … [Music] creates a system of apolitical, nonconflictual, idealized values. It is here that a child learns his trade as a consumer, for the selection and purchase of music are his principal activities' (Attali 1985: 110).

Radiohead is no exception to this collective desire for a refuge that may not provide much viable shelter. Thom Yorke has his quiver of contortions, from a trademark head shake to other verbal arabesques rarefied by the rock press into a familiar soup: 'Like a boxer delivering jab after jab, he sprays a series of ohh-ahh syllables over the calm seashore pulse' (Moon 2001). Given the band's stratospheric record sales and continual position as antirock rock stars, Radiohead's 'experimental' music and anticorporate message may not be as radical as it seems. As Thomas Frank warns via a somewhat virgin understatement: 'With their bottomless appetite for new territory to colonize, the [record] executives have finally come around to us' (Frank 1997: 160). Yorke may 'sing' about the plight of the economic subject in 'Dollars and Cents' ('We are the dollars and cents / And the pounds and pence / And the mark and the yen, and yeah / We're going to crack your little souls'), but how can we be sure that Radiohead, for all of its deliberately muddled articulation and innovative studio work, is not a tool of this same endlessly looping beat of the marketplace?

If Radiohead's August 7 2001 concert at New York City's Madison Square Garden means anything at all in a context violently reinscribed by the September 11th terrorist attacks on the Pentagon and World Trade Center, the band's counter-commercial rhetoric, along with its seemingly endless legions of fans, produce – and perhaps delight in – the flailing forms of a twilight postmodernism. Before that August 7 concert began, an anonymous female attendee, her neck inked with a perfectly mimetic barcode tattoo, pushed through the pack of less self-aware spectators to one of the many merchandise stands anchoring the arena's mezzanine. The contradictions of a cultural moment that assimilates everything into that vortex of duplication seemed fused into the program of vertical lines on her flesh as she thumbed through the rack of $35 T-shirts. Another nameless 'thumber,' seeking validation for her plastic identity, asked the attendant if a shirt with no discernible identifying text was 'actually' a Radiohead item.

The question is not so much what comprises an 'item' in the seemingly never-ending spectacle of Thom Yorke and company, but rather, what, within the protean rubric of commercialized resistance, does not. The allure of Radiohead's complex anti-establishment image, fueled as it is by its inventive music, emerges in the deliberate flood of schizophrenic images the band routinely deploys. Its 'Creep' days long gone, lead singer Thom Yorke rails in the show at Madison Square Garden against the inanities of his record company before launching into the song 'Talk Show Host;' he admonishes the crowd to buy an electric car, he dedicates *Kid A*'s 'Optimistic' (as one fan known as 'Rob aka Faketree' reports) 'to the boy who was shot and killed by police in genoa, italy. which i think is because the kid "tried the best he could"' [sic]. This reference to the July 21 2001 death of Carlo Giuliani at the hands of an injured carabinieri at the G8 summit must be viewed not in terms of its apparently counter-hegemonic content but, rather, within the matrix of signs reflecting other signs, of sentiments suffused into the cataract of instrumentality that surrounds all of Radiohead's attempts to destabilize corporate culture.

What has evolved into Radiohead's rebellious subtext finds inscription within the dialectic of the band's music, its position as an EMI/Capitol Records 'product,' and the methods by which popular culture dilutes all resistance into a mass of sanctioned rebellion, into pictures-of-cameras – hunting bears who are already captive. The Critical Art Ensemble, as early as 1994, warned that, 'The rate at which strategies of subversion are co-opted indicates that the adaptability of power is too often underestimated' (1994: 12), and while the lush, technological soundscapes of the *Kid A* and *Amnesiac* albums generate notions of possible displacement from the controlled excesses of the major record labels, the obstacles to such liberation remain considerable. Manipulating the image culture of a postmodernism that perhaps, as Frederic Jameson famously notes, masks an advanced form of multinational capitalism, Radiohead is caught within a dialectic of capital that invites a certain type of rebellion, where performativity eliminates efficacy – and despite a recourse to musical innovation and various guerilla media-manipulation tactics, those 'abrasive guitars' threaten to perpetually strum away into nothing.

In order to really *listen* to Radiohead's critique, a context must be firmly established; we will examine the authenticity of any radical displacement within the scope of commercial music through the band's virtual articulations, the viral marketing techniques used by its various 'handlers,' and an examination of Grant Gee's tour film *Meeting People is Easy*, in order to investigate the totalizing effects of corporate culture for a group whose praxis seems to be evolving toward a definitive break with traditional notions of commercialized resistance.

Das Capitol Records

With the incessant merger of record companies into the Big Five – Universal Music, BMG, Sony Music, Time Warner, and British conglomerate EMI – the latter enters its second century as the only one of the five major record labels to exist independently of a major entertainment conglomerate. As *The Nation*'s Mark Crispin Miller noted recently, the travails of these monster global media companies, notwithstanding any apparent antitrust protections, remain part of a larger capitalist fabric:

> The media cartel that keeps us fully entertained and permanently half-informed is always growing here and shriveling there, with certain of its members bulking up while others slowly fall apart or get digested whole. But while the players tend to come and go – always with a few exceptions – the overall Leviathan itself keeps getting bigger, louder, brighter, forever taking up more time and space, in every street, in countless homes, in every other head. (Miller 2002: 18)

As a subset of EMI, Radiohead's American label Capitol Records (along with British label Parlophone) finds itself always in the position of colonial administrator, dependent on the movement of larger multinational vectors.[1] And like any dutiful but territorial governor, the 'Hollywood and Vine' label continues to increase its own value to the industry through its stable of popular artists old and new, including Paul McCartney, Liz Phair, Pink Floyd, Coldplay, Bob Seger, and The Foo Fighters.

What increasingly separates the completely pre-packaged pop world (recycled for this current generation in numerous Boy Band/Sex Kitten incarnations) from the potential resistance of politically minded major-label groups such as Radiohead (or Rage Against The Machine) is not only that sense of self-reflexivity and cynicism that has come to characterize music in the postmodern era, but also a critique of record industry inequities. While eviscerating sorghum such as VH-1's *Behind the Music* routinely skewers the influence of record labels in the careers of musicians such as Rick James, TLC, or Milli Vanilli, the almost unwavering whine of the featured musician bears some affinity with Steve Albini's critique of new talent contracts: '[The band] has made the music industry more than three million dollars richer, but is in the hole $14,000 on royalties. The band members have each earned about a third as much as they would working at a 7-Eleven …' (Albini 1997: 176). Hip-hop acts, perhaps epitomized by the genre's current leader Jay-Z, are often skilled at elevating this I-Me-Mine critique (if only slightly) to a systemic level. Jay-Z rhymes in his recent hit 'Izzo (H.O.V.A.)': 'Industry shady it need to be taken over / Label owners hate me I'm raisin' the status quo up / I'm overchargin' niggaz for what they did to the Cold Crush / Pay us like you owe us for all the years that you hold us / We can talk, but money talks so talk mo' bucks.' The song, a paean to his modest nickname 'Hova' (as in 'Jehovah'), confirms his commodified pain that must no doubt accompany the profits from his record label, clothing company, and production house. If Jay-Z is a rhyming CEO unafraid to brandish his assets, Radiohead is ostensibly less comfortable with the caliber of its cultural capital.

The repetitive banality of the band's early records (mimicked continually by the depth of press coverage) ensured that these albums succumbed to a brand of colonized critique not so far removed from the rhetorical flourish of corporate rap. The throwaway cuts of *Pablo Honey* are barely worth mentioning, and while the band's sophomore effort *The Bends* (lauded by many fans made nostalgic by current 'experimental' Radiohead) invites a slightly more nuanced reading, it is difficult to sympathize with the 'alternative' travails of 'A cracked polystyrene man / Who just crumbles and burns' (from 'Fake Plastic Trees') once the traditional song structure finds its traditional 'alternative' video (Yorke wheeling around an artificially lit supermarket in a shopping cart). Regardless of this 'self-reflexive' content, as well as the band's success in stifling a Capitol Records remix of the track, the song and video fight music commercialization with all the success of a corporate Sisyphus shouting about the evils of his rock. The almost inability of *The Bends*' best work to clear the morass of the alternative rock formula has as much to do with a marketing structure that controls all flows within its multifarious media channels. Think punkfathers-cum-salesmen

William S. Burroughs and Allen Ginsberg in advertisements for Gap, and Yorke's assessment in a July 2001 article in *The Wire* is telling: 'you are right at the sharp end of the sexy, sassy, MTV eye-candy lifestyle thing that they're trying to sell to the rest of the world, ... if you're interested in actually being heard, you have to work within the system' (quoted in Reynolds 2001: 32). And the system, of course, is the media.

In Martin Clarke's 2000 biopic, *Radiohead: Hysterical and Useless*, any attempt by the band to articulate a counter-hegemonic viewpoint is completely diluted by the rhetorical solvent of Clarke's 'pop will save the world' sentiment. Reifying the narratives of consolidated resistance and hackneyed rock-star angst, Clarke notes that '[Thom's] distaste for multi-nationals and corporations is expressed in uncomfortable guitars and abrasive sounds' (Clarke 2000: 122). The tragedy is that Clarke means this with all the wide-eyed earnestness of an *NSync press pack.

Certainly, Radiohead has obviously attempted to break from these structures of complete consumption by the alternative rock machine at the same time that its music moves into less ostensibly controllable territory. Yet hyperbolic echoes of Clarke's sentiments endlessly dissemble throughout both mainstream and alternative press channels – powered by the band's five increasingly 'experimental' full-length studio albums and the most recent live offering, *I Might Be Wrong*; an army of b-sides; more online fan sites than most 'Big Five' record acts combined; and, most interestingly, the band's political statements meshed between the 'rock' of its newer 'antirock' and the hard place of the EMI/Capitol Records marketing machine. A few examples will help to illustrate this point.

In Ross's 2001 *New Yorker* piece on the band, 'The Searchers' (reminiscent of The Who's 'The Seeker' who 'searches low and high'), Yorke rails against the excesses of S.F.X., a promotion company whose venues Radiohead seeks to avoid. One of the band's three managers, Chris Hufford, grows 'impatient' in explaining to Yorke the reality of Radiohead's position within the marketplace. Yorke replies that 'the marketplace is where we sell records. This isn't the marketplace. It's an area of, I don't know, oversight' (Ross 2001: 87). Hufford tells Yorke that it is actually 'Capitalism,' to which Yorke responds with a cry of '*Bollocks!*'

From a June 13 1998 web chat, available in transcription from the press archive section of the 'Follow Me Around' fan site, Yorke deflects questions about Radiohead's new music as 'not really relevant,' in favor of promoting that weekend's Tibetan Freedom Concert. Yorke refers fans to Noam Chomsky before responding to a query about whether the United States government has any interests with China *beyond* trade policy: 'I think their hands are tied like with so many issues. By trade and powerful multinational corporations with vested interests. This has dictated much of foreign policy in the west since the second world war' [*sic*]. Earlier in the transcript, Yorke writes that a question about whether Radiohead's audience is actually 'getting the message' of the Tibetan Freedom Concert displays a 'patronizing attitude towards the audience.' Perhaps exasperated by the burdens of politics-as-such, Colin Greenwood relieves Yorke, closing the chat with several witty Beatlesesque answers to several vacuous Beatlesesque questions.

In the June/July 2001 issue of music magazine *The Blender*, a less serious Yorke chats about the band's promotional plans for *Amnesiac*: 'We are definitely having singles, videos, glossy-magazine celebrity photo shoots, children's television appearances, film-premiere appearances, dance routines and many interesting interviews about my tortured existence.' Quipping his way through the interview, Yorke also decries selling any Radiohead work to advertising agencies, and while rumors that the 'I Might Be Wrong' track from *Amnesiac* might be used for promotion of the 2002 Salt Lake City Winter Olympics, the band has recently allowed this same track, as well as the *Kid A* opener, 'Everything in its Right Place,' for use on the soundtrack (and in the film) of the Cameron Crowe movie *Vanilla Sky*.[2]

Limbless and helpless

Part of the perpetual 'sell' (and seemingly every other ideology, password, conformity plan, mutual fund prospectus, and snake-oil sales scam on the web) is also, always, perpetually, the contemporaneous internet presence of all manifestations of a product – in this case, the proliferation of a Radiohead marketing machine that threatens to all but subsume any individual song or album that the band releases. Its videos are archived on various websites, those songs and albums (often pre-release) can be found both on authorized promotional and quasi-authorized file-sharing interstices; and the physical detritus of their product – the record packaging, the 'secret' booklet under the polystyrene tray of limited *Kid A* pressings, and even the digital compact disc itself – reflects an apparently de-centered cyberspace housing.

In the same way that South African artist William Kentridge's charcoal drawings belie the complexity of production and erasure that informs his 'movies,' the physical aspects of the Radiohead phenomenon draw much of their significance from a virtual multivalence that simultaneously encompasses the music *and* its marketing. While many theoretical and popular analyses of the last decade have been devoted to discussions of virtuality, and a generation of college students has quickly absorbed the art of sitting in one place while pursuing a state of 'information nova,' there is also the concatenation of sites that index other sites, serving as interest-group mirrors for the suspicious 'featured sites' jumping to the top of the pre-selected search results, presumably because money has permeated a particular economic membrane.

The isomorphic utopias that characterized the ethic of early net applications and locations have changed into the transient, contemporary utopias-as-product. After Napster articulates itself, it begs to be colonized so that its ethic will, as Allucquère Rosanne Stone comments, 'last no longer than it takes for access to be sold off to private interests and milked for a profit' (1997: 66). The *virtual* Radiohead exists already as a 'real' commodity along with the physical – and this virtual body of work, no longer a mere addendum or convenient product location, but also the evolving product base itself, allows Burroughs' cynical 1951 prophecy to gain quite a bit of operational validity: 'Wouldn't it be booful if we should juth run together into one gweat big blob' (1985 [1951]: 100).

Because of this transfer of subjectivity away from passive subject who purchases product, to an 'active' 'construct' involved in the web life of the band, the official Radiohead website at www.radiohead.com, designed by band artist Stanley Donwood (whose nightmarish figures bear a slight affinity to Kentridge's angry CEOs), Tchocky (a Yorke alias), Chris Bran, and Tim Bran, scuttles the expectations of the fan-on-the-virtual-street looking for the latest long-hair-guitar-hero picture of Jonny Greenwood. Rather, the labyrinthine site mimics the modes of deterritorialization called for in the Gilles Deleuze – and Félix Guattari – brand of poststructuralist theory, yet abuses the traditional marketing of the obviously commercial Radiohead spaces (such as the Capitol Records site) through juxtapositions both witty and banal.

The would-be-Theseus websurfer can hook her twine to the doorway of counter-hegemonic hyperlinks and surf to such socially committed organizations as People & Planet, Corporate Watch, the media watchdog organization Fair, and the Free Tibet Campaign, among others. A second initial option allows the user to move the mouse over the decompressed crying minotaur mascot toward a page of 'blips' similar to the short promotional 'antivideos' that Joseph Tate lauds as useful deconstructions of the standard MTV-style video. The original 'blips' constructed to support the release of *Kid A* are short videos that feature Radiohead's former 'test specimen' mascot bears as 'either cartoonishly violent corporate sycophants or traumatized victims of surveillance' so that the viewer is 'asked to disassemble the object that distills a performer's presence for uniform portable consumption, only to find a text that decries consumption.' There is no question that the current roster of 'blips' (featuring both the test specimens and the newer crying minotaurs) is engaging and well conceived. Like the most insidious jingles of a subvertising culture gone wild, they dissent from the corporate video telos in admirable fashion. Additionally, Radiohead's official website at www.radiohead.com reverses the traditional order of 'socially concerned' pop-star agenda by connecting viewers *first* to the cause, and *second* to the product that is digitized with that look-at-me-but-don't-look-at-me irony.

The rest of the site meanders through somewhat more commercially relevant materials mixed in with social initiatives and various text/image labyrinths. The option 'escape' from the main menu page offers up another list of socially cognizant websites. Other links from the menu take the user to 'w.a.s.t.e. products limited,' Radiohead's merchandising arm, the Radiohead bulletin board, the 'I Might Be Wrong' video, or if the user is feeling a bit more cryptic, to 'imaginary prisons' (a text/graphic choose-your-own-adventure of sorts), a puzzle game known as 'Byzantine ziggurat,' and a page called 'three shapes' that runs Colin Greenwood's promotion for a 'D – J Required' show in Manchester along with a transcription and audio archive of a Noam Chomsky talk at MIT.

Opposed to this engaging but at times frustrating maze, the slew of unofficial websites feature almost everything else (and much overlap), and it would be useless to attempt even a partial list in this space. Yet, it should be noted that some of the unofficial sites post tidbits from the horse's mouth. In the December 11 2001 link to a 'Message From Thom,' Yorke (in a few scant lines) champions peaceful thinking, decries George W. Bush, calls for a World Court, and thanks 'everybody on w.a.s.t.e. for still listening and sticking with us and understanding the records we make.' Yorke's reference to w.a.s.t.e., which started out as the band's physical newsletter but has now evolved into the online merchandising outfit, refers to an important element of virtual conflation that reinforces the transformation of the 'fan base' into the 'economic subject' (of which more later). In the 'W.A.S.T.E. EMAIL LETTER #1'of October 15 1999, Colin Greenwood announces the new program:

> We've also opened our own store, called w.a.s.t.e on-line, which you can access through http://www.radiohead.com. There you can buy some lovely clothes, with designs by Stanley and Thom. You can also join our information service by clicking on 'join waste' at the front of the store. This will be another way to give you news, as well as keeping in touch with you – and you'll be able to change and maintain your own information, who you are and where you come from, as you see fit.
> We're doing this because we want to try and use this amazing communication thingie to natter directly to you and not via any corporate third party bollocks with spinning car ads ...

Greenwood's insistence that the user can 'change and maintain' her or his economic profile privileges a certain type of 'fan' – she or he who chooses to cease only 'reading' the seemingly defunct w.a.s.t.e. newsletter and enter into the interactive regime of web subjectivity. As the Critical Art Ensemble offers in the scenario of economic transaction that no longer refers to 'real' bodies: 'It is this body, a body of data, that now controls the stage' (1994: 59). The physical exists only in so far as virtual data and information justify the flesh.

Clearly, Radiohead is interested in disrupting the established flow of global capital. Yet whether there is any difference between the type of merchandising project that excises 'corporate third party bollocks' and the traditional yet unswervingly adaptive energies of the recording industry may very well be a moot question. For in cyberspace, the road to hell is not an information highway, but an artificial environment with no use for direct routes. The internet design ethic is in fact counter to such organization. The rhizomatic World Wide Web is meant to function even upon the amputation of a particular section. Coupled with this apparently de-centered system's evolution in the last decade as a full-service capital marketing platform, the once-physical roadways so necessary to human experience may become subject to greater and greater vortices of disrepair – with 'paved' becoming nothing more than an amputated concept.

Viral marketing

Before we analyze Radiohead's position within this system through *Meeting People is Easy*, we must take a brief detour to consider some recent marketing techniques executed by their by-no-means-apologetic handlers in the music industry – for Radiohead exists in a world of image marketing and spin that even The Beatles would be hard pressed to recognize *and* defuse through the pop song. The twenty-first century is an overlay of its previous incarnations, a feedback loop of feedback loops where control has penetrated into the brains and bodies of the global subject. Italian political theorist Antonio Negri and American academic Michael Hardt offer an important characterization of our new 'reality' in *Empire*; the work expands upon Michel Foucault's concept of 'biopolitics' – theorizing that current society is subject to 'biopolitical production' that works from the *inside* of the subject that has been colonized by a logic of power born partially from the success of the decolonization process. Explicit regulatory and disciplinary bodies established in the previous era of Modern sovereignty – whether manifest in the police, the family, the school, or the International War Crimes Court – now operate in concert with power mechanisms that have permeated into the global subject, so that power is not separate from its object, but is continually internalized, processed, articulated, and reduplicated in the life of each individual: 'Society, subsumed within a power that reaches down to the ganglia of the social structure and its processes of development reacts like a single body' (Hardt and Negri 2000: 24).

For Hardt and Negri, biopolitical power is one of the central aspects of 'Empire' – a transnational and suprapolitical regime that exerts itself through an unmediated (that is, a non-external mediation) connection to the multiplicity of global subjects. Furthermore, biopower collapses distinctions between superstructure and base so that production is integrated into the process at all stages. For our purposes, the economic production of the Radiohead system, typified in production, presentation, and consumption of product, can no longer be separated into constituent stages, leading to a system that Hardt and Negri identify as a field of life completely permeated by money:

> The great industrial and financial powers thus produce not only commodities but also subjectivities. They produce agentic subjectivities within the biopolitical context: they produce needs, social relations, bodies, and minds – which is to say, they produce producers. In the biopolitical sphere, life is made to work for production and production is made to work for life. (2000: 32)

While the complex arguments that Hardt and Negri deploy in suggesting resistance to Empire would also be impractical to synthesize in the space of this essay, we have taken up the concept of the biopolitical as completely invested in the life-production system to make a further distinction between global subjects that take productive control of humanity's merger with technology, *opposed* to the movement, in Empire, of a postmodernism that has consolidated itself through the manipulation of the market. Thus, Hardt and Negri proffer that a certain type of power exists in the virtual realm – championing circulation, exodus, and the intermingling of power flows, so that a counter-Empire 'multitude' 'can emerge as powerful and liberate themselves from a being that is invested hegemonically by capital and its institutions' (2000: 368). Assuming that the contradictions of Radiohead's project within its own careful articulations (as previously outlined) can be resolved in a manner that points toward even a limited mode of liberation, the action of the marketing machine – typified in its relation to Napster, Aimster, and most insidiously, the 'GooglyMinotaur' America Online Instant Messenger 'buddy' – works toward a continued dominance of the economic subject through the vectors of a product that is cast deliberately in the *image* of liberation.

Crucial to this industry project is the concept of viral marketing, the advertising culture buzzword of the late 1990s, exemplified by the proliferation of 'Hotmail.com' free e-mail accounts.[3] In *Web Marketing Today* from February 1 2000, Dr Ralph F. Wilson, an 'E-Commerce Consultant', outlines the basic schema of the viral process: it gives away what he deems as 'valuable' product, facilitates easy transfer to other economic subjects, multiplies in a way that allows the host servers to support the increased traffic, 'exploits' established user patterns, capitalizes on affinity networks of users, and finally, 'takes advantage' of existing resources that are separate from the virus. The latter principle, which proposes that websites promulgate the foreign virus so that the virus organization need not deplete its own resources, suggests the retro 'press release' model of business, where the original marketing message is carried, often as news content, by a plethora of respected entities that willingly incorporate it as legitimate 'content.'

The file-sharing service Napster, recently a site of considerable struggle between the record industry and artist copyright advocates such as Metallica and Dr Dre, has also played a valuable role in Radiohead's success. After the leak of the entire *Kid A* album to Napster three months before its release date, both die-hard Radiohead fans as well as the more casually curious listener could digest the 'weird, non-commercial album' without actually buying the music. Richard Menta (2000) observes that, paradoxically, the availability of *Kid A* on Napster did not dampen sales of the record, but propelled it to number one on the US album charts in its first week of release, beating 'the combined marketing efforts of Eminem, Madonna, Creed, *NSync and Britney herself.' Significantly, the record industry recoiled from crediting Napster because this would undermine its claim that the file-trading service infringes on copyright and 'gives' away the product (and thus, profit) that should 'rightfully' fall to the conglomerates. Menta correctly sees a more insidious telos of technological control:

> Big Music is not stupid. Many in the ranks see the promotional benefits Napster is having on them. At the very least, rising CD sales show it hasn't done anything to harm them. But what they don't like is an entity with such power that they don't control. Such an entity, they fear, can eventually undermine the profits that come with an oligopoly.

In the midst of the fall 2000 Napster lawsuits, Capitol Records struck a deal with the upstart Aimster file-sharing protocol in an attempt to control the flow of recorded music in a tentative manner. Designed to work with the America Online Instant Messenger application, although not officially sanctioned by AOL, Aimster advertises that the application 'allows you to be in control without complex overhead or controls. It can be as closed and private as you need' ('What is Aimster'). The deal provided a two-day 'window' in which Aimster was available with a 'skin' that presented a Radiohead-themed interface with an option directing users to a promotional website with a selection of Radiohead video files. Neither Aimster nor Capitol Records announced the promotion on their main websites, but the implication of the experiment, particularly in lieu of Napster's continued unauthorized *Kid A* trading, indicates the industry push to consolidate innovation and, of course, the successfully engendered 'desire' of innovation to embrace its would-be-legitimation with anxious arms. While the Capitol promotion provided tacit support to Aimster, and perhaps more generally to the larger cause of internet file trading, the smooth surface of corporate enterprise ensures that all initiative will eventually bow to its corporate masters.

Radiohead, for its part, has supported electronic distribution of its work toward the intermingling of market forces and nomadic interplay of power fluxes in line with the articulated, if contradictory, project of its political direction. The force of the multitude to instantly recognize and consume the music may be flattering to the band, but as viral methodologies increasingly indicate, the dialectic is no longer (and has never really been) a struggle between corporation and artist. Attali (1985) would locate the ease of electronic collection as a movement from the usage of music to the stockpiling of product – a harbinger of death signaled in the repetitive political economy of music. For Attali, collecting Radiohead cuts from Napster and amassing a collection no longer bounded by physical space or money (beyond the set-up and maintenance of computer networks) would allow the collector (or 'purchaser' or 'user') to 'freely' stockpile recorded material without deconstructing the system of product sales. In fact, this happened with *Kid A*'s Napster release, and as Attali writes in 1985:

> People will collect means for killing themselves ... just as they collect records, ... this sign will be the ultimate expression of a code of possession. It is inevitable, I

think, that this commercialization of death, represented in the commodity and stockpiled in the repetitive economy, will come to pass in the next thirty years. (1985: 126).

Nevertheless, Colin Greenwood tells the BBC's *Newsnight* program: 'We played in Barcelona and the next day the entire performance was up on Napster. Three weeks later when we got to play in Israel the audience knew the words to all the new songs and it was wonderful' (quoted in 'Radiohead take Aimster' 2000).

Napster does not weaken the recording industry, as Big Five rhetoric would have the consumer believe. This is but a ruse used to channel these new technologies into more easily controlled forms. Industry resistance to file-sharing networks assumes significance as a biopolitical mobilization of hegemonic control structures; as viral marketing, the attempt by Capitol (and the entire music industry) to authorize a particular service for Radiohead promotion, along with crediting (and presumably paying) that service for the privilege, establishes a regime in direct opposition to any counter-hegemonic possibility of the application. This tendency manifests in William Berquist's concept of postmodern capital organization (of which this Aimster/Capitol experimental virus is a symptom), characterized by the 'adoption of flexible structures and modes of interinstitutional cooperation to meet turbulent organizational and environmental conditions' (quoted in Hardt and Negri 2000: 152).

We are deliberately expanding Berquist's use of the 'institution' to represent not only the standalone instance of global capital involved in 'interinstitutional cooperation,' but also an interconnecting system of *many* organizations and industries that work like a physical World Wide Web for the production of life on a collective, internal level. The 'cooperation' uniting individual corporations in global-capital affinity groups is the exemplar of a virus that assumes control of *all* hosts. Future viral infections will be indistinguishable from the originating organism/company, which is no longer recognizable as such. As Radiohead seems to understand, the passage from conventional marketing to viral dissemination across virtual networks involves an internalization of the human–computer relationship. Yorke sings on 'Idioteque' from *Kid A*: 'Mobiles working / Mobiles chirping / Take the money and run / Take the money and run / Take the money ...'. 'Running' from the virus is also pointless. There is nowhere left to 'run,' due to the fact that 'legs' (along with 'hair' and 'arms' and 'pores') – all elements of the physical 'body' – have been radically trans-mogrified into data sets.

While the science-fiction connotation here is perhaps deliberate, it is not haphazard. The mini-website 'iBlip' that currently promotes *Amnesiac* and *I Might Be Wrong: Live Recordings* sets itself on the computer desktop as a smaller-than-normal browser window, seemingly disconnected from the 'main' content of the user. 'Friends' can host the 'iBlip' on their own website, or send the virus on to a 'friend' with the following pre-scripted e-mail message:

http://by.imedium.com/radiohead/amnesiac/76.html. Your friend has sent you the Radiohead iBlip, which gives you access to tons of Radiohead exclusives like music, video, a Radiohead desktop character, a Radiohead custom buddy that works in your instant messenger, postcards that arrive in the mail and much more. PASS THIS ON TO A RADIOHEAD FAN!

The apparent innocuousness of this viral marketing strategy, one that may coerce with bright colors, free material, and endlessly looped promotional beats from the two featured albums, breeds through a *voluntary* transference. Still, what proves most significant to the project of this virus is the Radiohead custom buddy, 'GooglyMinotaur,' an 'interactive agent' developed by Active Buddy, Inc., whose roster of like-minded Instant Messenger (IM) buddies also includes AgentBaseball, RingMessenger (for *Lord of the Rings* promotion), and LindsayBuddy to promote young 'singing sensation' Lindsay Pagano and her Warner Brothers debut album.[4] GooglyMinotaur, as an IM 'bot,' responds to real-language queries about its favorite band by providing consumers with instant access to sound-byte-sized 'information' on band matters. For instance, the query 'What is Jonny [Greenwood] like?' draws this instant response:

> **GooglyMinotaur:**   [jonny greenwood]
> personality
> key words: funny, erudite, impatient, splint, fringe
> other: hardly drinks. married. known as 'the dreamer' at school. likes
> buying clothes. wrote 'the tourist,' the final track on 'ok computer.'
> link: more jonny

Of course, GooglyMinotaur displays whatever answers are programmed to certain keyword questions – and the depth of information beyond teen-magazine press material, directions to purchase various Radiohead items, and an insipid Radiohead-themed hangman game, as one might expect, does not run very deep. (The jocular 'How does Thom feel about capitalism,' receives the reply 'I'm not sure if thom feel about capitalism' [*sic*].) Despite the banality of the interface, *Business Wire* reports that, as of November 19 2001, GooglyMinotaur had been added to 387,000 Instant Messaging buddy lists for a total of over 36 million messages (Entertainment Editors November 19 2001).[5]

The allure of this medium to Radiohead fans and other users is certainly conflated with the speed and efficiency of the device, but also, more significantly, the ability of users to perceive the information as 'personal.' After all, the 'conversation' occurs on a 'private' channel, and attendant to this fact the user exerts influence over the timing of the 'exchange.' Should the demanding boss walk in, the intimate fan/machine whisper can immediately be quieted. The concatenation of the remaining control mechanisms available to the IM user (as opposed to the commonplace invasions of other internet applications) provides, as with file sharing, an illusion of not only control-as-such, but also of an identity based upon false agency – allowing for communication to be *seemingly* conducted according to rules set by the participants, or at least codes that are 'universally' accepted.

This assumption could not be farther from the 'reality' of the Active Buddy situation. Stone (1997) argues that the 'Net Persona' evolves in such a way that fixed identity becomes illusory when the physical body is no longer a necessity of a transaction (either monetary or communicative), so that

> the Net persona is tacitly the real persona – when participants have become used to the idea that a Net identity cannot with absolute assurance be grounded in anything. So what we are observing is really a period of adjustment to unexpected consequences of innovation. (1997: 65).

For our purposes, any of GooglyMinotaur's hundreds of thousands of partners in 'communication,' of course, have recourse to the Net Persona anonymity of a screen name that need bear no resemblance to any 'real' name (or ethnicity, gender, or sex for that matter). While many users will no doubt interpret this relationship as one of 'freedom' in comparison to their other slavish net protocols, the dialectic is again illusory.

Even though AOL and other messaging platforms utilize screen names for users rather than the number identifiers of earlier systems such as ICQ, the potential for developing mass spamming programs is already inchoate along with the ability to translate user profiles into 'pure data' through the act of communication with a 'bot.' A July 28 2001 article in *The New York Times* warns of the 'control' that users must expend when confronted with unwanted IM messages:

> Even warnings on AOL's free service – the alerts that say, 'User "SexyGirl23" has sent you a message. Would you like to accept it?' – are a nuisance, according to John Carey, an adjunct professor at Columbia University's business school. He notes that some intrusions demand more than one answer to shut off. 'After the first I.M. window closes, a second one pops up saying, "You are not responding to SexyGirl23, is that correct?"' (Guernsey 2001)

It is not inconceivable that GooglyMinotaur's vapid 'hangman' game will eventually serve as an explicit data-collection device, or that all exchanges between 'real' IM users will become suspect after the physical body is completely effaced from the equation. Once all consumers are liquidated by their interaction with a specific IM buddy into a niche market number – gleefully and unknowingly updating their profile – 'who you are and where you come from', as Colin Greenwood once wrote, will no longer have anything to do with 'as you see fit.'

Furthermore, *Business Wire* reports that GooglyMinotaur's inception is not in conflict with Radiohead's other strategies, arguing that even before the release of *Kid A*, the band's official website would feature spontaneous recording and tour diary entries, and even the occasional unannounced streaming audiovisual performances of new material. With the creation of the Radiohead interactive agent, the band once again takes advantage of technology to enhance and expand its relationship with its fans.

Radiohead, we also learn, 'has long been one of the most proactive musical entities on the Web' (Entertainment Editors April 25 2001).

Here we see the erosion of control by the virus. This is not the generative aspect of biopower that Hardt and Negri locate in the possibilities of Empire, but the corruption of bodies that are beyond a physical measure, effaced into subroutines and potential data pits, transformed into an interface of binary numbers floating over the screens of the earth – the computer, the television, the retina. GooglyMinotaur, Aimster, and the 'iBlip' strategically invest the subject with the logic of internalized advertisement, personalized simply in the illusions of personalization, so that the private virtual mechanisms become colonized through the perpetuity of the 'private illusion.' If we all 'speak' to GooglyMinotaur, even simultaneously, it might be better, more personal – more 'real' – than retrieving our information from the same website no doubt cluttered by the likes of less-sophisticated Radiohead enthusiasts. Or, conversely, and according to form, our appreciation of the band's myriad 'proactive' resistance strategies might draw us away from the obvious banality of GooglyMinotaur, back into the viral labyrinth of 'real' Radiohead fandom. This corruption of personal choice through the nullification and constant transformation of a person into an economic subject, as Hardt and Negri discern, manifests 'in the perversion of the senses of linguistic communication. Here corruption touches on the biopolitical realm, attacking its productive nodes and obstructing its generative processes' (2000: 391). No matter where we point and click, the virus has eliminated the host.

Why not do your part and e-mail *that* message to a friend?

Pictures-of-cameras

The obvious argument is that this is all a bit counter-intuitive. After all, Radiohead is *just* a rock band (as the band often reminds us), not some sinister agent in a global conspiracy bent on partitioning its fans into economic subjects who exist only as data for the purpose of destabilizing the productive virtual possibilities that have arisen from globalization. The band's support of causes such as the Free Tibet campaign is well known and consistent. Surely, whatever viruses it carries must be better than the Britney Spears or Matchbox Twenty infection. Radiohead's strain may be *less explicitly virulent*, and the content of its art should be lauded for suggesting the space necessary to even discuss the possibility of resistance.

Finally, we are in a position to analyze some of Radiohead's production within this schema. This is not to make the band's work here clinical and completely academic. I listen to *Kid A* and *Amnesiac* voraciously (and to a lesser extent *OK Computer*), and often find myself 'watching' the music using the iTunes visual option on the PowerBook G4 generously loaned to me in my capacity as Assistant Professor of English by Lake Forest College. The irony of this activity (in light of this essay's discussion of virtuality and physical effacement) is not lost on me. I also remain somewhat unconvinced that what cheapens Radiohead's output is the wealth of quality music that eschews any sort of major label miscegenation. The argument that only the truly 'independent' artist speaks in our society remains naive in its assessment of any work as independent of marketplace concerns (or, more theoretically, biopolitical mechanisms), and also plays into a system of privilege and musical snobbery that makes product available only to a certain segment of the population (those with money, computers, access to 'authentic' channels, etc.).

Because there is no clear division between the corporate and the independent, a seemingly productive avenue for discerning resistance might lie in analyzing the prevalent modalities that defy the false binary and embrace the current global situation. This doesn't suggest that paying outrageous amounts of money to watch Bono and U2 prance under a giant lemon or shelling out 'filthy lucre' for the Sex Pistols reunion are viable solutions either. That brand of corporate rock is effective by virtue of its willingness to apply postmodern disruption strategies that defy binary schemas across new virtual networks so that difference can be convincingly collapsed toward *control of the 'rebel'-consumer-as-such*. This process, when located in products that not only eschew the corporate/independent binary dialectic but also revel in an articulation of liminal positioning that is fundamentally viral in approach, encourages a more insidious type of resistance that (in pixilated brilliance) channels the desire of the audience into greater modes of corporate complicity that appear – to the desiring mass – as greater modes of liberatory practice. Elsewhere I have called this strategy pictures-of-cameras, or 'POC': falsely disruptive image-gathering complexes that function with false agency.[6]

A 'camera' is placed in the hands of the user who, charged with notions of rebellion, invests the device with all of her desires. These desires are transmuted by the mechanisms that authorize the 'camera' into pure data, into just another picture of the economic subject collected in the digital flash pan. An illusion of renewed purpose and resistance masks the rapidly disintegrating physical body on which the control film and the contortions of the system are projected, erasing a limb here, installing a telescoping lens there, until the 'machine' against which we struggle has evolved into its next incarnation. It is important to note the ineluctable opacity of the entire process, and a brief look at Grant Gee's *Meeting People is Easy*, a tour film that straddles both the corporate machine and Radiohead's 'struggle' against that machine, offers a final point in our Radiohead analysis, a tentative identification of pictures-as-cameras.

The documentary focuses on the post-*OK Computer* media frenzy, and Gee's version of Radiohead (and by now it should be clear that we can only perceive versions or mutations) plays just this sort of false agency game with the analytical tendencies of the viewer who is no doubt already inaugurated into Radiohead's world of paranoia and press overkill. The film deploys the now familiar tropes of the commercial postmodern sensibility, enacted perhaps in the interest of 'resistance,' but popularized and endlessly packaged to the extent that Gee's jittery camera angles and nervous cuts deliberately call attention to their own use. Clarke's description of Gee's techniques (in *Radiohead: Hysterical and Useless*) feeds into the critique the film ostensibly offers: 'The film is in keeping with Radiohead's distinctive imagery as a band, chatting backstage in Barcelona, are viewed as an information over-load of text as newsprint scrolls down the screen' [*sic*] (Clarke 2000: 140). The difference between product and advertisement is effaced by more than the phrase 'You are a target market' emblazoned on the DVD cover. Provocatively, Gee's film points to the further elimination of distinction through the 'postmodern' quality of the edit, the ubiquity of the postmodern devices, as well as the rock press's incessant desire to locate Radiohead as 'edgy.'

The most compelling illusion of the early film is Radiohead's 'legendary' headlining gig at the Glastonbury Festival on June 28 1997. After numerous technical difficulties, Yorke calls out, 'Can you turn up the lights so we can see the people? 'cause we haven't seen them yet,' illuminating 40,000 people who are in a sort of supernatural thrall with the band, seemingly unaware of the technical problems. By most press accounts, this moment is a triumph for Radiohead. Clarke mimics the band's enthusiasm: 'It was clear that those present had seen a performance that would go down in rock history' (2000: 132); Randall does the same: 'What [Yorke] heard was the ardent roar of countless thousands … . For many of those in the crowd, it was a moment never to be forgotten' (2000: 246).

After this illumination, Gee begins to work his 'magic'; he edits a seamless transition from the lights hitting the audience at Glastonbury to show 34 of the tour, in Philadelphia on August 24 1997, where the band launches into an audience singalong rendition of 'Creep.' This *version* of Radiohead revels in this transcendent concert moment, which for the *Meeting People is Easy* viewer becomes an addendum that is unrecognizable as separate from the Glastonbury epiphany. Gee attempts to portray the band at its least self-conscious via this device. It *is* playing the 'pop' song that made it famous, a derivative piece of music that highlights the distance the band has traveled from that early subservience to the voracious appetite of the corporate machine. After Yorke, in the second verse, sings 'Whatever makes you happy,' a disembodied voice from the crowd yells back, 'You make me happy, Thom!' When Yorke reaches the line 'I wish I was special,' a voice responds with, 'You *are* special Thom!' Gee portrays this Glastonbury/Philadelphia symbiosis as the apotheosis of our heroes, the now artificially protracted Glastonbury moment that critics and band alike cite as exemplary of the whole 'insane' period, a high-water mark of that the great refusal, the eternal 'no' that scuttles power structures. The Philadelphia fans, linked with the epiphany of Glastonbury, now appear to recognize the inanity of 'Creep,' as a filmic triad of band, audience, and camera unite in the ironic deconstruction of the song's old political economy. Attali astutely notes that 'one participates in a pop music festival only to be totally reduced to the role of an extra in the record or film that finances it' (1985: 137), yet here the corporate financing structure is seemingly turned by Gee's edit back on itself, reversed like the negative of a 'fitter and happier' picture, stripped of all marketplace influence and returned to the primal realm of liberatory 'art.' For pictures-of-cameras to function in the postironic mode, these moments are meant to be simultaneously transcendent and false. Gee wants the audience to know that 'Creep,' and to a greater extent Glastonbury(-cum-Philadelphia), remain bound by the creativity that he uses in exposing the artifice. A meta-discourse of these staged and stylized moments creates the first condition of the POC: the recognition (often through the edit) that this sort of Glastonbury/Philadelphia transcendence is illusory.

The viewer is then forced to recognize a possible escape from the system. Gee can execute this function in keeping with Radiohead's 'distinctive imagery' while utilizing his position as director of the band's 'No Surprises' video (from *OK Computer*). In the music video, Gee's camera trains itself to the anguished Yorke's face, recalling one of Ingmar Bergman's close-ups from *The Seventh Seal*. Yorke's face is in a diving helmet, mouthing his paean to suburban reduplication as water rises from the bottom of the screen toward his mouth and nose. After the repetition of the word 'silence,' the water rises to cover his face, and Yorke, imbued with the Herculean strength characteristic of Gee's antihero, holds his breath for over a minute.

Part of Gee's project in *Meeting People is Easy* is to document the media circus following the *OK Computer* tour, as Radiohead 'find themselves in the strange/insane/seductive world of end-of-the-century celebrity, with thousands of cameras and microphones constantly siphoning little bits off them' (quoted in Clarke 2000: 140). Significantly, Gee exposes his own siphoning procedures as 'music video director' in a segment of the tour film detailing the making of the 'No Surprises' video. In this sequence, the viewer learns how Yorke struggled through multiple takes for the water shot, releasing the liquid from a pull-tab near his neck when he needed to breathe, and looking more and more exasperated each time. This reappropriation of the 'reality' behind the illusion of the 'No Surprises' video – couched as it is within the matrix of media performativity that distorts all reality for the band and, thus, the sympathetic viewer – establishes a tertiary level of representation beyond the official auspices of the media and the interface between Radiohead and its fans. In this new realm of pictures-as-cameras, the inability to resist is recognized as a construct that is analogous to the transcendent rock moment.

To derealize the postmodern spectacle (that of the music video) into some more essential 'reality,' Gee directs *Meeting People is Easy*, which clearly articulates Radiohead's disdain for the music industry and reveals the same artificiality (born partially from the camera techniques) at work in the tour film. For Gee, Yorke trained himself to hold his breath as a way of making all the unpleasantness of producing videos for the industry (of the 'contradiction' between music and money) disappear into the underwater silence. Gee, by pulling away the layer of artifice that his own 'No Surprises' video imposed on the unwitting consumer (just as Yorke executes the pull-tab) reveals that the fundamental question of resistance is not the rationale for radical action, but who or what constitutes the target within a matrix of complete corporate instrumentality. If Gee's music video (calculated by the industry to sell Radiohead records) can be deconstructed in *Meeting People is Easy* (as an apparent critique of the same industry), the revelation follows that the video now serves as a guerilla product made for the specific purpose of deconstructing the mechanisms of control in a manner that bestows 'control' on the viewer who consumes the tour film. The transcendent 'real' moment at Glastonbury is a cliché of the rock press and the camera for Gee; it cannot be trusted. So why not create complicity with the machine so that the disassembly of corporate product becomes a matter of performing the 'real' for the already cynical fan?

The pictures-as-cameras move from the distrust of transcendence *to the authenticity of controlled deconstruction*. The latter is no longer suspect, because if everything is a fabrication, the virus of collaboration must inhabit all participants in the system of image control (including Gee and Radiohead). Hardt and Negri observe the difficulty of categorically pinpointing the 'enemy': 'We are immersed in a system of power so deep and complex that, ... we do not know where to locate the production of oppression. And yet we still resist and struggle' (2000: 211). The POC capitalizes on this epiphany of collective complicity to transport the 'struggle' into the biopolitical realm of internal control. The enemy is not 'us' or 'them,' but the symbiotic mutation of all entities. Gee's version of Yorke, exasperated again by the press:

> I could give the demise of so many recording artists. Suddenly people start giving you cash as well. Soon you've got money and you get used to this lifestyle and you don't want to take any risks 'cause they've got you by the balls.

This second property of the POC is to require the destruction of the self (and the industry) that functions as a location for the viral replication of the commodity. Everything is suspect. The industry can't be trusted, but perhaps Gee's Radiohead, willing to indict itself as corporate flunky, can provide escape through its position as socially (and self) aware record industry subject.

Nowhere is this impulse to resist the media machine more metaphorically demonstrated than in one of Gee's central geographical images – New York City. Radiohead visits the Big Apple several times in the film and is even heckled outside a Manhattan club. In one memorable sequence following images of Thom in a lonely hotel room, Gee's camera gazes through another apparent hotel window at the Empire State Building. A sticker with the words 'I am not here and this is not really happening' adheres to the window, and as Gee's camera switches our view of the building from a variety of angles and distances around the city, the sticker vanishes and a flying insect crawls across the pane. The bug and building shift in and out of focus, superimposed and faded on different parts of the screen; the sticker appears again briefly at the end of the segment, and the three elements echo that earlier triad of representation: the band in the sticker, the city in the building, and the 'probing insect intelligence' of the music business in the fly. The enemy appears only by triangulation through Gee's constantly shifting window 'screens,' and we know from his filmic manipulations that the sticker might be nothing more than a piece of paper superimposed on a lens, the Empire State Building could be derived from a picture book or old movie, and the insect, that exemplar of the music business, which like Beelzebub sets these evil events in motion, might be nothing more than a construct of the consumer, perhaps not a fly at all anymore, but a projection of a bug lost somewhere else, already dead and reborn on the crest of the rising genetic tide. Still, the illusion of resistance is in the least pliable of the objects. The POC, after identifying the falseness of the transcendent rock moment, establishing the viral reduplication of an enemy that has infiltrated the cells, and suggesting that 'authenticity' might be born from creating and deconstructing the virus within each of us, now suggests a more dire quality of replication. Smash the bug and the building might fall; action, deconstruction, and resistance must only be taken within the scope of response that appears liberatory, but still allows the virus to continue its mutation.

    In the final moments of *Meeting People is Easy*, after another performance in New York City, one of the silhouetted band members says, 'Well we fucked that up,' as the group enters the backstage room. Busily snapping away, a man with a camera, an image of that false agency, that tired old cliché of the rock press, is told by an unidentified voice, 'Hey chap. I mean, camera chap, I think you should stop now … I think it's the end.' Gee's sound and picture track snaps to black as the word 'End' settles into the bottom middle of the screen. Moments later, of course, the picture returns in a new scene (under the scrolling credits) for one final live rendition of 'Exit Music' – so that the legion of fans cans be assured that Radiohead's struggle with the corporate enemy will never end. Yorke sings passionately, 'We hope that you choke, that you choke …' Yes, this may be false transcendence, but it's all that's available right now, and somehow, because Gee's Radiohead is always deconstructing its own complicity in the recording-industry system, this final song is also a healthy bit of auto-destructive rock energy. The 'you' that will 'choke' perhaps represents both the recording industry that authorizes the replication of the Radiohead phenomenon, as well as the band itself that is complicit in the process. Gee makes it abundantly clear that everyone is in danger of choking. Everyone feels her lungs fill up with liquid, and *yes, it is difficult to hold one's breath for very long.* Yet Thom does it, Gee does it, and the viewer can do it too ...

The pictures-of-cameras have channeled resistance away from the physical body of the potentially rebellious multitude, and into the virtual body of the alienated, differentiated consumer. This arrangement is entirely comfortable in its discomfort for the music industry and the other mundane suburban vectors that require a certain type of 'resistance' to eventually replicate the economic bourgeois class of a bodiless, virtually communicative populace.

So we've come to the conclusion of the essay, where I, the dutiful cultural studies academic, resolve these problems of over-coding, of viruses, of physical bodies eliminated by the insidious pictures-of-cameras regime that authorizes corporate control of global flows in spite of its own snarling, apparent refusals. So, to be fair, Radiohead is no different in the improbability of this rebellion thus far than any of its peers. The band invites a 'higher' level of discussion due to the explicit content of its work, and the intriguing music from *Kid A* and *Amnesiac* to the present in ambient tracks such as 'Kid A' and 'Pulk/Pull Revolving Doors.' Perhaps the obvious hope is that Radiohead's articulation of these issues points toward a praxis that might establish a resistance strategy worthy of its intent.

Yet perhaps, as Frank remarks, academic resolutions follow their own pattern:

> For years the culture industry has held up for our admiration an unending parade of such self-proclaimed subverters of middle-class tastes, and certain scholars have only been too glad to play their part in this strange charade, studying the minutiae of the various artists' rock videos and deciding, after long and careful deliberation, that yes, each one is, in fact, a bona fide subversive. (Frank 1997: 154)

Perhaps Frank is right and it will be easy enough for us to make the case that the virtual multitude have a basic right to reappropriate their relation to the control machine. Perhaps everything is just fine. Just pretend, as Yorke suggests in 'How to Disappear Completely,' that *you are not here and this isn't really happening.*

I've done my part already; all you have to do is sing on after the closing credits.

Notes

1. Two proposed mergers, first with Time Warner in late 2000 and then with BMG in early 2001, were scuttled by regulatory concerns about further consolidation of the oligopoly. In the wake of EMI's divestiture from the Thorn company in 1996, Eric Nicoli was brought in as chairman of EMI in 1999 to find a partner for the standalone company. While EMI and its erstwhile partners were unwilling, or unable, to sell the larger assets that would have been necessary to receive regulatory approval, EMI remains an attractive steak to a media conglomerate salivating for a cut of the music industry.

2. Radiohead recognizes that this dialectic between 'independence' from an explicit corporate 'sell-out' machine and the staccato swipe of the credit card remains hopelessly synergistic. In the typical rock press-style book *Exit Music: The Radiohead Story*, Ed O'Brien defends the band's practice of 'total' recording control as a way to minimize the fair to middling fluxes of the pop world: 'The record company's got you. If a band has a successful album and then they start making records that don't sell, that's when they've really got you, because they've given you this taste of what it can be like, and they're like, "Now you're not selling, we're going to tell you what to do." It would be scary if that happened' (Randall 2000: 240).

3. The concept is relatively simple, and perhaps loosely analogous to 'word of mouth' advertising. Hotmail offers free e-mail accounts with a self-advertising tag at the bottom of every free message which encourages every recipient to follow suit, presumably signing up for a free account and, like the exponential reproduction of a virus, spreading the Hotmail gospel across the endless interweaving corridors of the internet. Bombardments of banner ads and frame windows, advertising offshore gambling, sex lines, and DVDs, are the 'price' users must pay for their free service when using the Hotmail-style interfaces, and in conjunction with the spam that eventually infiltrates each account, these viral initiatives piggyback on their brethren, derealizing the host beyond even the inured familiarity of an original mutation.

4. I was uncertain how to initially access these various buddies without going to the Active Buddy website. A colleague's ten-year-old daughter, Ruth Perret-Goluboff, had easily memorized all of the buddy names, and quickly added them to my IM buddy list.

5. Significantly, the success of GooglyMinotaur has helped Active Buddy push its service as a promotion device for all types of information at all levels of cultural awareness. Lindsay Pagano may be relatively unknown, but certainly, 'her' IM bot, along with the requisite videos, saccharine singles, and other media promotions, can easily 'rectify' that situation.

6. See my forthcoming essay, 'Cell my Last Words Everywhere: Filmic Fiction in Leni Riefenstahl, Jean Genet, and William S. Burroughs,' in *Literary Modernism and Photography* from Greenwood Press.

Chapter 3

The Aura of Authenticity: Perceptions of Honesty, Sincerity, and Truth in 'Creep' and 'Kid A'[1]

Carys Wyn Jones

> The real problem I had was with the 'identify' bit ... Even now, most interviews you do, there's a constant subtext: 'Is this you?'
>
> Thom Yorke (quoted in Reynolds 2001: 32)

Music asks its own questions of truth, and the criteria by which we judge it are loaded with assumptions and ideologies. One of the most debated words used in this discourse is 'authenticity.' Authenticity in art music usually denotes a branch of musicology (and its effects) that attempts to faithfully recreate the music of centuries past. As such, it has the luxury of a clear, but ultimately illusory, object to which to be authentic. For popular music, this is only a minor implication of the word, partly as recording technology has left us with artefacts that represent (and in some cases are the same as) the original object, and also because the oldest music of this type is only decades, rather than centuries, old. Instead, the authentic is situated in intent, affect and effect, and through questions of sincerity, integrity, truth, and achievement. Such authenticity is always contingent and the constellations of meanings signified by authenticity are highly contested.

Radiohead is interesting from this perspective as it is generally perceived as occupying the oxymoronic position of possessing mainstream integrity, although this in itself immediately makes it an obvious target for criticism. The purpose of this study is to use concepts of authenticity to analyze the music of Radiohead, but also, conversely, to use Radiohead as a tool for understanding authenticity. Given the large number of parameters on which notions of authenticity operate, I have decided to limit this study as much as possible to readings of just two songs, which carry rather different markers of authenticity. 'Creep' (first released as a single in the UK in September 1992 and rereleased far more successfully in September 1993) was responsible for drawing in a great many fans. 'Kid A' (the second track on the 2000 album of the same name, from which no singles were released) is a fairly typical song from an album that allegedly lost the band many of its fans, but was also roundly defended by others. I shall use these two songs to explore how certain usage of words, voice, music, and performance give Radiohead the redolence of authenticity that its fans and also often the press ascribe to it, before situating these readings in existing models of authenticity in popular music proposed by Grossberg, Fornäs, and Moore.

Perhaps the clearest (and most useful) definition of authenticity in this context is that given by Fornäs, as the idea that the authentic is 'the genuine or the honest expression of a subject' (Fornäs 1995a: 99). However, my usage of the term in this study also recognizes Moore's assertion (2002: 209–25) that authenticity can be, and is, used as a synonym for 'real, honest, truthful, with integrity, actual, genuine, essential [and] sincere,' and in so doing I am dissolving some of the difference and distance that Mazullo (following Trilling) places between sincerity and authenticity (Mazullo 1999: 3–7).

Authenticity spins a tangled, sticky, and rather fragile web through general discourses on popular music.[2] The most common use for which the concept is employed in popular music is in matters of value judgment made when a central role is given to the singer/songwriter. In this, the nineteenth-century ideal of the artist, as described by Trilling (in his study of sincerity and authenticity), is pivotal:

> What the audience demands of the artist – really demands, in its unconscious desire – and what the artist thinks it ought to be given … [is] the same thing: … the sentiment of being. The sentiment of being is the sentiment of being strong … such energy as contrives that the centre shall hold, that the circumference of the self keep unbroken, that the person be an integer, impenetrable, perdurable, and autonomous in being if not in action. (Trilling 1972: 99)

Trilling further suggests that the characteristics of the sentiment of being are 'self-sufficiency, self-definition and sincerity.'

The crux of the matter rests on what is considered to be the greatest asset of popular music, which is its strength and immediacy of emotion. As Gracyk succinctly puts it, 'No emotion is beyond the pale. But faked emotion is' (Gracyk 1996: 224). This suggests a concept of authenticity that demands a singer who writes and performs her own songs about her own emotions and experiences in an honest and sincere manner. However, this very simple model immediately encounters problems when applied to actual songs.

The case of 'Creep': words, music, voice, and performance

Music expresses something, something very human. It does not, however, incorporate a readily discernible and universal set of relational meanings, and therefore, as a means of communication, is somewhat vague at best. However, most songs (almost by definition) have words, and so this would seem to be the most logical place to start an investigation of the sincerity of a song.

'Creep' (*Pablo Honey*, 1993)[3]

1. When you were here before,
    Couldn't look you in the eye,
    You're just like an angel,
    Your skin makes me cry,
    You float like a feather,
    In a beautiful world,
    [And] I wish I was special,
    You're so fucking special
    [chorus] But I'm a creep, I'm a weirdo,
    What the hell am I doing here?
    I don't belong here.

2. I don't care if it hurts,
    I want to have control,
    I want a perfect body,
    I want a perfect soul,
    I want you to notice,
    When I'm not around,
    You're so fucking special,
    I wish I was special.
    [repeat chorus]

3. She's running out again,
    She's running out …

4. Whatever makes you happy,
    Whatever you want,
    You're so fucking special,
    I wish I was special …
    But I'm a creep,
    I'm a weirdo,
    What the hell am I doing here?
    I don't belong here,
    I don't belong here.

In this state of artificial detachment from both singer and music, it is clear that we have no means of knowing for certain if these words are an account of the author's experiences. However, to some extent the sincerity of the words might be gauged in terms of their overall coherence. Accordingly, nothing in the lyrics of 'Creep' seems explicitly contradictory, and so it is reasonable to assert that, on this level at least, no overt deception is evident.

Most song lyrics are, of course, written in the first person, giving an immediate impression of being the sentiments of the singer. The presence of a second-person character, provided it is not an oblique reference to the self, strengthens the individualism of the singer by introducing a clear boundary between the self and others. The moment in which the second-person character is transformed into the third person shifts the perspective (and perhaps complicates the internal coherence of the song a little), but only serves to compound the autonomy of the singer.

Although the veracity of the narrative created is uncertain, certain words help to connect the singer to lived experience. The lyrics contain corporal manifestations ('eye,' 'skin,' 'cry,' 'hurts,' and 'body'), and also emotional signifiers ('happy,' 'wish,' 'want,' 'hurts,' 'control,' and 'soul') which all testify to the experience of the author. The strength of feeling is exacerbated by the use of swearing ('fucking' and 'hell'), although the presence of such language also has the secondary function of simply being appealing to its intended audience. However, the abstraction of these lyrics from the voice and music changes their nature, and therefore it is necessary to restore them to their natural environment in order to support and augment these readings of sincerity and honesty.

Song words are articulated both through a melody and a voice. Both of these give the words resonance and power, but can also contradict the apparent meanings of the lyrics, and so it is necessary for all the elements of a song to cohere in order to convey the impression of candor (although such coherence can also simply be a criterion for positive value judgment as a separate issue to that of authenticity). The voice is especially important, as the instrument of most direct expression, and it must carry signifiers of authenticity in order to be accepted as sincere.

To sound like yourself, you need to *not* sound like anyone else. A unique, autonomous artist must have a correspondingly singular voice. Frith suggests that it is possible to 'identify with a song whether we understand the words or not, whether we already know the singer or not, because it is the voice – not the lyrics – to which we immediately respond' (Frith 1987: 145). But a singing voice is always constructed, as the necessity of manipulating the pitch of the voice renders it the focus of exceptional attention. In this sense, there is no such thing as a 'natural' singing voice.

Although this song is responsible for Radiohead's early success, Thom Yorke's voice is rather less distinctive on 'Creep' than on later songs, with shades of an American accent on lines such as 'I don't belong here'. This could be read as a result of absorbing American pop music in his youth, as a deliberate reference to the grunge music that proliferated around this time or even as a subtly sarcastic spin on the lyrics. Conversely, there is no denying that even at this stage it has a certain quality to it that is unique to Thom Yorke. Beyond the assumed individuality of the voice, however, methods of expression necessarily tend to be more universal, as particular emotions must be codified in order to be understood by others.

The timbre of the voice on 'Creep' is rather flat, but it is the flatness of deadened emotion rather than that of un-involvement. A more assertive voice would contradict and falsify the emotional power of the words, and so deflated cynicism is here a marker of truth (if not sincerity, which is a word a little at odds with cynicism, although even the most negative of sentiments can be sincerely intended). 'Fucking special' is perhaps given more emphasis than the surrounding words, but not so much that it gives the phrase an overtly sarcastic spin that would undermine the integrity of the singer's emotions. This is not to say that the potential for sarcasm is not latent in the song, as will be explored later, and the room left for cross-reading of the song would very much depend on the site of reception. However, the most notable exception to the flat delivery style occurs during the third section, when the voice rises to cry out the words 'She's running out …'. The force, volume and somewhat open quality of the voice at this point is exceptional within the context of the song, giving credence to Frith's assertion that it is the voice, rather than words, that really conveys emotion. Although 'She runs, runs, runs, runs, runs, runs' is not a profound statement, the emotional impact of the voice renders the line engaging. This burst of emotion corresponds with the shift to the third person, and thus the strongest emotion only emerges when the singer takes a rest from self-deprecation. After this point, the voice is cracked and weary, again supporting both the words and the perception that a real emotional investment has been made in the song by its singer.

The agreement of lyrics and voice is compounded by the music. A simple four-bar, 4/4 chord progression 'I/III/IV/iv' (G/B/C/c) is repeated endlessly during the course of the song, reflecting the talking-in-circles narrative.[4] Equally, the low self-esteem expressed in the words is corroborated by the relatively weak chord structure of 'I/III/IV/iv' as opposed to employing a more conventional or stronger sequence such as 'I/III/IV/V.' The weak 'iv' chord coincides with the particularly baleful lyrical constructions of 'your skin makes me cry,' 'you're so fucking special,' 'I don't belong here,' and 'I want a perfect soul,' but also, more importantly, concurs with the emotional release after the last scream of the third section.

Similar to the need for a voice to be unique is the demand for originality often bound up with notions of authenticity. Each song should be an expression of a singular self. The similarity of chord sequence between 'Creep' and the Hollies song 'The Air that I Breathe' is usually mentioned as a case against originality, and often, by extension, authenticity. But other features can redeem its singularity, such as the second 'voice' provided by the lead guitar of Jonny Greenwood. Pairs of crunched chords give momentum to the chorus, and the guitar gives melodic support to the high emotion of the third section; but the guitar does not contradict or overwhelm the main voice. For an emotion to be deemed sincere in this context, it is essential that all the musical elements are in affective agreement.

With such markers of sincerity as these, the recording process must not be perceived to be putting any aural barriers between the performer and the listener, and the song has a sound quality redolent of live performance (helped in the case of 'Creep' by slightly uneven rhythms). Perceptions of truthfulness would demand that the singer's voice and emotions are her own to recreate, and so live performance is an essential tool in providing proof of the artist's integrity; it also carries with it another range of signifiers of sincerity.

'Strong emotion evinced in performance testifies to the extremity of prior experience on which both the song and performance are based' (Bloomfield 1993: 17). The honesty of a performer is calculated in the amount of effort, range of body language, and general appearance displayed by the singer. Live performances of 'Creep' are recorded on two of the three 'official' Radiohead films. The first of these, *Radiohead: Live at the Astoria*, is an apparently straightforward account of a live performance recorded on May 24 1995, and contains many indicators of emotional effort (or at least the appearance of pain). Wearing what appear to be his everyday clothes, jeans and a long-sleeved T-shirt, Thom Yorke shuts his eyes in concentration, clutches the microphone stand and reacts to the lead guitar entry as if it is sending electric shocks through his body, causing him to recoil. The whole of the second verse is rendered with his body doubled up as if nursing a kicked stomach, and the effort that goes into the soaring 'She's running ...' section is unmistakable, as he takes huge gulps of air and belts out the line, arm outstretched and hand shaking. The next few lines see him doubled up once more, his voice reduced to a barely audible whisper, his hunched figure silhouetted against harsh white light and his face bowed low in defeat. There is little here to undermine the overall statements of the song.

Recorded two years later, in 1997, *Meeting People is Easy* presents a rather different picture. This film is a montage of footage of the band shot over the course of a year, following the release of the album *OK Computer*. Filmed and edited by Grant Gee, *Meeting People is Easy* is a highly atmospheric and fragmentary account of the band that uses a variety of different film techniques to capture live performance, backstage conversations, press interviews, hotel rooms, and a stream of different cities (usually seen through tour bus or hotel windows). Radiohead's music features as background sound for the most part, but 'Creep' is exceptional in that it is afforded footage of two live performances, and both show Thom Yorke visibly detached from the emotion of the song. In the first clip (sur-titled 'Show 34 – Philadelphia – 24.8.97'), the performance is joined at the beginning of the second verse, and Yorke is not even singing. He appears to be chewing on something, then turns his back on the audience. After a few moments, he turns back to face them, and, with an apathetic shrug, holds out his microphone to the audience, who proceed to sing. At this, Yorke's face contorts into a wry and obstinate grin, and he seems to acknowledge someone in the audience, before eventually picking up the song again at the second chorus and (ignoring the guitar entry, although the lighting effects do not) then building up to a harrowing rendition of the third section. The melody at this point is in such a high register and the sound so open (particularly the vowel sound of 'run'), that it demands effort and engagement in order to be performed at all. However, once he has returned to the lower register of the final section, his voice is dripping with sarcasm and atypically hoarse, and he stands quite normally, not doubled up, but backing away from the crowd, in the direction of the drum kit.

In the other clip of 'Creep' on *Meeting People is Easy*, the camera approaches from a lobby, and travels up the corridor, passing under a *défense de fumer* sign, to find Thom Yorke a distant figure silhouetted against harsh white stage lighting, just visible over the heads of the audience. He is rounding off the end of the first chorus, in a manner apparently similar to that of the performance at the Astoria. However, as he launches into the second verse, his personal distance from the song is thrown into sharp relief as the lights change, making his features visible. Rather than displaying the emotions suggested by the song, he is performing a series of mimes, clutching his fist, displaying his biceps, thumping his heart, pointing at the crowd, and doing muscleman poses to the guitar interjections. Clearly Yorke does not mean what he is singing. But do we conclude from this that he is therefore insincere (and, by these criteria, inauthentic), or consider that what might once have been an expression of self is no longer applicable? If a subject can change, then so too (perhaps) can markers of authenticity.

The case of 'Kid A': words, music, voice, and performance

'Kid A' (*Kid A*, 2000)[5]

1. I slip away
    I slipped on a little white lie

2. We got heads on sticks
    You got ventriloquists
    We got heads on sticks
    You got ventriloquists

3. Standing in the shadows at the end of my bed
    Standing in the shadows at the end of my bed
    Standing in the shadows at the end of my bed
    Standing in the shadows at the end of my bed

4. The rats and children follow me out of town
    The rats and children follow me out of town
    Come on Kids

As with 'Creep,' it is fundamentally impossible to know if unadorned lyrics are expressions of lived experience. However, in the case of 'Kid A,' this becomes almost irrelevant. Although a subject presents itself in the first section, it is already slipping away. Without a context, the little white lie could be a sign of corruption or remorseful confession. However, the words of the second section (with their heads on sticks and ventriloquists) suggest that this is either not entirely serious or the meanings are rather heavily codified; neither approach is especially compatible with the notions of authenticity generated by 'Creep.'

It is quite difficult to know what to make of these lyrics, and it seems unlikely that restoring them to their vocal and musical setting will necessarily reveal them to make much more sense than they do as bare poetry. The ventriloquists, bedroom shadows and Pied Piper references cautiously suggest images of a nightmare childhood. However, it is very hard to locate the position of the singer, slipping away, holding heads on sticks, in a bed or at the end of it, and leading the small folk out of town. It has a certain inner coherence, but one that relies somewhat on incoherence. The music augments the childhood themes of the words with simple chiming keyboards and the chirping of computers on an alien adventure, however this is cut through by a driving and disjointed drum machine and blocks of ambient sound. If the voice is thought to be the most humanizing element of a song, then by this measure 'Kid A' is almost inhuman. While it is still recognizably Thom Yorke's voice, the vocal line on 'Kid A' has been fed through a synthesizer (vocoder) rendering it utterly emotionless and detached. The treatment of the voice makes it sometimes dull and sometimes rasping. However, it also makes the words virtually indecipherable. Some words stand out, especially 'We got heads on sticks,' but it is more the quality of sound produced by the words, rather than their meanings, that seems to be important here. This can either be interpreted as an act of disowning the lyrics of the song (and by earlier criteria rendering them insincere), or as an attempt to convey a very different emotion, one that is impossible to express through previously used styles. In his book *Cultural Theory and Late Modernity*, Johan Fornäs proposes a notion of authenticity that can be employed in this context to account in some measure for the continued perception of Radiohead's music as being an honest expression of emotion.

> Only a reflecting subject can be made 're-sponsible' for what she says and does ... An adult individual can form expression with more sophisticated means than cries and screams, in other languages than the mother tongue and in more genres than those inherited from childhood. The appropriation of foreign tongues and styles is often a crucial means to express deep inner states better than is possible with the tools inherited from childhood or the parental culture. Secondary socialization is not only an outward progression to widening competences, but also a striving to integrate and develop the contradictory unconscious sides of one's subjectivity. Its tools may well be extremely modern and artificially constructed, as long as they manage to connect to the inner subjectivity in question. (Fornäs 1995b: 275)

This would appear to be the case in 'Kid A,' which imbues emotion, but it is an abstract emotion, feelings at arm's length. If the guitar-band sound of 'Creep' is taken to be the mother tongue, then use of synthesizers, computer-generated noise and garbled, fragmentary words is an act of secondary socialization, and thus an attempt to describe a different side of the self to that expressed in 'Creep.'

'Kid A' fails by many measures of authenticity described during the discussion of 'Creep' above. The lyrics are (hopefully) not taken from actual, corporal experience; a strong, autonomous subject is not created during its course; no physical effort is heard in the voice, nor any extremes of emotion portrayed through the melody; Yorke's unique voice has been treated to the extent that it is barely recognizable; live performance seems out of the question.[6] Yet, if the measure of authenticity is to be understood as the extent to which a song is an honest expression of the artist's self, 'Kid A' could be seen to succeed far more than 'Creep,' operating on a far more complex and reflexive plane.

To say that we cannot know, only guess, the honesty of a singer as has thus far been suggested is fundamentally but not completely true. Most highly successful singers are also celebrities who construct subjectivities not simply though their music but also through mass media. If we wish to be satisfied that a song is autobiographical, we often need only consult a magazine, switch on the television or log on to the internet. This pushes the boundaries of required coherence even further, as a song must now be authentic in its own right, in the context of the album, in the context of other music, and in the context of its creator, whose life may well be described in a series of paperback biographies in your local bookshop.

Acts of observation change the object under observation. The aura that has built up around Thom Yorke, partly through his music but mainly through the mass media, has been formed through combination of his vocal personality, his physical appearance, and general character. In his case they gel particularly well, as his fragile, damaged voice is mirrored in his slight, fragile-looking body and drooping, damaged eye, and his reputation for thoughtfulness, obstinacy, and pessimism perpetuated by the press. As a whole, they make an icon. An icon has a (larger than) life of its own, independent of its nominal embodiment, and is allowed to change only by leaps rather than increment. And so a schism occurs between Thom Yorke the icon and Thom Yorke who experiences mundane, everyday life; and so the demand for a singer/songwriter to be true to themselves begs the question: 'Which self?'[7]

Thom Yorke not only cuts a very troubled figure in the media, but also generates a mass of contradictions about himself and his music. Interviewed in *The Wire* on *Kid A* and *Amnesiac*, he says:

> The real problem I had was with the 'identify' bit ... Even now, most interviews you do, there's a constant subtext: 'Is this you?' By using other voices [such as on the vocodered 'Kid A'], I guess it was a way of saying, 'obviously it isn't me'. (quoted in Reynolds 2001: 32)

Yet, elsewhere in the same interview, he describes the way in which he incorporates political statements into his work:

> It's all so part of the fabric of everything, even the artwork ... I was really conscious of not wanting to use a sledgehammer to bang people over the head with it. It's pretty difficult to put into songs. In a way you have to wait until it's a personal issue or experience. (quoted in Reynolds 2001: 30)

So the songs can still matter to him and be honestly intended, while allowing him to assume alternative subject positions.

The demand for authenticity in popular music makes sense in light of its role in identity formation for the listener. And it is in reception that such meanings as those described above are formed (although the degree to which this is reckoned as true has been highly debated since Barthes' 1977 'Death of the Author').[8] Equally, the demand for consistency between Thom Yorke the singer and Thom Yorke the icon is understandable (but not necessarily realistic or even desirable) in this context. If Radiohead's music is important to a fan, it must also be seen to matter to Thom Yorke. This is especially true of sad or serious songs, which form the backbone of Radiohead's music. It is often easier to empathize with songs of loss and disappointment, as more people are more accustomed to losing than winning, but the statements of the songs would be undermined if the public perception of their creator was one of an untroubled, unconcerned, and thus apparently untruthful individual.

Modeling authenticity / situating Radiohead

All elements of a song, including tone, timbre and inflection of voice, musical structure, and lyrical content, are positioned in the head of the listener in a set of precariously balanced relationships of perceived honesty and deception, sincerity and insincerity, truth and falsehood. It is far easier to tip the balance with one perceived falsehood than with a lone instance of truth. That which is perceived as the most authentic is usually also the most highly privileged.

Authenticity plays an important role in value judgment and certainly the word has moralistic overtones. Most of the problems generated by the notion of authenticity in popular music are caused by its lack of definition. Very generally it is employed as a synonym for truth, but this word has its own range of contextual meanings, including truth to self or situation (honest, sincere, actual, genuine), a true spirit (constant, rightful, trusty), or true popular music (typical or exemplar of the style).

An obvious answer would be to reject meta-narratives of authenticity, and to simply leave intact small, situational instances of perceived integrity, sincerity, and truth. And yet this too is misleading as all judgments happen interrelationally, and an overall coherent picture is always built up around a single referent that accommodates all facets of its articulation in our known world-view. To deny this mini meta-narrative is as misleading as it is to say that authenticity is a fixed term unchanged by culture and the passage of time. The problem, however, is how to create a coherent model of authenticity that accounts for the relativistic, inwardly contradictory, and changeable concept that is left. Models and frameworks are necessary for comprehension, but often change the object of study. And so, although sporadic mention has been made of theorists of authenticity in the text so far, I have left discussion of various models proposed until after an exploration of the two songs, and will now look at how they are reflected within previously constructed frameworks, and in turn reflect back on such structures.

Three such frameworks have been suggested by Grossberg, Fornäs, and Moore, although Fornäs bases his model on Grossberg's, and Moore in turn on Fornäs's. Each is a tripartite division of the subject area, and each maps on to the web of authenticities from a slightly different angle. In 'The Media Economy of Rock Culture' (1993), Grossberg splits authenticity into three main stylistic threads, those of hard or folk rock ('the ability to articulate private but common desires'), dance (the 'construction of a rhythmic and sexual body') and postmodern ('linked with the self-consciousness of art'). However, these categories are presented in the context of his belief that there has been an irreversible 'erosion of ... the ideology of authenticity' (Grossberg 1993: 202–3, 186). Within such a broad division of the field, 'Creep' would seem to fall mainly into the first category, and 'Kid A' is a reified child of Grossberg's postmodern sensibility, 'simultaneously ironic and cynical, celebratory and horrified' (Grossberg 1992: 206). However, this (implicitly outdated) model is afforded little attention compared to (what he proposes as essentially an extension of the third category) 'the logic of authentic inauthenticity':

> You have to construct particular images for yourself and adopt certain identities but, according to the logic of authentic inauthenticity, you must do so reflexively (not necessarily self-consciously, one can just as easily take it for granted) knowing that there is no way to justify the choice. The only authenticity is to know and even admit that you are not being authentic, to fake it without faking the fact that you are faking it. (Grossberg 1992: 206)

Authentic inauthenticity has four variants, which are classified as 'hyperreal,' 'ironic,' 'sentimental,' and 'grotesque' inauthenticity (although largely only the first two are of use in this particular instance).[9] Hyperreal inauthenticity

> distrusts and often rejects the very fact of affect itself, not only the specific form of any affective investment. It is staunchly neutral, refusing to affect itself. Its tone is bleak, its practice super-objective. Portraying a grim reality in all its dismal, gritty and meaningless detail, with no affective difference inscribed upon it, is the only statement possible ... no narrative voice is capable of any judgement or discrimination.

The use of vocoder in 'Kid A' satisfies many of these qualities, neutralizing their most affective instrument (although fascinating for the opportunity it affords Jonny Greenwood to 'play' Thom Yorke's voice and thus create a dual subjectivity). However, the words do not present meaningless detail or grim reality (rather a grim fairy tale), but the vocal tone is surely bleak, and its practice objective to the point that another person is in control of its pitch and direction.

Ironic inauthenticity 'refuses to make any distinctions between investments on any basis … Although it seems to celebrate the absence of any centre or identity, it actually locates that absence as a new centre … It celebrates the fragmentary, the contradictory, the temporary.' Certainly 'Kid A' is fragmentary, the disjointed rhythmic pulse suggests the temporary, and little sense of the identity or position of the singer is established (with a real case to be made that this is not Thom Yorke at all, but a role he has adopted that he can equally well shirk). However, were this absence of centre (in this case Thom Yorke) to become a permanent feature of Radiohead's music, it is questionable as to how long its music would continue to appeal. It may not always be possible or desirable for a song to be an attempt at subjective expression, but this does not diminish the continuing power of such an approach as a general strategy.

Turning Grossberg's term on its head, 'Creep' would seem to be an example of inauthentic authenticity if considered in this context, bearing few markers of ironic distance, reflexivity or fragmented identity. The fact that this song met with great success at around the same time as Grossberg was declaring a decline in more traditional notions of rock authenticity would seem to negate his argument, and yet the band's arrival at 'Kid A' some seven years later might be seen to redeem or even confirm his suspicions.

Fornäs reinscribes Grossberg's discarded rock/dance/postmodern categories, by removing the genre-specific division and suggesting instead *subjective* authenticity (source and reception truth-to-self), *social* authenticity (criteria functioning at the level of group interaction), and *cultural* or *meta*-authenticity (the level of symbolic expressions) (Fornäs 1995a: 107). Fornäs also stresses the close relationship between the authentic and the reflexive, which has already been demonstrated within the discussion of 'Kid A' above. Following both Grossberg and Fornäs, Moore has rewritten the terms to produce a 'globalising' model of 'first person authenticity' (the music's truth to the musician), 'third person authenticity' (broadly speaking, the music's truth to other styles, genres, or texts) and 'second person authenticity' (the music's truth for the listener) (Moore 2002: 211–20). This model continues the trend of becoming progressively non-specific in order to encompass all styles of music.

As the focus of this study is very much centered in the first category of both Fornäs's and Moore's models (which differ in detail rather than overall idea), the other two types from both models are useful here mainly to indicate other directions that could be taken. However, these models are united in their rejection of a traditional notion of authenticity stemming from 1960s rock (but actually an amalgam of different ideologies), which privileges the white, male, guitar-based, 'naturally formed' rock group as somehow intrinsically more authentic than any other combination. This is true to the extent that the style of 'Creep' could be seen almost to be positively discriminated against for being a product of such a combination.

Fornäs's five genre case studies suggest different ways in which authenticity is construed within distinct genres (namely karaoke, rock/pop, rap/toast, house/techno and avant-garde/montage), suggesting that authenticity is articulated through different parameters in each of these genres. This is a useful and informative approach, but its application to the case of 'Kid A' highlights the problem of genre hybrids when categorizing authenticities. Authenticity is still a general concept that has to be re-evaluated with every case of both song and listener.

Taking 'Creep' and 'Kid A' to be representative loci of Radiohead's general trajectory in terms of musical style (which I believe they are), I will suggest finally that changing markers of authenticity is an essential tool in maintaining credibility, both in terms of perceived honesty of expression (as a marker of the authenticity of the naive can only hope to succeed for a limited time) and also as a sign of the still-desirable notion of artistic originality and progress, absorbing authenticities of other genres, and becoming increasingly reflexive in the perpetual challenge to maintain 'a certain mobility in the service of stability' (Grossberg 1992: 209). A certain gesture can only be accepted as authentic once, and can only be returned to when there is distance achieved from its first utterance.

Both the problem and the value of the concept of authenticity in popular music is that the word generates a multitude of implications and sites of authentication. It is the tension that such models as Grossberg's, Fornäs's and Moore's generate when mapped on to actual songs that is often most revealing, and so such models are more useful if they undergo constant evolution rather than be declared suddenly extinct. By examining 'Creep' and 'Kid A,' it has been possible to identify some of the large number of threads of authenticity generated by two songs, but this study has ultimately only managed to hint at the vastness of such a web of authenticities that is woven through music and its related discourses.

Notes

1. I would like to thank Dr Kenneth Gloag for his comments and role as a sounding-board during the writing of this essay, earlier versions of which have been presented at Cardiff University and at a Royal Musical Association Research Students' Conference (Salford, January 2003).
2. Moore admirably attempts to bring many of these threads together in a (partially historicized) summary of some of the many musicological approaches to the term in recent years in Moore, A.F., 'Authenticity as authentication,' in *Popular Music*, 21/2 (2002), 209–25.
3. These lyrics are taken from the CD booklet for the *Itch* EP (1994), a collection of live and alternative versions of *Pablo Honey* album and b-side songs, released in Japan. (The liner notes for *Pablo Honey* do not include any lyrics.) These supplied lyrics are a little curious, partly because the version they accompany is the 'clean' radio version that substitutes 'very' for 'fucking,' but mainly for the fact that the first horizontal ellipsis ('…') covers the words to the climax of the song ('She runs, runs, runs, runs, runs, runs,' banal out of context, but positioned at the musical highpoint), whereas the second ellipsis has no significance whatsoever.

4. This is something of a over-simplification, as there are also 7ths added by the voice, and the iv chord could be heard as a rootless diminished 7th with an added 11th, but the overall effect is simple.
5. These lyrics are a combination of words from the concealed booklet in *Kid A*'s CD case and direct transcription from the song.
6. 'Kid A' *is* performed live, but rarely and sporadically. At a performance in Belfast on May 19 2003, Thom Yorke overcame the difficulty of performing words cloaked by a vocoder on the record by over-enunciating the lyrics (almost to the point of sarcasm). This sense of playing games seems to pervade all aspects of Radiohead. Although live performances of 'Kid A' are rare, they are probably still more frequent than live performances of 'Creep,' despite the latter's continued popularity.
7. Thom Yorke was ranked 16th in a list of 'The 100 Greatest Stars of the 20th Century' in *Q*, 155 (August 1999), 43–74, nestling two places above Bono and one below Michael Stipe. The 'Greatest Star of the 20th century' was John Lennon.
8. See Barthes' 'The Death of the Author,' in *Image, Music, Text*, trans. Stephen Heath (London: Fontana Press, 1977): 142–8; see also Burke, S., *Death and Return of the Author: Criticism and Subjectivity in Barthes, Foucault and Derrida* (Edinburgh: Edinburgh University Press, 1992).
9. This and the following paragraph use quotations from Grossberg 1992: 227–34.

Chapter 4

Radiohead and the Negation of Gender

Erin Harde

In the music industry, gender – through constructions of sexual identity in lyrics and performance – constitutes the greater part of a band's image and contributes to its success. Consider the stage antics of rock legends past like Mick Jagger, or the staggering number of today's blonde pop tarts, whose bare tummies are not an uncommon sight. Then there is Radiohead, a band seemingly devoid of gender. From the time of Radiohead's debut with *Pablo Honey* to the enigmatic *Amnesiac*, it has challenged fans and critics with the evolution of its art and image. The Oxford, UK, quintet began with rock that explored traditional gender relations and constructions, in however obscure and neurotic a manner. With *OK Computer*, *Kid A*, and now *Amnesiac*, Radiohead began a complex exploration of social, psychological, and political issues. Its departure from the traditional topics of sex and gender indicate that for this band, they are altogether a non-issue. Thus, Radiohead is conspicuously non-gendered, and through lyrics, videos, live performance, and image, Radiohead – and Thom Yorke in particular – constructs the image of the androgyne.

While the band members have never identified themselves as androgynous,[1] neither have they worked to portray an overt or specific sexuality or gender identity. This negation of gender is anomalous in an industry hyper-concerned with representations of sexuality, clearly defined through sound and image. Radiohead's experimentation[2] with sound and image came not with its last three albums, but with the first two. It released two traditional rock albums and then evolved into the band it is today, one that is devoid of sexual categories and restraints.

Androgyny in popular music did not originate with Radiohead. Consider the 1970s trend of glam rock and transvestism, where David Bowie assumed the androgynous persona of Ziggy Stardust.[3] While Bowie is still a popular artist, his method of androgyny as an art form is infrequent among today's musicians, possibly because the gray areas of sexuality make people uncomfortable. However, the musicians who dwell in these gray areas are the ones who accomplish the most interesting music, both lyrically and melodically. For instance, on *Kid A*, the album sweeps along until 'Treefingers,' a pretty, but surprising and unpredictable song; it's an interesting and challenging inclusion. Mainstream pop music tends not to invite listeners to become interested, only pacified. Radiohead transcends musical boundaries because it is entirely unconcerned with sex or gender. Its members need not cross-dress, or assume sexually ambiguous personas to accomplish androgyny, because their music is non-gendered and their image is non-sexual. Radiohead's success is perplexing, especially considering that the band works in an industry that necessitates exploitive sexuality in order to achieve success. The answer may simply be that Radiohead challenges accepted ideologies in the music industry and provides an alternative art form amid a sea of tired stereotypes and prototypes.

When an artist defies gender boundaries, there will inevitably be animosity because androgyny was, and still is, an alien concept. Check out a top 20 singles or albums chart and it seems that many of today's music fans will search for something they can readily identify with or at least sing along with, instead of something that will challenge their identity and sexuality. The members of Radiohead, however, have never identified themselves as androgynous people or as performers of androgynous music, nor have critics or fans seemed concerned that the band is oblivious to gender identities. This observation may prove that if sexuality is not front and center, it is altogether a non-issue, and for Radiohead this is a distinct possibility; its androgynous music is covert and unintended, and while its music may be the most rebellious in the current scene, it presents itself as a subtle rebellion. By identifying with the androgynous, Radiohead rebels creatively, and thus effectively. Whether it intends to do so or not, Radiohead tests the boundaries set up by the decadent glam rock androgyny of the 1970s, and is thus able to transcend the boundaries of the music industry. In a *Spin* Radiohead interview, Zev Borow writes that when a Capitol Records insider first heard *Kid A*, he said 'it's amazing, but weird, there aren't any radio singles, and they hate doing press ... Roy Lott [Capitol president] is going to shit' (Borow 2000: 114). None the less, the company still produced *Kid A*, even though Radiohead remained steadfast in its ambition to create an album that catered to its members' artistic expression rather than the company's expectations.

Radiohead identifies with the androgynous not because its members assume traits from both genders, but because they negate gender altogether. Every album following *The Bends* develops themes that are separate from sex and gender. Granted, the band is comprised of men and you can't expect to see five hermaphrodites walk on-stage. Considering, however, that sexuality is a big selling point of successful bands and artists in the contemporary music scene, Radiohead is astonishingly alien. Although androgyny promotes the ideal of eliminating the dichotomy of gender, many critics still rely on that dichotomy to define androgyny. In *Hollywood Androgyny* (1993), Rebecca Bell-Metereau gives a thorough survey of transvestism in hundreds of different movies, but her definitions of gender-bending are hardly adequate. Men and women in drag are still identified as men and women, and their target audience are either the opposite or the same sex. With Radiohead, however, the band's image and intended audience are ambiguous, so androgyny must be a concept that has more depth than simply cross-dressing. Sandra Bem comments that 'limiting a person's ability to respond in one or the other of these two complementary domains thus seems tragically and unnecessarily destructive of human potential' (Bem 1976: 50). Consider Patti Smith and her androgynous voice and image.[4] Had she become the corporate sex kitten that is now portrayed by many current divas, she could hardly have made the impact that she did. Radiohead's music responds to neither gender and thus the music can fulfill its potential.

When deciphering Radiohead's image, it is the third and fourth albums and stage performance that should be considered rather than the individual band members' personal image. *OK Computer* and *Kid A* are significant because there is nothing gendered about them, in fact, there is nothing human about them; they are cold and impersonal. *OK Computer* detours from its predecessor *The Bends*, and embarks on a journey that is skeptical about technology, politics, and human contact of any kind. This dystopic journey continues with *Kid A*, a title that claims no identity, no gender, no labeling. Likewise, Radiohead performances as seen on *Meeting People is Easy*[5] greatly deviate from a traditional rock performance, though Thom Yorke once claimed, 'I never wanted to be in a rock band,' and with his non-traditional patterns of performing, this becomes evident. Bem says 'consider, first, the androgynous male. He performs spectacularly. He shuns no behaviour just because our culture happens to label it as female, and his competence crosses both the instrumental and the expressive domains' (1976: 58). This works particularly well if one is to consider the performance of typical male rock rhythms that have a steady beat with the inevitable climax in the final chorus. There are no surprises when The Rolling Stones perform; the audience expects Jagger to hump his way across the stage in every performance, and he doesn't disappoint. With Radiohead, there are few presuppositions about the performance and, as Bem says, the performance is spectacular; no one has any idea what to expect. Yorke's performance is remarkable; he is convulsive in the more demanding songs and mystical in the slower, passionate songs as though he's communicating with the audience as a supreme entity. While climax is often inevitable in Radiohead's songs, it is one of emotional overload rather than the sexual energy that is central to so many of the band's contemporaries. And, in all Radiohead songs, there is more than one climax, and thus Bem's theory is applicable, if only in a carnal way.

Because Radiohead does not rely on the gender norms so commonly practiced by other artists, it is curious it reigns as such a popular band. A solution to this can be found in Simon Frith's and Angela McRobbie's 1990 article 'Music and Sexuality.' The authors discuss the extremes of male music: 'cock rock' and 'teenybop.' The former includes artists like Jagger, Roger Daltrey, and Robert Plant, who 'are aggressive, dominating, and boastful, and they constantly seek to remind the audience of their prowess, their control' (1990: 374). Teenybop includes the boyband genre, whose exponents all have four or five members who represent 'the young boy next door: sad, thoughtful, pretty, and puppylike'

(1990: 375). Cock rock targets men and teenybop targets adolescent girls, but this excludes a significant percentage of the population. Because Radiohead does not rely on extremes, its music presents a dichotomy. The music is strange and alienating, but also provides an alternative to the music that relies on social and sexual ideologies. Cock rock unites men as a collective, all roaring and grabbing their crotches in unison; teenybop singles out young women, making them feel special and loved. Androgynous music does neither, but rather encourages the audience to decipher their own feelings about the music. I expect that Radiohead's brave ventures into unknown territory could have just as easily failed, but because the music is so strong and intelligent, it succeeded in spite of its rebellion.

Because Radiohead identifies with the androgynous, its music takes precedence over gender. According to Bem, the androgyne is a model of perfection, and she claims that 'an androgynous personality would thus represent the very best of what masculinity and femininity have each come to represent, and the more negative exaggerations of masculinity and femininity would tend to be cancelled out' (1976: 51). If gender is canceled out, then the artists are afforded the unique opportunity of being concerned strictly with the quality of music; they need not toy with their image in order to be successful. Bem's assertion fails to clarify what the best of masculinity and femininity is, but it is unlikely that there is universal agreement on the best or worst qualities of each sex anyway. Trying to decipher which elements of both sexes Radiohead represents is far too subjective a task, but by subverting gender stereotypes, which the band undoubtedly does, it allows Radiohead, and its fans, to focus on the music instead of gender requirements.

The fact that music is Radiohead's main agenda, however, does not mean that its sexuality must be undermined. In fact, while Radiohead's lyrics are devoid of the erotic, I argue that their performance can still be sexual.[6] Robert G. Pielke says:

> There is every reason to believe that an androgynous society would actually enhance sexuality, both quantitatively and qualitatively. Since the traditional sex roles (gender) have served to restrict the sex drive in every conceivable way, their removal would inevitably serve to encourage a much freer and more abundant sex life than ever before. (Pielke 1982: 191)

Thus, Yorke's abstinence in his lyrics makes for a greater possibility of sexuality. Radiohead's misuse and non-use of gender leave greater opportunities for the performance and the audience's relation to the performance. But not all critics welcome androgyny as a reality. Mary Anne Warren comments that 'other feminists object to the ideal of androgyny on the grounds that it is utopian and visionary rather than pragmatically useful' (1982: 180). While this is true on a daily social basis, 'utopian' and 'visionary' are concepts that can benefit music. Utopian/dystopian literature is fascinating and Radiohead capitalizes on the genre in its images and lyrics. The very title *Kid A* conjures images of Huxley's mass-produced, assembly-line Alpha children. The concepts in *Kid A* have been swirling around in classic dystopias like *Brave New World*, More's *Utopia* and Orwell's society governed by Big Brother. The album is visionary because it translates these startling novels into startling music, both in lyrics and melody. Perhaps androgyny is utopic rather than pragmatic in contemporary society, but in music these elements can only encourage a provocative discourse.

Because androgyny is perceived as a utopic concept, it can also be recognized as a mode of escapism, especially when in the hands of Radiohead. Stella Bruzzi comments that Virginia Woolf 'presents androgyny as a utopian ideal, as a sexless state that can guard against repression' (Bruzzi 1997: 200). Woolf was interested in both the uniting of the masculine and feminine intelligence and an actual meshing of sexuality, as demonstrated in *Orlando*. In Woolf's opinion, 'to be truly creative one must use the "whole" mind. In keeping with this, the greatest writers are 'androgynous': they use and harmonize the masculine and feminine approaches to truth' (quoted in Bazin 1973: 3). This theory is applicable to writers of music, and should be considered in a discussion of *OK Computer* and *Kid A*. While Woolf presents readers with androgyny as a beneficial state, Radiohead presents listeners with a darker vision. The band's androgynous image is refreshing, but within the lyrics, androgyny is not the pleasant invitation that Woolf extends. *OK Computer* and *Kid A* contain the same dystopic elements as Orwell's novels: no passion, no love, and no gratuitous sex. Radiohead execute these concepts by exercising sound and vocals that are as strange as the 'Subterranean Homesick Alien.'

OK Computer and *Kid A* present chaos via rhythms and vocals; there are no traditional patterns of cock rock, teenybop, or anything in between. Granted, in retrospect, *OK Computer* now seems tame after the release of *Amnesiac*, but as the third and fourth albums assert Radiohead's androgyny, they will be my focus. Zev Borow defined the album as 'a predominantly ambient experiment largely absent of guitars, traditional song structures, and lyrics, it still manages to sound distinctly Radiohead: cerebral and haunting, sweeping and fierce' (Borow 2000: 111). 'Distinctly Radiohead' is an oxymoron and with it Borow admits, maybe boasts, that it is not a band that can be defined and organized. According to Mac Randall, the band was never easily categorized: 'these Oxford kids, none of whom could be mistaken for strict purists were already mixing and matching their favourites with little regard for genre lines' (Randall 2000: 27).

Ironically, *Kid A*'s first track is 'Everything in its Right Place,' which hints at society's neurotic need to label and compartmentalize everything. The title track features Yorke's voice rambling incoherently through a synthesizer, which produces a terrifying effect, though the lyrics 'We got heads on sticks / You got ventriloquists' are more disturbing. Yorke's character is a robot in this song, claiming full agency as it identifies itself among the controllers, the ones who are speaking for others, not the ones being spoken for. As a robot, Yorke claims the unsexed androgynous voice, and thus the sexual beings are the dummies and the androgynes/agents are the ventriloquists. The robot is also featured in 'Fitter Happier' on *OK Computer*, which lists the rules on how to be 'more productive.' This character is the voice of society, spitting its rules and expectations back at it. When social norms are reiterated without a smiling face behind them, they are revealed as superficial: 'favours for favours / fond but not in love.' Androgyny has the ability to deconstruct social traditions and show them for their real value.

Just as androgyny is still not an accepted gender, or state, and thus remains outside contemporary gender boundaries, the character or narrator of many Radiohead songs and videos is also an outsider and has difficulty communicating with others. In 'Everything in its Right Place,' Yorke repeats 'what, what is that you tried to say?' Kate Bornstein has posited the theory of 'gender defenders' or 'gender terrorists.' These are people for 'whom gender forms a cornerstone of their view of the world' (1994: 74). Bornstein explains that for these people there are only two genders, with no gray areas in between. Gender terrorists cannot communicate with those who dwell in the gray areas. Quite often throughout *Kid A* there are two dynamics: the group and the individual. The two are rarely found together. In 'The National Anthem,' only the group exists, but in 'How to Disappear Completely,' only Yorke exists, moaning and wandering by himself. What makes these songs androgynous is the fact that there are no gender identifiers, only pronouns like 'us' and 'me.' The collective and the singular form a pattern that runs through *Kid A*; the album does not qualify as a concept record like Pink Floyd's *The Wall* or Led Zeppelin's *Houses of the Holy*, but there is a narrative. The listener understands that the singer is a man, but Yorke's voice never slips into a distinctly masculine or feminine pattern of singing due to the incorporation of falsettos, which except for a few bands like Queen and Supertramp is rare in rock and alternative music. This factor makes Yorke's characters quite pathetic; they are often alone.

When conventional themes are used, the end result is disaster. Consider 'Idioteque,' where Yorke asks 'who's in a bunker / women and children first,' one of the rare cases when gendered nouns are used, but they are used in a chaotic context. Men and women often appear in the songs with an apocalyptic vision.[7] Yorke draws the line between his character and society when he sings 'I laugh until my head comes off,' showing that he does not empathize with humanity. In 'Morning Bell,' the topic is divorce; it divides the furniture, the clothes, the couple, and, finally, Yorke wants to 'cut the kids in half.' Whenever anything 'normal' in regard to relationships and gender is the focus, it proves to be a nightmare. Not once do the lyrics embrace the conventional. Just like in 'Everything in its Right Place,' this song's protagonist cannot communicate: 'I wanted to tell you but you never listened.' The final song on *Kid A* is a love song that deliberately fails. It features lyrics like 'red wine and sleeping pills,' 'cheap sex and sad films,' 'stop sending letters / letters always get burned.' Because the albums dwell so often in the androgynous state, the odd emergence into acceptable traditions of sexuality inevitably fails. The band doesn't know how to be normal even if it wanted to. The lyrics of the final song are all romantic notions that fail before they are out of Yorke's mouth.

With the gay – in all senses of the word – use of androgyny in the 1970s, there was the optimistic factor of companionship, though never a defined companionship.[8] Ironically in 'Optimistic,' Orwellian concepts are evident in Yorke's lyrics. 'You can try the best you can' is reminiscent of *Nineteen Eighty-Four* slogans. 'Living on animal farm,' eerily brings forth the disturbing image of people being nothing more than 'fodder' for social politics, whatever they may be. Just like Kid A, these characters are reduced to objects, parts of a machine, no identity and no gender, which presents the more disturbing side of androgyny and leaves little wonder why mainstream love songs are so popular. 'Optimistic' also contains the lyric 'I'd really like to help you man,' which is immediately followed by 'nervous messed up marionettes.' While the meaning of this juxtaposition is debatable, I suggest the latter lyric is the assessment of not just the 'man' in the former lyric, but of humans in general. Thus, the group dynamic takes on that of the singular androgyne because marionettes are wooden dolls on strings, non-sexual inanimate objects; they have no agency.[9]

Radiohead's aural landscapes make for a sublime but difficult experience. On 'In Limbo,' a rather significant title, Yorke declares, 'I'm lost at sea. Don't bother me.' That's where he wants to be, away from the chaos of the normal, in a world that has no boundaries. *Kid A* itself was built through a process without boundaries. Yorke claims that 'I stopped relying on extremes to get me through when *OK Computer* finished. It made me nervous that the music was not coming initially from extremes' (Borow 2000: 118). Yorke's extremes include those of gender and, once he learned to work apart from them, his music became uninhibited, which is evident on *Kid A*. Thus, music that is created outside of extremes is initially intimidating for the artist and fan, but eventually rewarding for both.

Radiohead's videos are as disparate from mainstream trends as their music. Often, pop videos are focused mainly on the band or artist, whether they simply lip-synch, assuming the role of a character in a story, or in live performance. Radiohead's band members are rarely in the spotlight of their videos; often they are seen only in cameos. Consider 'Paranoid Android,' 'Just,' 'High and Dry' (US version), and 'Karma Police.' In the animated 'Paranoid Android,' two characters are followed through a day as they encounter many strange sights. In a bar, a man dances on a table with a small head jutting from his stomach. At the table, looking disgusted, are the five members of Radiohead. Despite the chaos around them, they sit back in their chairs calmly shaking their heads. Eventually, Jonny Greenwood's cartoon points the mutant dancer toward the door. Just as in the lyrics, their respective characters in the videos do not partake in the action or interact with the group. In 'Just,' perhaps one of the most frustrating videos ever created, a man brings an entire crowd to the ground with one sentence which is never revealed. Where are the members of Radiohead? They are looking down from a nearby apartment window, just observing. In 'High and Dry,' a story takes place in a diner in which a couple find themselves with a bomb in their takeout. Radiohead? They are sitting at a nearby table, the only ones in the diner not singing the song. Yorke smiles briefly at a child in the washroom, an androgynous child in a unisex washroom, but is interrupted as a man bolts out of the stall. For the most part, the band is again just observing. Finally in 'Karma Police,' a car pursues a man, perhaps the man 'who buzzes like a fridge.' Yorke shows up in the back seat as the singing Greek chorus, breaking down the video's events for the audience.[10] Yorke subverts the role, and is uninvolved and neutral to the point of being bored. Upon the conclusion, when the man has set the car on fire, Yorke has disappeared because his part has ended. What conveys androgyny in these videos is partly the fact that the members of Radiohead play distant observers, not really part of society, but more the fact that sex and gender are absent, aside from blips like the flasher in 'Paranoid Android.'

Incredibly, despite their defiance of accepted traditions in music, Radiohead has thrived and become an icon in the contemporary music scene. I believe the feminist theory of 'othering' plays an interesting role in this phenomenon. Judith Butler says that 'by defining women as "Other", men are able through the shortcut of definition to dispose of their bodies, to make themselves other than their bodies – a symbol potentially of human decay and transience, of limitation generally – and to make their bodies other than themselves' (Butler 1968: 616). If 'women' is replaced with men or women who exist in accepted sexual roles, then Yorke must not abide by mortality. Because Radiohead does not explicitly identify with either sex, it does not identify with the consequences of sex, like transience. Its sexual counterparts, Britney Spears and Ricky Martin, are the 'Other' – they are physical and thus must age and die, or at least succumb to the reality of being a fad. Sheila Whiteley also confronts the idea of the immortal androgyne but applies it to Mick Jagger: 'veiled or on stage, Jagger remains an idealised representation of himself: 'Jumping Jack Flash', the eternally youthful androgyne, focus of every possible sexual appetite' (Whiteley 1997: 92). I question if being the 'focus' of every sexual appetite makes one an androgyne. Just because Jagger appealed to straight, gay, and bisexual people of both sexes does necessarily mean he was and still is an androgyne. His presence is largely of a horny male singing traditional rock songs with lyrics that were hardly challenging. Jagger and The Stones are still popular, but the most common thing heard about the group in the media is how old they are; while still revered, they don't have that certain mystery and nuance about them that surrounds Radiohead. And as Radiohead continues to defy music and gender boundaries, it will endure as a musical icon, and rightly so.

Among sociologists and psychologists, androgyny is hotly debated as something that is either healthy and practical, or destructive and unrealistic. Music critics and theorists, however, tend to agree that androgyny in music is interesting and different. As demonstrated by Radiohead, androgyny is not detrimental, but rather allows artists to experiment, test themselves and test the audience. Radiohead's androgyny is non-sexed, but as I have shown, can still have a sexual effect on the audience despite a lack of sexual content in lyrics. Radiohead focuses on the apocalyptic, and subtly reveals the possibilities of androgyny. This band is invaluable to a music scene where lookalike, soundalike musicians plague fans with the mundane. Radiohead challenges listeners with its brave new sounds and difficult lyrics, and will continue to do so as it reinvents itself through its music for years to come.

Notes

1. The *OED* defines androgynous as having a partly male and partly female appearance or having an ambiguous gender. I find this rather inadequate and, for the purposes of this essay, understand androgyny as a state that distorts gender either by combining the genders or negating them depending on the cultural markers of gender such as dress, voice, and gesture. Kate Bornstein (1994) makes the distinction between gender ambiguity, a refusal to fall within a prescribed gender code, and gender fluidity, a refusal to remain one gender or the other.
2. Because the sounds and lyrics of *OK Computer*, *Kid A*, and *Amnesiac* are not consistent with traditional, straightforward rock melodies, one might argue that these are the albums ripe with experimentation. However, because its non-traditional albums outnumber the traditional, I argue that Radiohead's first two albums occupy a liminal space and that with the latter albums it found a space that it is comfortable working in.
3. In a 1987 *Rolling Stone* interview, journalist Kurt Loder claimed David Bowie was the 'Pioneer Androgyne' because he defined the 1970s glitter rock transvestism.
4. While Patti Smith is now faded to an influential avant-garde ghost, her impact is clear. One only needs to consider R.E.M.'s 1996 hit 'E-Bow The Letter,' which features moaning vocals from Smith. 'Who is that?' young fans asked, many surprised to discover that those haunting vocals came from a woman. Smith's androgyny was pronounced not in elaborate sexually ambiguous personas, but simply by assuming an image that was natural and neutral, no make-up, just her philosophical lyrics and tenor vocals.
5. *Meeting People is Easy* is a 1998 Radiohead documentary by Grant Gee, which includes portions of performances and interviews.
6. Gender roles are not a part of Radiohead's image and performance, but this does not mean fans must ignore their own sexuality. Anyone who has seen a Radiohead show knows how involved the band members become with their music, which can make for an intense and sexy experience.
7. The third verse in this song predicts 'ice age coming.'
8. Consider Bowie's song 'Rebel Rebel' about two lovers. The sex of the lovers is not identified, but it doesn't need to be in order for the song to be passionate.
9. I don't mean to suggest that androgynes are inanimate in any sense, or even non-sexual. The point is that the lyrics are comparing humankind to puppets, not intelligent, sexual beings. To be fair however, Pearl Jam, a band that easily fits in the 'cock rock' category, has a similar lyric on 'Mankind.' The chorus runs 'It's all just inadvertent simulation a pattern in all mankind / what's got the whole world fakin it.'

Here is a parallel to the pattern of the group dynamic on *Kid A* as well as the conveyed meaning of 'marionette.' Thus, bands opposite Radiohead on the sexual spectrum may also recognize the stale, non-gendered aspects of society, but they don't identify with them through performance and image. During the early 1990s, Eddie Vedder was a sex symbol; you might see fans lusting after Thom Yorke, but chances are, it isn't because of his looks. Radiohead makes the observation Pearl Jam does, but actually lives it as a band.

10. The Chorus originated in Ancient Greek drama. The character was not part of the action, but provided insight and commentary on the events and characters.

Chapter 5

To(rt)uring the Minotaur: Radiohead, Pop, Unnatural Couplings, and Mainstream Subversion

Greg Hainge

In his article 'Deleuze and Popular Music,' Ian Buchanan contends that pop acts as a refrain in the Deleuzean sense of this term, which is to say that

> like the tick, [it] is composed of three functions. It comforts us by providing a 'rough sketch of a calming and stabilising, calm and stable, centre in the heart of chaos'. It is the song the lost child, scared of the dark, sings to find his or her way home. The tune also creates the very home we return to when our foray into the world grows wearisome. (Buchanan 2000: 183)

This notion of popular music providing a comforting center may appear to be somewhat problematic when applied to the music of a band such as Radiohead, however, whose music has always dealt in somewhat unhomely themes that evoke spaces of alienation and dysfunction rather than centers of calm. None the less, if one examines the way in which audiences have embraced Radiohead's early songs of dysfunction, and none more so than the anthemic 'Creep,' it is entirely feasible to apply Buchanan's formula to Radiohead. The chorus of 'Creep,' for instance, is eminently singalongable; whether every member of the audience repeating its hyperdysfunctional sentiment relates to it in some way, finding solace in a sense of identification, or whether the lyrics are often emptied of their content in the act of repetition, becoming merely an accessory to the melody, is ultimately unimportant, for in both cases the sense of home that Deleuze finds in the refrain is achieved.

With its last two releases, *Kid A* and *Amnesiac*, however, Radiohead seems to have problematized the creation of this kind of homely space considerably in a number of ways. First, and most obviously, the musical experimentation that seems to have occupied the interim period between *OK Computer* and *Kid A/Amnesiac* has produced two albums that stray far from the guitar-based rock that previously characterized the band's music; a move that, while drawing large amounts of critical acclaim in the press, appears to have alienated certain sections of the band's long-standing fan base. Nor is it only the instrumentation that has undergone a transformation; Thom Yorke's lyrics on these last two albums do not, for the most part, follow a verse/chorus/verse/chorus structure, while his vocal style and the studio manipulations of the vocal line (which is often digitally skewed from its natural expression or else far further back in the mix than previously) often render it difficult to understand individual words or phrases – as in 'Kid A,' to name but one example.

Second, if it can be said that pop acts as a refrain for contemporary audiences, it might also be said that the very notion of popularity inherent in pop as a product intended for mass consumption colludes in this aspect of it. In other words, just as the predictable nature of the refrain is what provides the listener a sense of recognition that creates a homely space, so conformity to the conventions and axiomatics of the mainstream to which any band commanding a high level of commercial success inevitably belongs reinforces this feeling of home through a reassuring sense of familiarity. Although some might protest that not all artistic expressions that achieve a high degree of commercial success are necessarily a mainstream expression, that a minoritarian expression within the majoritarian commercial sphere is still possible, an examination of the functioning of the mainstream will vindicate this apparently contentious statement; for when an apparently non-conformist expression emerges that generates commercial success equal to or greater than conformist mainstream acts, the parameters of the conventions of the mainstream expand outward to encompass this new expression, which consequently loses its anticonformist potential and becomes acceptable. This movement can be thought of in terms of Deleuze and Guattari's analysis of the mechanisms of capitalism which reterritorialize any instance of deterritorialization. As for empirical examples of what this might mean, we need only think of grunge, an anti- (or, rather, a-)fashion statement that became integrated within the mainstream as the commercial success of bands such as Pearl Jam and Nirvana brought it to the masses, and that eventually ended up on the catwalks of the major fashion capitals of the world. We can even find an example in the music of Radiohead itself, for in a recent interview drummer Phil Selway has stated, 'When *The Bends* came out everyone went on about how uncommercial that was. Twelve months later it was being hailed as a pop classic. The record company were worried there wasn't a single on it – and we ended up with five Top 30 hits from it!' (*Uncut* August 2001: 58).

In almost every aspect of its dealings with those industry channels through which the potential commercial success of a band is maximized, however, Radiohead, while remaining popular (although perhaps not as popular as its record company executives would wish it to be), has not conformed to the conventions of the mainstream in which it is situated; on the contrary, as time progresses it appears to be attempting ever harder to confound every expectation an audience might have of a mainstream band and blatantly to contravene every record industry axiomatic in the book. We shall first, then, analyze the ways in which, both musically and artistically, Radiohead at the outset of its career did indeed collaborate with mainstream expectations, in spite of the band's apparent 'alternative' (and thus marginalized from the mainstream) credibility. We shall then turn to the two antipopulist movements of the latter part of the band's career evoked above, before suggesting that recurring elements in the artwork of *Kid A* and *Amnesiac*, and in the accompanying promotional tools, may, in fact, be considered as a coded avowal of this deliberate move away from the mainstream.

That Radiohead's first two albums, *Pablo Honey* and *The Bends*, are made up entirely of songs structured according to a verse/chorus/verse/chorus pattern is incontrovertible, and while the rushed recording process of *Pablo Honey* produced fewer 'classic' tunes whose refrains would be hummed as the auto-objective soundtrack to thousands of individual existences, the fruits of Radiohead's first excursion into the truly creative territory that it has claimed as its own, *The Bends*, soon became recognized as a pop classic bursting with choruses begging to be ruminated repeatedly in the mouths of millions. Musically, then, even if these albums express, especially in their lyrical content, a sense of alienation, dislocation, and dysfunction, *Pablo Honey* and *The Bends* proffer a space of home in which a sense of order against the chaos of the outside can be found, a space consonant with the 'Deleuzoguattarian' analysis of the relationship between music and the refrain. For Deleuze and Guattari, 'the *refrain* is properly musical content, the block of content proper to music,' for 'music is a creative, active operation that consists in deterritorializing the refrain. Whereas the refrain is essentially territorial, territorializing, or reterritorializing [and] music makes it a deterritorialized content for a deterritorializing form of expression' (Deleuze and Guattari 1987: 299, 300). In organizing musical expression around itself, then, the refrain creates a territory that can be inhabited by the listener; the punctual structures of most pop songs, which are often variations on a pre-conceived formula, examples of 'diversity within homogeneity,' as Buchanan suggests, invoking Bourdieu (Buchanan 2000: 187), follow this rule to the letter and can thus shelter the listener from the terrifying sense of alienation that the chaos of the modern world and global politics can instill in individuals *even when*, as we have suggested, this very chaos, alienation, and dysfunction forms the thematic content of such songs.

The artwork of these two albums reinforces this sense of home. The booklet accompanying the CD of *Pablo Honey*, for instance, has as its front cover what could well be the very epitome of a comforting image: a baby's face surrounded by candy covered in brightly colored hundreds and thousands – both of which evoke a sense of nostalgia for childhood – from which spread out the yellow stamens of a flower. Similarly, the inside pages of the booklet comfort the listener/reader by presenting him/her with exactly what is expected: a numbered list of song titles; a picture of the band looking suitably like English (which is to say, slightly geeky, almost androgynous) rock stars with their regulation skewed poses, sucked-in cheeks, pensive-verging-on-inquisitive expressions, and featuring Thom Yorke in a *de rigueur* pair of retro (almost kitsch) wire-framed

CHiPs-style sunglasses; a centerfold picture of the band *in mediis rebus*; a 'weird' and yet at the same time amusing photograph of a palm-green velvet cushion on which is taking place a stand-off between a lizard and a plastic crocodile, an image that itself might be said to invoke the same movement from primordial/ primitive expression toward a homely territory that we have observed in music's relationship to the refrain; thanks and credits, and then, finally, on the back cover, a composite photograph of an anonymous urban streetscape at night, tinted in bright colors that lend it an air of almost menacing irreality, but that is seen through the frame/projection screen provided by two figures standing one behind the other, barely touching yet furnishing each other, in their proximity, feelings of melancholy and solace.

The booklet that accompanies *The Bends* does not follow quite such an orthodox pattern. Rather than taking the form of a stapled folding booklet, it is a concertina of paper that, once unfolded, reveals, on one side, the album's song lyrics (which, obviously, facilitate the reader/listener's ability to internalize the refrain) interspersed with innocent, childish, entirely non-threatening drawings and, on the other, the artwork. This artwork is made up of four different sections: the front cover is an image adapted from medical photographs of a slightly androgynous figure shot from the shoulders up. There is something unsettling about this image, which evokes a sickly atmosphere: yellowy-green hues suggest a state of anemia, while two white circles on the chest appear to be heart-monitor pads. In spite of this, however, the ultimate effect of the image is one of solace, for the expression on this face can be read only as one of sublime bliss. The two middle panels of the booklet's artwork are made up of brightly colored, abstract, highly pixelated images, which appear to have been shot by a security camera and on top of which have been superimposed enlarged details of the childlike scrawled drawings and lyric fragments from the booklet's reverse side. The overall effect is fragmented yet ultimately coherent, for these images seem to obey the aesthetic compulsions of a self-sufficient design function rather than perform a narrative role that might leave them open. The final panel of this artwork comprises six images, which apply the surveillance-camera aesthetic to rock-star portraits (although darker, more serious versions than those of *Pablo Honey*) of the five members of the band, and one other image of a distended globe set against a conference room scene that, although seemingly out of place and implicitly political, does not ultimately distract us from the homely function of the portraits that allow the listener to put faces to the sounds.

OK Computer, at first glance or listen, would appear to have disturbed the homely space created by pop in its musical experimentation and coherent single concept, which deals with alienation in a world of global politics and postindustrial technology. As Simon Reynolds notes in *The Wire*, this was the album 'where Yorke and co started to complicate the anthemic qualities of their earlier music in earnest by deep immersion in such avant staples as Miles Davis's *Bitches Brew*' (2001: 28). Indeed, according to Reynolds, *OK Computer* was in many respects antipop (or, at least, anti-Britpop), the very antithesis of Oasis's 'anti-intellectualism and vacant hedonism' (2001: 28). If *OK Computer* is thought of in this way, then the cover art of this album may also appear, at first, explicitly to reinforce this interpretation. Composed of a collage scene that presents a complex, seemingly impossible elevated highway intersection, illustrations from an aircraft safety card, blurred figures and white scribbles, this cover art appears to show the very epitome of alienation in a technological universe. Most significant for the present analysis, however, is the inclusion on this cover of the words 'Lost Child,' which are repeated twice and figure under a logo of a child crying. If pop, in its use of the refrain, does indeed give the lost child a song to sing to find his or her way home, then surely this album with its lost-child logo will not proffer such a way home and refuse the territorializing function of the refrain. Or perhaps not. For the rest of the booklet, using these same motifs, seems to show us how to insulate ourselves against the technological world *by having faith in it*. Page 2 shows an illustration from the airline safety card in which we see a man blocking an aircraft exit having observed flames outside while a text advises us: 'Jump out of bed as soon as you hear the alarm clock!! You may also find it useful spending five minutes each morning saying to yourself: "Every day in every way I am getting better and better". Perhaps it is a good idea to start a new day with the right frame of mind!' Page 3 shows a family (cut from a 1960s photograph) smiling and looking up at a large statue of Jesus over which has been drawn the taxi and take-off path of an airplane, the take-off clearance zone (that point at which all passengers place their faith in technology) being situated directly over Jesus's heart. Pages 4 and 5 show complex-looking electrical circuit diagrams, scribbles, lyric fragments, logos indicating undrinkable water, scenes of domesticity (a 1960s photograph of a woman applying paste to a sheet of wallpaper and a drawing of a couple eating dinner at a table) and a smiley face logo under which sits the word 'tasty'. Page 6 gives the lyrics to the album's first song, 'Airbag,' which again shows how the technology that harms us also saves us:

> >in a deep sssleep of tHe inno$ent /~~completely terrified~~
>   am born again
> >in a fAAst geRman CAR
> i'm amazed that i survived
>   an airbag saved my life

The following pages continue this transcription of lyrics; most notable for the present analysis is 'Exit Music (for a film),' which asks that someone 'sing us a song / a song to keep us warm / theres such a chill sucha CHILL.' The artwork throughout the rest of the booklet, meanwhile, retains the fragmented form of collage with its resultant sense of dislocation, but places within that space many symbols of home: a silhouetted family holding hands; an architectural three-dimensional drawing of a house; childlike drawings of a house; a blurred doll shape; a holiday photograph; a childish drawing of stick businessmen shaking hands; and, finally, an illustration of an underground train platform and a photograph of the tail section of a plane, which is to say pictures of two modes of communal commuter transport that take people to and from home.

The back cover of the booklet, on which can be seen a book, the pages of which are covered in the same kind of cut-and-paste and scribble design as the rest of the artwork, and on which is written the track listing of the album, only reinforces this interpretation. This book is positioned on a background of clouds as seen from an airplane and, in the top right-hand corner, a photograph of a single tree on top of a hill highlighted against a brilliant blue sky with perfect cotton-puff clouds. Ultimately, there may be no deep significance to this, but the contrast of the stark simplicity of nature with the scrawled- and scribbled-on book is striking, and suggests that there is perhaps meaning to be found here. While it is obviously composed of many different texts and layers, there appears to have been an attempt here to paint over all of this book's different layers with white-out (which retrospectively makes us reinterpret the white scribbles throughout the artwork of the booklet) so as to leave a blank canvas on which the essence of this product – the song titles – can be presented in such a way that it mirrors the beautiful simplicity of the tree and the sky, and is thus similarly able to provide a calm and stable haven from chaos.

This examination of the back-cover art of *OK Computer*'s booklet might serve as an entry point into the analysis of its music also – although, as we shall see, this striving for simplicity may ultimately be its downfall. Even though the musical experimentation of *OK Computer* arguably pushed the boundaries of guitar-based rock further than they had ever gone before, beyond the parameters and genres previously referenced, stretching to 'DJ Shadow; The Beatles; Phil Spector; Cocteau Twins; Ennio Morricone; Miles Davis; Can [and] Krzysztof Penderecki' (Dalton 2001: 58), the overall effect is far from cluttered as all of these layers and the different technologies used are fused into a series of songs that are (deceptively) simple and conventional in their structure and that can, almost without exception, be internalized as a homely territory. The obvious exception to this possibility comes with 'Fitter Happier,' a monologue spoken by a computerized voice behind which can be heard abstract musical scribblings. Again, however, the lyrical content of this song merely instructs us how to be fitter, happier, and more productive within modern society, how to insulate ourselves against the modern world through a desensitizing conformity to it. Spoken by a robotic voice and ending with the grotesque image of 'a pig in a cage on antibiotics,' the song obviously wishes to denounce the dehumanization that society is undergoing in the technological era, the false sense of community that market forces create. We are told not to drink too much, to get on better with our associate employee contemporaries, to eat well, care about animals, set up a standing order to a charity, to be fond of someone rather than love them, generally to be more sensible and less reckless. *OK Computer* is conceived, I would imagine, as the very antithesis to this kind of conformist and desensitized life, it is supposed to be an expression of the genuine angst, alienation, and dislocation that is born of living in an overly complex world. Indeed, David Cavanagh, writing in *Q* magazine, describes it as 'an encapsulation of what it's like to feel terrified by the times' (2000: 96), but it is because it is voicing such terror that ultimately both the artwork and music create spaces of home as a refuge against this fear, and it is for this reason, not simply because it is just *so* good, as Cavanagh continues, that there could exist a 'party atmosphere in the stalls as Radiohead played their complex elegies in half-lit reverie' (2000: 96). The overall effect of *OK Computer*, then, as Nick Kent points out, is one of identification thanks to its 'insinuated struggle to find a humane set of values amid the numbing paraphernalia of the lap-top mind-set' (2001: 60). In painting over their many intertexts with a big white Radiohead brush, in reducing all of this album's various musical and political layers to beautifully simple songs whose lyrics are distilled into soundbite portions, the effect upon the listener can be quite different from that intended, for the sense of home that emanates from the refrain is still what dominates in spite of moments of genuine horror. Symptomatic of this is Yorke's later disavowal of this album; as Simon Reynolds notes, 'touring and promoting the album for much of 1998 convinced Yorke that it was still too mired in rock tradition, too epic' (2001: 28).

Radiohead's music videos from their first three albums can be seen to follow this same pattern for they generally adhere to a standard format, presenting the band on stage (as in the videos for 'Creep' and 'My Iron Lung'), or else performing the song in a setting that serves merely as a backdrop and space of presentation for the music (as is the case with the swimming pool in 'Anyone Can Play Guitar,' the roof in 'Stop Whispering,' the Oxfordshire exteriors in 'Pop is Dead,' the trailer park in 'Street Spirit,' the desert exterior in 'High and Dry' (UK version), the hyper-generic supermarket in 'Fake Plastic Trees,' the studio in 'Lucky,' and the glass anechoic/suffocation chamber in 'No Surprises'). A few videos created for *The Bends* and *OK Computer* do attempt to push the boundaries of the music video genre, but ultimately even these create a sense of closure with a pseudo-happy ending. The man in the street in the video for 'Just,' for instance, achieves a kind of apocalyptic communality with all of those around him; Robin in the video for 'Paranoid Android' is carried away from his place of persecution by an angel in a helicopter while his persecutor, the leather G-string wearing, ax-wielding masked businessman, is, having cut off his own legs and arms and fallen into the river, saved by topless mermaids who wrap him in swaddling clothes and carry him away to a safe haven in a tree. The video for 'Karma Police' is perhaps the one from these three albums that pushes the conventional boundaries of the music video genre the furthest, for it plays with the relationship of the song to the image as an extra-diegetic or intra-diegetic element, Yorke sometimes mouthing the lyrics as they are sung, sometimes not. Similarly, the diegesis itself plays with the conventions of the thriller genre from which it is drawn: Yorke climbs into the back seat of a driverless car that chases after a man running down a road; the man falls to his knees, exhausted; the car reverses and pauses, waiting for the moment it will accelerate toward him to kill him; the man, however, notices a trail of petrol on the road, fumbles for his lighter and drops it on to the petrol trail, which chases after the car now reversing down the same road; finally, filmed from inside the car, we see the engine burst into flames as the camera pans round to where Yorke was previously but is no more. Starting *in media res*, this video contravenes the conventions of the genre that it springs from, for we are unable to establish a good guy and a bad guy just as we are unable to comprehend why Yorke is seen singing only occasionally while he is heard singing constantly. All of these open questions, however, are closed off by the time we have finished watching the video, for we are enclosed by the clever reversal of the diegesis that brings it full circle and, not knowing what gave rise to this strange scenario, merely relieved that neither the mysterious man nor Thom ended up hurt.

Commercially, throughout the period in which Radiohead released these three albums, it also seems to have behaved pretty much as any artist signed to a major label should: the band members gave interviews (even if Yorke often did so begrudgingly and made no secret of this fact to his interviewers), gave photographers free rein to present them as they wanted, made videos suitable for heavy MTV rotation, and toured extensively. Radiohead's official website was, at this time, perhaps the element of its marketing machine that strayed furthest from the path of a well-behaved band, becoming increasingly difficult to navigate, increasingly text-based, and increasingly political as time went on. In most respects, however, Radiohead, although undoubtedly idiosyncratic, comported itself, happily or not, as a mainstream artist, providing its audience with the sense of familiarity that we have suggested this majoritarian realm creates.

Radiohead's collusion with the marketing machine set in motion to promote its next album, *Kid A*, however, was to be far less cooperative. An initial absence of interviews, no videos, no singles, just a few short video blips with snatches of songs and abstract images (later revealed as elements of the album artwork), a 'logo-free' tent in which to tour – a move likely truly to upset the apple cart of today's music industry in which product placement and endorsement is almost as endemic as in Hollywood – and a series of computer-manipulated portraits in *Q* magazine that can only have been intended as an anticelebrity act of provocation, each member of the band being starkly lit to the point of slight over-exposure, the irises of their eyes tinted sickly yellow. (Yorke has said of these photographs: 'I'm sick of seeing my face everywhere. It got to the point where it didn't feel like I owned it. We're not interested in being celebrities, and others seemed to have different plans for us' (*Q* 104).) As Jon Pareles has written in his review of *Amnesiac* for *Rolling Stone*, 'Acting like a bunch of artists – not, as in most current rock, a business consortium touting a consistent product – Radiohead continue to slough off the style that made them standard-bearers for anthemic Brit pop in the 1990s.'[1] Some have viewed this anticorporate stance with great cynicism. In an article entitled 'Are Radiohead Dirty Great Hypocrites?,' for instance, Andrew Collins writes:

> Rock'n'roll is the wrong place to look for acts of true subversion. Though its roots lay in the empowerment of teenagers and the upturning of conservative orthodoxy through jive, popular music is no more about subversion than the Cheltenham & Gloucester building society. The minute a band submits to a record company – big or small – it becomes part of the system, a cog with a bad haircut. Which is why Radiohead putting out an album with no discernible singles on it and refusing to have their photo taken for *Q* has not brought the record industry to its corporate knees. Indeed, it helped fire *Kid A* to the top of the charts, both here and in America. They – and EMI – must have laughed until they blew champagne bubbles out of their noses – and looking back over the year 2000 their attitude is the rock issue that rankles above all others.
>
> Granted, we should be glad that a record as difficult as *Kid A* is a mainstream hit. It gives us all hope. But I can't help but feel uncomfortable with Radiohead's anti-marketing pose. Manufacturing an 'event' by doing hardly any interviews and not putting out a single is no more subversive than saturating the press and putting out one single before and two after (as they did for *OK Computer*). To recall the great CJ [a character in the British TV comedy series *The Fall and Rise of Reginald Perrin*]: they didn't get where they are today by not doing promotion or being photographed. Radiohead are world famous because, among other things, they are signed to Capitol in the States, toured constantly for about four years and supported R.E.M. (and because they promptly re-released 'Creep' when it looked like it would sell in '93). Now, as Thom Yorke never hesitates to tell us, Radiohead are tired of the corporate rock merry-go-round. They're opting out.[2]

Through an analysis of the music and artwork of *Kid A* and *Amnesiac*, as well as of recurrent imagery in its new website and the internet-only video for 'I Might Be Wrong,' however, we shall endeavor to show that it truly is Radiohead's intention with these albums to opt out of certain aspects of the mainstream (which is not to say by any means that they do not want to sell any albums), to problematize their relationship to the refrain, and not, therefore, to create a space of home.

For the recording of *Kid A* and *Amnesiac* – the material for both albums was recorded in the same sessions – Radiohead entirely reformulated the conception of what a band is. Whereas previously each member had had a specific role to play, the band's increased reliance on studio methods and electronic instrumentation meant that its usual five-piece combination of voice/guitar, guitar/keyboards, guitar, bass, drums and other recording norms went out of the window. As David Cavanagh notes:

> Many of the qualities of *OK Computer* – particularly the amazing guitar sounds and the masterful use of dynamics – are absent from *Kid A*. Also absent from some of the songs are certain members of Radiohead themselves. It was an album made in an entirely unfamiliar fashion: no time constraints; very little pre-written material; a great deal of bewilderment and fear. 'In terms of the relationship between the five of us, everything was up for grabs last year,' Selway reckons. 'It was a case of trying

to see what different musical approaches there were – whether they were appropriate, whether we were prepared to do them and whether we could find something to agree on.' (Cavanagh 2000: 98)

Indeed, as Cavanagh's interview with the band shows, the new conception of what purpose the individual members of a band such as Radiohead served would entirely reformulate the whole rock-band ethos. Leaving their egos and individual roles behind, there would be even less room on *Kid A* for the rock-star posturing seen in the booklets of *Pablo Honey* and *The Bends* than on *OK Computer*:

'If you're going to make a different-sounding record,' [O'Brien] says, 'you have to change the methodology. And it's scary – everyone feels insecure. I'm a guitarist and suddenly it's like, well, there are no guitars on this track or no drums. Jonny, me, Coz and Phil had to get our heads round that. It was a test of the band, I think. Would we survive with our egos intact?'

For O'Brien it meant a complete rethink: he would hardly touch a guitar in 1999. Selway, too, wondered if he had a valid contribution to make to Radiohead's music any more. Colin Greenwood concedes the album didn't start to take shape for him until earlier this year. As for Greenwood's brother Jonny, the lead guitarist once described as a 'chronic upstager,' he is thoroughly low-key on *Kid A* and plays guitar on only a couple of tracks. (Cavanagh 2000: 100–1)

Nor was it only the roles of the band members that would be radically rethought; their songwriting methodology, song structures, and arrangements would also undergo a quantum shift. As Cavanagh notes,

Partly because Yorke was unable to complete any songs, and partly because he'd had a Warp revival, he would sometimes bring demos to the studio that contained only a programmed drum sequence or an interesting sound. Perfectly legitimate procedure if you happen to be Massive Attack, but a bit of a head-scratcher for a three-guitar band like Radiohead. And since few of the songs that evolved from Yorke's demos had distinct verses or choruses, it was hard to work out the basic arrangements, hard to see where the guitars should go, and hard for the musicians to know whether they were making headway or wasting their time. (Cavanagh 2000: 100)

In this 'self-*deconstruction*' of the band, as Simon Reynolds termed it in *The Wire* (2001: 26), of all the elements transformed, the most radical transmogrification – and the one that would most upset the band's previous punctual use of the refrain and its homely territory – would be that brought to bear upon Yorke's vocals. As Reynolds writes,

Discarding or tampering with the two elements most celebrated by fans and critics alike: their guitar sound, and Yorke's singing and lyrics[,] *Kid A* is largely devoid of guitars, with Jonny Greenwood preferring to play the Ondes Martenot ..., write arrangements for string orchestra, or even play the recorder. ... As for Yorke's singing, on *Kid A*/*Amnesiac*, studio technology and unusual vocal technique are

both applied to dyslexify his already oblique, fragmented words. Yorke has said he
will never allow the lyrics to be printed and that listeners are expressly not meant
to focus on them. (Reynolds 2001: 26)

Many critics, and indeed the band, seem to be at pains to stress that, although
emerging from the same sessions, *Kid A* and *Amnesiac* are two very different
creatures even if they issue from a similar mental space. '*Amnesiac* is about
seeing really awful things that you try to forget and can't quite. Whereas *Kid A* is
deliberately trying to keep everything at a safe distance,' Yorke has said (Watson
20001: 46). '*Kid A* is like you pick up the phone, you call somebody, and there's
an answering machine on the other end. With *Amnesiac*, you get through to that
person. And you're engaged in the conversation,' the band's graphic designer,
Stanley Donwood, has commented (O'Brien quoting Donwood in Fricke 2001a:
48). 'The effect [of *Amnesiac*] is like *Kid A* turned inside out. ... On *Kid A*, Yorke
often sounded like a ghost trapped inside an ice sculpture. On *Amnesiac*, he sings
in front of the music with confrontational intimacy,' writes David Fricke, who
also sees this latter album as more of a return to Radiohead's previous style of
making and arranging music (2001a: 48). *Amnesiac* 'appears to build a bridge
between its sister album's *avant*-noise post-rock soundscapes and more
traditionally recognizable pop forms, from acoustic ballads to big band jazz,'
suggests Stephen Dalton (2001: 45). But, as Simon Reynolds and Ian Watson
realize, in spite of the differences between the two albums, they are in many
respects one of a kind, neither one of them ultimately marking a return to more
conventional pop structures, neither one, then, in the context of the present
analysis, allowing for the creation of a homely space. As Steven Wells has written
in the *NME*:

> The bad news is that the new Radiohead album has apparently been ruthlessly
> purged of anything that might even vaguely resemble a good pop song. Sigh! It
> seems my work is still not finished so, Thom, listen up, man! Pop songs are good!
> They make the world go round, they put a spring in your step and they give the
> grocer's boy something to whistle as he cycles around the village on his trusty old
> boneshaker delivering sausages, bananas and Anal Intruder vibrator batteries to the
> denizens of middle England. You fucking SNOB! ... Why not just do your job
> properly? You know the score. Hook, verse, chorus, verse, chorus, fiddly middle
> eight bit and/or screaming guitar solo, verse, chorus, and get the fuck out of there.
> Thank you ladeez an' genelmen! Radiohead have left the building! ROAR! You
> know, good ole rock'n'fuckin'roll! Which, now that you've got yourself sorted out
> gymwise, would have angry and optimistic lyrics. As opposed to all that self-
> indulgent, self-pitying, depressing, mawkish and downright bloody boring
> miserablist toss you were churning out when you were a couch potato.[3]

And as Watson comments – somewhat more calmly but still dispelling the notion
that *Amnesiac* is more listener-friendly or, rather, more old-Radiohead-fan-
friendly – even though this album contains some moments which are arguably
more accessible and melodic,

the sequencing of the songs and often bleak lyrical tone makes *Amnesiac* a very troubling album indeed. Where *Kid A* eased you in with the comforting warmth of 'Everything in its Right Place' and rewarded you after that draining emotional journey with the serene beauty and reassurance of 'Motion Picture Soundtrack,' *Amnesiac* is a far more desolate experience. Opener 'Packt Like Sardines in a Crushd Tin Box' marries an unsettling clutter with a sense of tired defeat. 'Pulk Pull Revolving Doors' is creepy and unnerving, like lapsing into an insomniac fever. 'Like Spinning Plates' places you at the eye of the storm, moving from panic, confusion and despair to a realm beyond language and reason where all you know is you want to be sick and you want to get out right now, right now. And 'Life in a Glasshouse' uses the admittedly gorgeous jazz meanderings of veteran trumpet player Humphrey Lyttelton and chums to chart complete and utter disaster. (Watson 2001: 48, 50)

It is perhaps this notion of 'despair [and] a realm beyond language and reason where all you know is you want to be sick' that will best facilitate our own analysis of these two albums. All of these ideas, of anguish, the loss of controlling reason and sickness, are reminiscent of Antoine Roquentin's existential crisis in Jean-Paul Sartre's 1938 novel, *Nausea*. In this book, Roquentin undergoes a kind of breakdown following his realization of the terrible contingency of the universe. Having understood that his existence is no more justified than that of the objects around him, the material world loses its sense of fixity, becomes capable of touching him and provoking in him a dreadful sense of nausea as the universe around him enters into a dizzying state of flux. Roquentin's proposed solution to this terrible anguish is to write a novel, an artistic expression which would be entirely self-sufficient, containing in its very coherence and internal necessity its own justification. This solution comes to him after he realizes that the one thing that can make his nausea go away is a jazz song he hears in the café he frequents. This song seems to him to have an internal coherence and justification, for every note in its melody needs to be in its place for the melody to work. *Kid A* and *Amnesiac* are born of this same kind of realization, out of this kind of traumatic space that is created when all of those pre-givens and rational methods of categorization previously used to order existence disappear, leaving in their place a gaping chasm. Indeed, Yorke has explained the title *Amnesiac* through reference to the Gnostics' belief that 'when we are born we are forced to forget where we have come from in order to deal with the trauma of arriving in this life' (David Fricke in *Rolling Stone* August 2001: 111), and has described the track 'Pulk/Pull Revolving Doors' as expressing 'the feeling that everywhere you're going all the time, there could be a trapdoor absolutely anywhere and you don't know where you're going to end up next. And you're pretty certain you're not going to come back to where you were' (David Fricke in *Rolling Stone* August 2001: 46).

The music that Radiohead has produced on *Kid A* and *Amnesiac*, then, far from constituting a solution to this sense of disorientation – as does the jazz song for Roquentin – serves merely to express this sense of being lost, to give voice to the space of trauma that modern man can feel when faced with a global economy in which the individual can have little effect. Nowhere is this more apparent than in the existential, anguished manifesto of impossibility that appears at the top of each page of the limited edition book version of *Kid A*, and that reads:

NOBODY LIKES NOTHING
I CERTAINLY WISH WITH ALL MY HEART IT DID NOT
EXIST
BUT WISHING IS NOT ENOUGH
WE LIVE IN THE REAL WORLD WHERE NOTHING DOES
EXIST
WE CANNOT JUST DISINVENT IT
NOTHING IS NOT COMPREHENSIBLE
NEITHER YOU NOR I HAVE ANY HOPE OF
UNDERSTANDING JUST WHAT IT IS AND WHAT IT DOES
IT IS HARD TO KNOW IF NOTHING IS ACTUALLY
NOTHING
AND THUS DIFFICULT TO KNOW IF A POLICY OF DOING
NOTHING IS SUCCESSFUL
NOTHING
HOWEVER EFFECTIVE IT MAY HAVE PROVED UP TO THE
PRESENT
CAN HARDLY CONTINUE TO DO SO INDEFINITELY
IF I HAD TO CHOOSE
BETWEEN THE CONTINUED POSSIBILITY OF NOTHING
HAPPENING
AND OF DOING NOTHING
I WOULD UNQUESTIONABLY CHOOSE THE LATTER
OR THE FORMER

Far from an existential affirmation of infinite possibility born from the void, Yorke and Radiohead voice with *Kid A* and *Amnesiac*, as Simon Reynolds puts it, 'contemporary feelings of dislocation, dispossession, numbness, impotence, paralysis; widely felt impulses to withdraw and disengage that are perfectly logical, dispirited responses to the bankruptcy of Centrist politics, which ensure that everyone remains equally disenchanted and aggrieved' (Reynolds 2001: 30).

The apparent emotional coldness that many felt in this new, more electronic phase of Radiohead's career, then, might be said to convey more truly than did *OK Computer* the sense of genuine terror that the technological era can inspire, 'the feeling of being a spectator and not being able to take part' (Reynolds 2001: 30). Even though many fans and critics have received *Kid A* and *Amnesiac* as enthusiastically, if not more so, as the band's previous albums – although with undoubtedly fewer superlatives than were heaped upon *OK Computer* – every aspect of the conception and creation of these albums seems to be directed toward disallowing any kind of comfort zone or recognizable *point de repère* – as David Fricke has written, 'the whole point of *Kid A* is that there are no sure things, in pop or anything else.'[4] Simon Reynolds sees this intent at play particularly in the treatment of Yorke's vocals:

> Bored with all the standard tricks of vocal emoting, Yorke decided to interface voice and technology and develop what he's called 'a grammar of noises'. The first two tracks on *Kid A*, 'Everything in its Right Place' and the title track, are especially striking in this respect, almost a declaration of intent. The words are drastically processed in order to thwart the standard rock listener mechanism of identify and interpret (the very mode of trad rock deed and meaningfulness that *OK Computer* had dramatically revived). (Reynolds 2001: 32)

Although Reynolds' subsequent comment that the frequently heard charge against *Kid A*, that it contains no tunes, is 'absurd' since 'actually, almost every track on the album is structured like a song' (2001: 32) would seem to counter this analysis, it should be remembered that we have, in our definition of pop, forged a link between pop and the mainstream. For Reynolds, writing in *The Wire*, a magazine that prides itself, as Reynolds points out in the very same article, on 'championing mavericks and margin dwellers' (2001: 26), *Kid A*'s tracks may indeed all appear to be fairly conventional songs. For the mainstream, though, even if these tracks are admired, they are not songs in the strict sense of the term, and present difficulties and problems of interpretation because of this.[5] Reynolds may lament this fact and name its causes – 'the mixed response *Kid A* garnered in the UK revealed how the Britpop era has weakened the rock audience's (or more likely, the rock media's) ability to handle anything not blatantly singalong' (2001: 32), he writes – but it remains true. Take, for instance, David Cavanagh's brief description of *Kid A* in *Q* magazine:

> *Kid A* is 48 minutes long, stunningly beautiful, frequently bizarre and wholly engrossing. It begins with a fabulous electric piano song played by Yorke, follows that with the oddest Radiohead track ever, veers off into something even odder, brings you back with the loveliest orchestrated ballad in years, wanders away on some unexplained errand for a while, returns with two guitar songs as uncanny as they are exceptional, goes suddenly very dark and inhospitable for about five minutes, reaches out for you as though nothing had happened and eventually bids you farewell in a halo of harps and choirs. There has never been an album like it. (Cavanagh 2000: 169)

Kid A and *Amnesiac* create this feeling of expansiveness and grandeur, which is both beautiful and terrifying, by erasing all punctual coordinates of the refrain that attract music around a stable center. 'I'd completely had it with melody,' says Yorke, 'I just wanted rhythm. All melodies to me were pure embarrassment' (Cavanagh 2000: 100). Forsaking that very aspect of music which, for Roquentin and the average listener, provides a space of solace, a sense of recognition, Radiohead presents a series of distant plateaus difficult to approach. Sing 'Creep' in your head, right now. Now do the same with 'Just.' Now again with 'Karma Police.' Now try it with 'Kid A,' or 'The National Anthem,' or 'How to Disappear

Completely,' or 'Motion Picture Soundtrack,' or 'Pyramid Song,' or Pulk/Pull Revolving Doors,' or 'Dollars & Cents,' or 'Like Spinning Plates,' or 'Life in a Glasshouse'. See?

This feeling, Yorke has stated, is 'all so part of the fabric of everything, even the artwork' (Reynolds 2001: 30). Indeed, the booklet for the regular version of *Kid A* is composed almost entirely of a series of epic sweeping landscapes stretching into the distance, always *away* from the viewer and with no points of reference. There are no houses, nothing that looks like a home. The family on the center pages, dwarfed by the white cliffs before them, are not holding hands but separated in their stunned contemplation of this expanse. The distant hills behind which, after a long trek, may lie home are unapproachable, for the orange glow of the sky lets us know that whatever lies beyond them is ablaze. The cartoon teddy bears standing on a mountain do not welcome us either, their evil eyes and sharp teeth, straight out of a child's animated nightmare, warning us to stay away.[6] It is these last two elements of the artwork in particular that are taken up and developed in the limited-edition book version of *Kid A*. Made of thick cardboard pages, like a child's book, we are presented with painted versions of landscapes similar to those in the regular *Kid A* booklet: white hills and distant forests lit by the orange glow of fires; distant, monolithic, unclimbable rock formations. But in addition to these vistas, we are presented with larger versions of these unapproachable spaces of home hinted at in the regular booklet: one page features a series of apartment blocks, but they are on fire; one page features a pet cat (or is it that cuddliest of wild animals, a polar bear?), but it is so deformed and its teeth so sharp and long you would never try to pet it; one page features the evil toothy grinning teddy bears, one of whom has come closer but remains hostile. While this book in its very form may then appear to provide a nostalgic space of home, a chance to revisit lost childhood, just as do the music-box tinklings with which 'Kid A' begins, the childhood it evokes is one of trauma that we do not wish to go back to.

Another detail of the artwork of both of these versions of *Kid A* is very significant for the present analysis. We have suggested, talking about the artwork of *OK Computer*, that the various layers of text and reference that go into the composition of *OK Computer* are painted over so as to reduce the complexity of the whole. The procedure on *Kid A* is somewhat different, for while the whitewashed landscapes of the artwork of *Kid A* also feature hardly legible text, it is apparent that these texts are not underneath the white but have, rather, been scratched into it. It is as though these texts – which may or may not bear any relation to the lyrical content of the album, it matters little – are an attempt to inscribe meaning on to a vast primordial landscape, to make an individual mark on the incommensurable, an attempt that is doomed to failure just as, musically, Yorke's voice on *Kid A*, that element of any song which affords the greatest chance of identification, struggles to break through the vast expanses of sound, his syntax broken and dyslexic.

Yorke's voice ultimately, then, as was his avowed intention, becomes merely another textural element of the instrumentation in *Kid A*'s landscapes and does not act as a bearer of meaning.[7] If the artwork of *Kid A* does indeed reinforce this analysis, then two of its other illustrations also become highly significant. Toward the end of the book version, for instance, there features an oil painting of a face seen from so close up that it is barely recognizable as such, appearing rather to be pure texture, a set of random brush strokes. Rejecting the identification afforded by lyrical content in favor of a textural use of the voice, could this picture not also symbolize the denial of the identification with the face of the individual members of the band (what Deleuze and Guattari call faciality), the surpassing of their individual ego boundaries into constituent elements of a group? And if *Kid A* refuses meaning and punctual forms in its music, could the reason for this not be found in the painting on the book's back cover, a series of three scarlet shapes resembling war planes above which figure the words:

WE WILL NOT HESITATE TO CARRY OUT WHAT HAS
BEEN THREATENED
THIS IS NOT OVER UNTIL ABSOLUTE UNCONDITIONAL
SURRENDER
AND COMPLETE MEETING OF ALL DEMANDS
THERE WILL BE NO FURTHER WARNING WHATSOEVER
AIRSTRIKES ARE IMMINENT

Faced with the possibility of such absolute power and destruction, how can meaning be possible, how can any safe haven, any sense of order, any semblance of home be achieved, *Kid A* seems to ask us.

Amnesiac, as has been seen, presents a somewhat different scenario musically, but one that ultimately wells from the same traumatic space as *Kid A*, which similarly denies us a sense of home. The main difference between these two albums, as has been seen from various quotations, is one of perspective: whereas the vocals on *Kid A* are far back in the mix and disturbed through processing, on *Amnesiac* they are brought to the fore. Even though Yorke's lyrics are heard more easily, then, this does not mean for one second that they are more *comprehensible*. Far from espousing the kind of explicit political messages found on *OK Computer*, *Amnesiac*'s lyrics are made up of paranoid soundbites, often repeated in a mantra-like fashion, that unveil a deep sense of persecution and lack of protection or home:

I'm a reasonable man, get off my case, get off my case, get off my
case.
There are doors that let you in and out but never open.
Come on, come on, you and whose army?
I might be wrong, I might be wrong, I could have sworn, I saw a
light coming home.
I want you to know he's not coming back, Look into my eyes / I'm
not coming back.

Where'd you park the car, Clothes are on the lawn with the
furniture
Cut the kids in half, Cut the kids in half
Once again, I'm in trouble with my only friend.

Just as *Amnesiac* welcomes us in to its unhomely spaces musically, so the
artwork situates us in the space of trauma so that we are 'standing in the fire,'[8] at
the heart of the now absent center. Fragmented street maps, blazing buildings,
towering skyscrapers seen from the bottom up, interweaving power cables and
Escherian drawings of arches and staircases all appear to give sets of punctual
references and coordinates with which to orient ourselves, but ultimately have the
opposite effect, creating that same sense of being lost and dislocated felt in *Kid
A*. Evoking a lost sense of a calm and stable center that was once present, the
limited-edition book version of *Amnesiac* (from which the regular version is
drawn) also contains many drawings and fragments of text (some of which are
drawn from the album's lyrics) that express feelings of fear and paranoia so
extreme they verge on pathology: one page figures the phrase 'ARK,
complacence. rivers rising. whispering electronics, private security. in LOndon.
Rooms where you are forgotten. mental home' and then the word 'sectioned'
repeated again and again; on another can be seen the words 'my former self
????????????? ... scare the crows ??????????? ... HE SMASHED'; later, 'i am
citizen insane' is typed as a mantra, *à la mode de The Shining*'s Jack Torrance,
and so on, and so on. Almost all of these pages, meanwhile, show dark pencil or
pen drawings of scenes of violence, dark looming buildings, twisted trees with
ghostly branches,[9] a graveyard with hollow faces on every tombstone, men with
no eyes or eyes sewn shut, and childhood monsters that have emerged from the
closet, all of which are furiously scribbled with obsessive-compulsive attention to
detail. Inside *Amnesiac*, where a funeral pyre burns what looks like a rag doll
while the toothy grinning evil teddy bears are closer than before, this time bearing
large mallets, we appear to be in that traumatic space of lost childhood that lay in
the distance in *Kid A*.

One figure stands apart in the midst of all of this fear: the weeping Minotaur.
The closest *Amnesiac* gets to a logo, the weeping Minotaur figures throughout the
book – on the front cover (for even if this weeping figure has no horns, horns are
scribbled on to it inside the book and on the cover of the regular version of
Amnesiac), on the library card insert as the symbol of the Catachresis College
Library, and at the center of its heraldic shield, overlaid on top of some sections
of pathological text, blown up to various sizes, drawn over the book's *ex libris*
stamp and, most significantly, in a doodle that shows him dreaming of one of the
grinning bears holding an ax at the scene of a massacre.

The weeping Minotaur also features prominently in Radiohead's new official
website on which can also be found the same disturbing, nightmarish images of
buildings, ghosts, and trees as in the booklet, but used in animated form as short
blips. While some of these looped blips invoke the legend of the Minotaur by

Figure 5.1   'minotauralley.mov.' Music video. Dir. Chris Bran

animating labyrinthine passages and cityscapes, the weeping Minotaur (named as such on the website) figures in two blips of his own. In one of these he is quite simply weeping (Figure 5.1), while in another flash animation we are invited to torture the Minotaur by moving a pitchfork over him with our mouse, an action that makes him cry and moan as the line plotted between the anger and revenge axes of a graph increases (Figure 5.2). Rather than constituting another element of the unhomely, nightmarish space evoked in *Kid A* and *Amnesiac*, the weeping Minotaur represents, I would like to finish by suggesting, the unhomely space that Radiohead have come to inhabit within the homely space of the mainstream. What prompts this suggestion is a drawing in the *Amnesiac* book that shows a version of the Minotaur (this time the GooglyMinotaur, a slightly less sad, more scared and confused looking version of the monster that the band's record company website has done its best to turn into a cute, friendly, homely icon)[10] next to an angry-looking media man with clenched bared teeth (Figure 5.3). In order to conjecture as to why this might be significant, however, we will have to remind ourselves of the myth of the Minotaur.

Struggling with his brothers to ascend the throne of Crete, Minos decides to pray to Poseidon for a snow-white bull as a sign of approval of his reign. He promises subsequently to sacrifice the bull as a sign of subservience to the gods, but when Minos sees the beautiful creature that emerges from the sea, he covets it for himself and sacrifices the best bull out of his own herd instead. Furious at this act of betrayal, Poseidon makes Minos's wife, Pasiphaë, fall in love with the white bull. The bull rejects her advances, however, until she commissions the architect, Daedalus, to build her a wooden cow into which to crawl and fool the bull into mating with her. The offspring of this

experiment # 6
torturing the minotaur

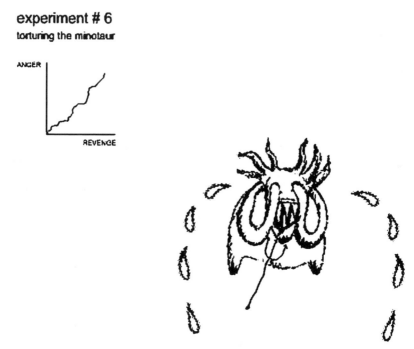

Figure 5.2   Website image

unnatural coupling was the Minotaur, a monster with the body of a man and a bull's head and tail.

This monster caused great terror and destruction in Crete, so Minos summoned Daedalus and ordered him to build a gigantic labyrinth to contain the Minotaur. Once he was trapped there, every year for nine years seven youths and maidens from Athens were sent into the labyrinth for the Minotaur to feast upon. Hearing of this atrocity, Theseus offered himself as a sacrificial victim and went to Crete in order to kill the Minotaur. Once there he met Ariadne, Minos's daughter, who fell in love with him and promised him the means to escape from the labyrinth provided he would marry her. This he promised and Ariadne gave him a ball of thread, which he was to tie to the labyrinth entrance and unwind behind him as he advanced through the maze. Once inside, Theseus came across the sleeping Minotaur, beat him to death and led the virgins to safety.

It is entirely feasible and not too far-fetched to find in this legend an allegory of Radiohead's career. Like many bands wishing to make a career out of music, Radiohead's initial enthusiasm at being signed up by a major record label soon soured, as one of the band members recalls: 'We were in Leicester Square going, "Yeah, we've signed!" Then driving back to Oxford in the pouring rain, the clouds were gathering, already starting to worry and panic, how are we going to do this?' (*Uncut* August 2001: 48). This panicked reaction no doubt had to do, in

Figure 5.3   Website image

part, with the realization that a contract such as this would inevitably put them in a position of subservience with regard to their record company, that there would be deadlines and many other constraints with which they would now have to comply. As Stephen Dalton notes, 'early in 1992, EMI took the band aside for a makeover conference. They were given a £300 clothes budget and told to sharpen up their act' (Dalton 2001: 48).

Their subservience to the record company's expectations was only partial, however, for while they played the part of the consummate rock stars – as has been seen from the above analysis of representations of the band on the first two albums' artwork and their compliance with the promotional machine during the first three – musically Radiohead appeared to be veering into ever-darker and more experimental territory unlikely to please most A&R men. (Even if we have maintained that *OK Computer* ultimately retains a conventional form, it is none the less conceptually outside of the parameters of the mainstream industry's expectations. Indeed, when Capitol, the band's US label, heard *OK Computer*, it reduced sales forecasts from two million to 500,000.) Up until this point, the parallel with the legend of the Minotaur remains true, then: Radiohead, like Minos, not delivering 100 per cent on its promise of subservience after having been handed the keys to success. From *OK Computer* onward, however, the legend is somewhat modified, since Radiohead's apparent betrayal of the record company gods turned out to be far from a bad thing for the record company in terms of sales. *OK Computer* sold 4.5 million copies worldwide and was widely acclaimed as a masterpiece. It is thanks to these sales figures that Radiohead was allowed to do as it pleased for its next album, *Kid A*, the band's brief being merely to take as long as it needed to produce whatever it wanted. What the members of Radiohead subsequently did, as we have seen, was to hole themselves up in a studio with no pre-givens, no pre-written material, no points of reference, a labyrinth in other words. The ultimate product of this long period of gestation was, then, the result of an unnatural coupling: the marriage of the mainstream record industry – which normally prizes predictability, efficiency and sales figures above all else – with genuine artistic experimentation, which cannot be rushed and whose commercial potential cannot be gauged.[11] Perhaps this is why the Minotaur figures so prominently in the artwork of *Amnesiac*, why the limited-edition book version is explicitly referred to as a labyrinthine structure, why the pages of this book are used as labyrinth walls in one of the website's blips and why the Minotaur is seen trapped within these same walls in the new internet-only video for 'I Might be Wrong' (Figure 5.4). If there is anything at all in this hypothesis, then this might also explain why, for this new video, Thom Yorke himself suggested intercutting shots of the Minotaur with shots of himself performing the song,[12] for *Kid A* and *Amnesiac* would thus become the song of the Minotaur, offspring of an unholy union, confined to a labyrinth.

Why, though, is Radiohead's Minotaur weeping? By all accounts, the period of creative activity that was the genesis of *Kid A* and *Amnesiac* has left the band happier than ever before. The image of the weeping Minotaur in a labyrinth

Figure 5.4   'I Might Be Wrong.' *Amnesiac*. Parlophone, 2001. Music video. Dir. Chris Bran

should not be read as a self-pitying reflection of a whinging group of individuals in an extremely privileged position, therefore, but rather as indicative of the band's current creative state. The labyrinth, we have suggested, being an infinitely complex structure that hides a dead end or further possibility at every turn, is the creative space within which Radiohead confined itself in an attempt to retain/restore its musical and emotional integrity after the grueling period of corporate whoring that followed the release of *OK Computer*. From within that space (given to the band by the record company to stop it from self-destructing, just as the labyrinth was built to stop the Minotaur destroying the town of Crete) it has managed to create a genuine, emotional expression symbolized by the Minotaur's tears – to cry is perhaps the most unreflexive, primordial response in the human vocabulary of emotions. This expression, while echoing the sense of alienation and unhomeliness with which its genetic space inevitably instills it, is not, ultimately, an unhappy one. Indeed, precisely because the labyrinth is, by definition, a space in which familiarity (the very essence of a home) is impossible, because it is a space of the unknown, a space where there are no givens and no expectations, it is a haven of calm from the mainstream which – far from being a comforting, homely space as it would normally be – had become a hostile place for the band. This is why the media man standing next to the GooglyMinotaur looks so angry, and this is why both *Kid A* and *Amnesiac*, while both rejecting the homely coordinates of the refrain and mainstream expression, while both being somehow unsettling, are also capable of inspiring ecstatic, almost transcendent, feelings of joy. 'People build themselves their own mazes that they can't get out of ... but no, I'm not negative,' Yorke is quoted as saying.[13] If it is to survive within the mainstream space in which its commercial success

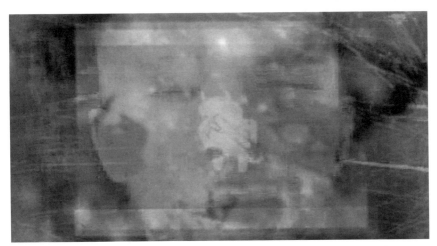

Figure 5.5 'I Might Be Wrong.' *Amnesiac*. Parlophone, 2001. Music video. Dir. Chris Bran

necessarily places it, and which is also necessary to its very survival, then, Radiohead should perhaps not try to escape its self-imposed labyrinthine exile at the very heart of the mainstream, cos it ain't over 'til the Minotaur stops crying.

Notes

1. Available online at: http://www.rollingstone.com/recordings/review.asp?aid=2042419&cf=236, accessed August 31 2001.
2. Available online at: http://www.q4music.com/features/fullfeature.cfm?ObjectUUID=8F01B66F-CB7B-11D4-9CDA000629DEBDC3, accessed August 31 2001.
3. Wells, Steven, 'Banging On Radiohead About ...', *New Musical Express* (July 15 2000), available online at: http://www.greenplastic.com/articles/nme07152000.html, accessed August 31 2001.
4. Fricke, David, review of Radiohead's *Kid A* for *Rolling Stone*, available online at: http://www.rollingstone.com/recordings/review.asp?aid=64764&cf=236, accessed August 31 2001.
5. See Steven Wells's comment in the *NME*, quoted above.
6. An article in the *Silicon Alley Reporter Magazine*, 41 (April 2001) notes that 'Radiohead's death-bear icon has roots in a bedtime story Stanley [Donwood] once told his daughter.' Available online at: http://www.greenplastic.com/articles/siliconalleyreporter2001.html, accessed August 31 2001.
7. On Yorke's desire to instrumentalize his voice, see Reynolds 2001: 28.
8. Yorke quoted in *Rolling Stone* (July 2001), 50.
9. The drawings of twisted trees with sinewy branches and roots are very reminiscent of descriptions of the tree root that provokes such terror for Roquentin in Sartre's *Nausea*.
10. At the band's label website, http://hollywoodandvine.com/radiohead/, it is currently possible to 'Befriend the Buddy! Add the GooglyMinotaur to your buddy list for all things Radiohead,' or else get the Minotaur as an 'instant messaging buddy icon.'
11. It is of vital importance to realize – as critics such as Steven Wells and Andrew Collins have not – that this latter phase of Radiohead's career truly is the result of a marriage between the mainstream and *avant-garde* experimentation, and not indicative of a desire completely to abandon commercial success. As Yorke has said when asked if he could live with the contradiction existing between his anticorporate rhetoric and the fact that his band is financed by a huge media conglomerate: 'Not really, I'm pretty touchy about it ... . But if you want to actually have your record in a shop, then you've got no way round it because you have to go through major distributors and they've all got deals and blah blah blah. There isn't a way round it. Personally, one of the reasons that I wanted to be in a band was actually to be on the high street. I don't want to be in a cupboard. I write music to actually communicate things to people' (quoted in *Uncut*, August 2001, 61).
12. One shot is particularly significant as a melancholic portrait of Yorke enters into a dissolve with the weeping Minotaur, the latter fading into the very center of Yorke's face (Figure 5.5). The video is available in its entirety in streaming format at the band's official website, http://www.radiohead.com, accessed August 31 2001.
13. Yorke quoted in *Uncut*, August 2001, 66.

Chapter 6

'Ice Age Coming': Apocalypse, the Sublime, and the Paintings of Stanley Donwood[1]

Lisa Leblanc

Nobody likes nothing
I certainly wish with all my heart that it did not exist
But wishing is not enough
We live in the real world where nothing does exist
We cannot just disinvent it
Nothing is not comprehensible
Neither you nor I have any hope of understanding just what it is and what it does
It is hard to know if nothing is actually nothing
And thus difficult to know if a policy of doing nothing is successful
Nothing
However effective it may have proved up to the present
Can hardly continue to do so indefinitely
If I had to choose
Between the continued possibility of nothing happening
And of doing nothing
I would unquestionably choose the latter
Or the former

Stanley Donwood, Kid A Special Edition book

Since Radiohead's release of *The Bends* in 1995, Stanley Donwood has been working collaboratively with the band, creating an iconographic language, and providing a strong visual analog to the music. The work is not done in isolation, or as an afterthought, but rather develops in conjunction with the music, and the result is a complicity between the two. They support and complete one another, one picking up where the other leaves off, creating a visual and auditory whole.

Thematically, the works focus on anxiety with an almost gradual progression of ever-increasing dread. On *The Bends*, the music and artwork convey the individual's anxiety and insecurity in contemporary society, emphasizing a personal fear of inadequacy, of being unable to act or effect change, or to make a meaningful contribution. The conflict between the desire to participate in social activism and the reality of being the complicit participant in a consumeristic world is encapsulated in the juxtaposition of the lyrics and the artwork. 'I wish it was the sixties / I wish I could be happy,' sings Thom Yorke on the title track of

The Bends. Donwood echoes the sentiment in the artwork through the childlike scrawls of birds with their heads in the ground, or a sketchy human-like figure with his head in a bubble. There is a sense of denial and inadequacy in these works. While the formal rendering of this early artwork is rather literal, the underlying message sets the thematic groundwork for years to come.

On 1997's *OK Computer*, the anxiety is turned toward the community, manifested as a societal fear, through a false sense of security and the impending doom of suburban life. The conflict between the desire to embrace technology and the fear of letting it overcome our existence is clear in both the artwork and the music. The iconography is familiar, symbols that we have seen before, comforting elements of a basic visual literacy. They are stylized figures of men and women on public washroom doors, hazard labels on household cleaning products. Donwood relies on the language of wayfinding icons, those we see in subways and malls, guiding us through our lives, showing us the way out, to send us in the proper direction, to steer us clear of danger. While their form is clearly familiar, their content makes the familiar seem strange. They are at times authoritative and guiding, and at other times oppressive and alarming. They warn and protect, and offer help and reassurance. Although many of them are drawn from that familiar bank of images we carry with us – warning signs preparing us for the danger that lies ahead – these icons, instead of warning us of High Voltage, or Poison, are life warnings. Beware what lurks behind the clean and shiny surface, question everything: 'Thin Ice,' 'Lost Child,' 'Against Demons.' They tell us to proceed with caution, at our own risk, we are being alerted, we are being told to pay attention.

The music sounds a similar warning bell. We are asked to question the very things and activities through which we are meant to find comfort, our home ('such a pretty house / such a pretty garden'), ambition and prosperity ('a job that slowly kills you') ('No Surprises'), and our family ('so lock the kids up safe tonight / shut the eyes in the cupboard') ('Climbing Up the Walls'). Yet, instead of our finding comfort in the things we have been taught to cherish and strive for, they become the very impediments to our freedom and happiness. You may only be able to pay for that pretty house by working at a job that is unfulfilling, stressful, and compromising. And while you might be able to raise your children in a lovely suburban neighborhood, you can only guarantee their safety by locking the house up tight and setting the alarm.

On *Kid A* the anxiety becomes global. To make this shift, Donwood moves beyond confined and sterile cityscapes to monumental landscapes, replacing the impending doom of suburban life with the melting of polar ice caps and the threat of global destruction, focusing on our anxiety about the world we live in. Through a different medium, and a colossal scale, Donwood leaves behind sinister suburbia and walks straight into the apocalypse. As Donwood explains, 'I wanted to make big paintings because I'd spent so long making little pictures on a computer, mostly for *OK Computer*. All that pointing and clicking was driving me crazy. So I wanted to really go crazy.' In the following pages I will discuss how Donwood renders tangible and makes credible the threat of the apocalypse, sounding a clear warning, by eliciting the sublime.

While anxiety continues to be a prominent concern in the *Amnesiac* Special Edition book, its formal manifestation takes on the appearance of a statement of facts, or scientific evidence, rather than a warning. Both musically and visually, anxiety returns in full force on 2003's *Hail to the Thief*, only to confirm the strength of the theme.

The sublime

The esthetics of the sublime refer to the attainment of a state of being, an emotional, perhaps even spiritual, response experienced in the mind between the imagination and reason. In the mid- to late-eighteenth century, Edmund Burke and Immanuel Kant sought to define the esthetics of the sublime so as to correspond with the Enlightenment ideals of the period.

Burke suggests that the passions of self-preservation, those of pain and danger, the fear of sickness and death, elicit the strongest human emotion, that of the sublime. 'Without all doubt, the torments which we may be made to suffer, are much greater in their effect on the body and mind,' and therefore, catastrophic events in nature, such as earthquakes or hurricanes, often elicit the sublime, causing a fear of pain and suffering by their sheer unpredictability, magnitude and destructive force (Burke 1971: 58–9). For Burke, fear and distress are causes of the sublime, and lead to a sense of powerlessness and astonishment.

For Kant the sublime is 'a feeling of imagination by its own act depriving itself of its freedom by receiving a final determination in accordance with a law other than that of its empirical employment' (Kant 1952: 120). Kant defines his theory from a mathematical perspective, proposing that when the viewer is faced with, for example, the soaring heights of a mountain, astonishment is achieved by the mind's inability to quantitatively conceive of the mountain in its entirety; its scale is beyond the mind's comprehension. Unable rationally to understand what it sees, the mind is left trying to complete the representation of the mountain through the freedom of imagination, yet, frozen in a state of astonishment, is deprived of its ability to do so. Out of this conflict, the viewer attains a state of the sublime. As Gilles Deleuze explains:

> The Sublime thus confronts us with a direct subjective relationship between imagination and reason. But this relationship is primarily a *dissension* rather than an accord, a contradiction experienced between the demands of reason and the power of the imagination. This is why the imagination appears to lose its freedom and the feeling of the sublime seems to be a pain rather than pleasure. But at the bottom of the dissensions the accord emerges; the pain makes a pleasure possible. (Deleuze 1984: 51)

Our sense of astonishment in the face of nature has faded in the last century. It is difficult for the scale of a mountain to elicit the sublime when that mountain has been scaled by a growing number of people, photographed from airplanes and helicopters, its dimensions accurately mapped and charted by satellite. As our quantitative, mathematical, and scientific ability to demystify grows, our sense of astonishment, and consequently of the sublime, diminishes. The dissension between reason and imagination weakened, the imagination no longer struggles to complete the representation, as our mind is now continually provided with the quantitative information required to finish the picture.

In the twenty-first century, possible sources of the sublime – the fear of sickness and death, pain and danger – have taken on apocalyptic proportions, through the scale of our cities, the pervasive ecological threat to our planet, the fear of nuclear annihilation or chemical warfare, the spread of contagious diseases, genetic manipulation, and terrorist destruction. The news media feed us an endless supply of statistics and quantitative information regarding the effects of such apocalyptic possibilities. While we may be horrified by the potential destruction, we seem unwilling to believe that such an apocalypse is possible. As Deleuze further explains, 'Imagination thus learns that it is reason which pushes it to the limit of its power, forcing it to admit that all its power is nothing compared to an Idea' (Deleuze 1984: 51). The Idea of the apocalypse, its conceptualization, is so powerful that it is beyond the imagination. The power of this Idea overwhelms the imagination and problematizes the representation of the apocalypse, making it impossible to imagine.

Art forces us to use the power of imagination to create a dissension with reason, and provides a representation of the unrepresentable (in our case, the apocalypse) in such a way – through form, content, and juxtaposition – that once the dissension emerges, the sublime is attained. Burke further explains, 'When painters have attempted to give us a clear representation of these very fanciful and terrible ideas, they have I think almost always failed; insomuch that I have been at a loss, in all the pictures I have seen of hell, whether the painter did not intend something ludicrous' (Burke 1971: 109). Consequently any such attempt at mimetic representation is subject to ridicule due to the limitations of imagination. The representation of the apocalypse must therefore be believable as an Idea for it to elicit the sublime. Can art provide a means of eliciting the sublime by rendering tangible and making credible the threat of the apocalypse?

The *Kid A* paintings

Painted over a period of a year, when Radiohead was recording its fourth and fifth albums, *Kid A* and *Amnesiac*, this series of large, dark, and dirty paintings by Stanley Donwood is in stark contrast to the whitewashed sterility of the computer-manipulated *OK Computer* works. The paintings are simultaneously the logical thematic progression from, and the surprising formal antithesis to, Donwood's previous work – they are as similar and different as siblings. The *Kid A* paintings make tactile the scratched, layered, erased, and inscribed surface of the *OK Computer* works, adding a sculptural dimension to the latter's smooth and shiny surface.

All but two of the paintings in the series are landscapes, descendants of a well-established English tradition. But these are not your grandparents' pastoral Constables, where the subjectivity of representation results in a calm and idyllic landscape. They have a closer affinity with the turbulent work of J.M.W. Turner, through their formal aggressiveness and socio-political commentary on a myriad of twenty-first-century concerns. However, unlike Turner's landscapes, which are full of movement, Donwood's are static. They convey the sense of time standing still, a film set to pause, where pressing play would resume the action, and complete the destruction. Like newsreel footage, where the camera allows the action to be stopped, and then replayed over and over, in slow motion, until the reality of the event is forever etched in your mind, you repeatedly watch the scene unfolding before you, incapable of believing it is really happening.

According to Burke, the power of the sublime lies in its closeness to reality. For Turner however, 'the sublime and the ridiculous are often so nearly related that it is difficult to class them separately. One step above the sublime becomes ridiculous and one step above the ridiculous makes the sublime again' (quoted in Gowing 1981: 783). It is a difficult line to tread, and where it seems as though Donwood may fall into the ridiculous, it begs the question whether he intends his representations to be closely related to reality. If so, how can he convey this reality without seeming preachy or, worse, ridiculous? 'We're not scaremongering / This is really happening,' Thom Yorke shouts in 'Idioteque.' Is he being sincere? Are we meant to take this seriously?

Despite the overwhelming use of white, and its western connotations of peace and purity, the landscapes are dark and foreboding, blood-red skies, and stark, cold vistas, where coniferous forests and skyscrapers loom in the distance, and where no human presence remains. Donwood explains, 'I wanted the battlefields to be empty – everyone had gone. Nothing left but memories and bloodstains' (Donwood, January 12 2003, interview with the author). The only remaining living creature is the recurring sharp-toothed bear. The world seems to have entered a nuclear winter. There are definite, sometimes clear, more often scratched and erased, recurring visual elements, such as field patterns (former farmed lands of plenty) and pyramids (symbols of the glory of 'civilization'), and, of course, the skyscrapers (modern symbols of power), forest, and bears. The sky often has the appearance of being simultaneously ablaze with fire and light, and shrouded by a dark postapocalyptic cloud. There is nothing warm and fuzzy about these paintings, and yet there is nothing sterile and cold either. These are not intimate scenes, they are landscapes of colossal destruction, cities on fire and abandoned.

Donwood states:

> I'd been fascinated with a memory I had of seeing some paintings when I was small
> … From a distance the paintings looked beautiful, like jewels scattered in mud. But
> close up they showed hundreds of killings, lots of white men in red coats killing
> almost naked black men. I suppose they must have been triumphal Empire-era
> paintings – they were very big, as I recall. (Donwood, January 12 2003)

While perhaps inspired by memory, these images cannot be classified in the
tradition of historical paintings. These events have not happened, but are
simulacra, scenes of an apocalyptic future.

In their children's book format, the paintings read like a story, a Grimm fairy
tale that begins, in the first three paintings, with the slow destruction of the
cityscape, and the tenuous survival of nature seen in the representations of forests
and fields. These three paintings act as an introduction to the story, inviting the
reader into the narrative: this is what we know, the world looks like this, fields
and skyscrapers and forests. Nothing is unfamiliar. Buried under the surface,
barely visible, like archeological evidence, are the traces of the story once told,
now erased, and forever unknown. In *Snow Accident* (Figure 6.1), under the red
and yellow sky ablaze over a dark coniferous forest, is a heavily inscribed white
field. The story continues in *Snow Evidence* (Figure 6.2), in the whiteness, which
appears to be engulfing the city, the foreground stained red; and in *Dead Fields*
(Figure 6.3), in the gray shadowy remains of the city to the bottom left of the
painting. As Donwood explains:

> The polytex was applied with sticks and knives, and moved about with my clothes
> and my boots. When it was half dry I scratched stories into it with an old biro and
> a knife. Then when it was a bit more dry I smoothed the writing over to make it
> pretty much illegible, but rubbing soot into it afterwards made the words reappear,
> sort of. (Donwood, January 12 2003)

Like the iconography of the *OK Computer* works, Donwood starts from a familiar
point of reference, from the known, and alters it to the point where our perception
of the familiar seems strange. We know these landscapes that invite us into the
story. They are cleverly positioned to provide us with a sense of security, they are
recognizable, we might even have a feeling that we've been there. We readily
accept them at face value and walk into the story without hesitation. But on closer
inspection, the paintings seem strange, something is not right. The landscapes are
empty. Nobody is there.

The following four paintings reveal the apocalypse. *Untitled* (Figure 6.4)
begins the sequence with the most descriptively apocalyptic scene, crammed city
skyscrapers aflame,[2] dripping with debris, a swimming pool filled with blood, and
an immersed human figure. Again, the sky over the city is dark and gray. This is
not the gray of storm clouds, but rather the suffocating gray of a nuclear winter.
A faint reminder of humanity's glory, and its sullied history, remains in the small

Figure 6.1   *Snow Accident*, 1999–2000. Artex, soot, burnt wood, acrylic on canvas, 72 × 72 inches

sketchy pyramids in the center. The grotesque and indistinctive skyscrapers of our mega-cities now dwarf the magnificence of the Giza pyramids. The block-like uniformity of the buildings is in sharp contrast to the unique character of the pyramids, which remain intact amid the destruction. In the whiteness, to the right, is the shadowy outline of two bears. The bears are recurring figures in this series, perhaps a reminder of nature's precarious position in the face of twenty-first-century 'progress.' Much like *Snow Evidence* (Figure 6.2), where the city has encroached on the rural environment, the bears in this painting have been forced into the outskirts of the city, their environment destroyed by ever expanding urbanization, their natural habitat diminished to the point where they too inhabit our mega-cities.

In the foreground is an unrecognizable human figure, featureless and drowning

Figure 6.2 *Snow Evidence*, 1999–2000. Artex, soot, burnt wood, acrylic on canvas, 72 × 72 inches

in a sea of melted polar ice caps, his very life-force being expelled from his dying body. Behind him is a red square, a representation of a blood-filled swimming pool. Donwood says the idea is from the graphic novel *Brought to Light*, where the protagonist explains how the CIA calculates casualty figures by counting swimming pools, based on the premise that every human being holds one gallon of blood in their body, and a swimming pool holds 50,000 gallons (Carson and Walters 2000).

In *Twenty-Four Hours* (Figure 6.5) a surviving bear has taken on mammoth proportions, he is large and baring an angry, toothy grin. In this fairy tale, the bear is not the comforting teddy that we snuggle to help us fall asleep in the frightening darkness, he is the antagonized bear of the forest, dislocated, angry, relying on instinct for survival. He dominates the landscape, the rows of houses dwarfed by his presence, their order and symmetry in contrast to the mayhem of

Figure 6.3 *Dead Fields* (detail), 1999–2000. Artex, soot, burnt wood, acrylic on canvas, 72 × 72 inches

the landscape. Just above the rows of houses is a red-stained pyramid, still standing, but separate from the three shadowy pyramids in the top-center of the painting. In the distance is the field pattern, dotted with new growth, with trees, rebirth in the aftermath. Above the bear is another blood-filled pool. We might be glimpsing at the state of the globe after the destruction, barren, save for an angry bear, and humanity's debris.

Bear Forest (Figure 6.6) is stained and blurred, as if by tears dripping from the heavens, the calm of the blues somehow in disturbing harmony with the bilious yellow, with all its connotations of rust and urine, the detritus of the organic and the inorganic. The screaming, growling bear, awash in blue, trapped in the corner, distanced from the three other small bears, sperm expelled from him as from the human figure in *Untitled* (Figure 6.4), taken from him by violence rather than through orgasmic release. He is distressed, his aggression a manifestation of his perilous situation, isolated and deserted.

In *Get Out Before Saturday* (Figure 6.7) we are faced with the aftermath of apocalyptic destruction. Icebergs stand on the horizon, the foreground awash in charred remains, littered with what appears to be the debris of countless electrical poles. The pyramids are gone, as are the field patterns and skyscrapers, but the

Figure 6.4   *Untitled* (detail), 1999–2000. Artex, soot, burnt wood, acrylic on canvas, 72 × 72 inches

forest is still visible in the distance. In the sky floats a haloed skeletal figure, ears, eyes, and teeth reminiscent of our recurring bear. In the foreground stands the lone, ghostly shadow of humanity. In the surface, now black, are the traces of the story. Records and memories soon to be erased and forgotten, history doomed to be repeated should we be given a second chance.

Donwood has used an iconography based in the knowable to represent the countdown to the apocalypse. Does he manage to avoid the ridiculous? More to the point, do the paintings manage to elicit the sublime? As representations of the apocalypse, the paintings in this series tread the line between the sublime and the ridiculous. These cataclysmic events being clearly beyond mimetic representation, Donwood starts with what we know – landscapes, bears, cityscapes – and turns them on their head. Conflict arises between reason (what is the likelihood of angry bears taking over our cities, then being annihilated along with humanity's architectural wonders?) and the power of imagination (is it not possible that the polar ice caps will melt, and polar bears will be carried down on ice floes to the cities, and skyscrapers will be aflame because we destroyed the world with war and nuclear weapons?). The representation of the apocalypse may seem a little ridiculous, but the idea is always a little bit possible.

Figure 6.5   *Twenty-Four Hours*, 1999–2000. Artex, soot, burnt wood, acrylic on canvas, 72 × 72 inches

By making the strangeness of the apocalypse seem oddly familiar, does Donwood manage to avoid the ridiculous and attain the sublime?

There is a conflict between these images as six-foot-square paintings, and as reproductions on compact disc packaging, not only on a formal level, but also on an ideological one. On the one hand the paintings are aggressively large, their surface textured to the point where 'you could cut yourself on them if you tried' (Donwood October 3 2001); on the other hand, they are reproduced in a children's book format – with its thick board pages amply illustrated and accompanied by a short text – that is small, intimate, and glossy.

Few contemporary visual artists have access to such a vast audience, through a commercial vehicle like compact disc packaging, whose main purpose is to help move units, to increase sales. Donwood is relying on one of the very tools he

Figure 6.6   *Bear Forest* (detail), 1999–2000. Artex, soot, burnt wood, acrylic on canvas, 72 × 72 inches

abhors, consumerism, to get his warnings across. Yet without access to such a widely distributed medium, fewer people would be reached.

Individually the paintings do not elicit the sublime. However, as a series, in their children's book format, the narrative placement of the works in a linear sequence offers a different perspective. The first three paintings in the series, *Snow Accident*, *Snow Evidence*, and *Dead Fields*, represent clearly recognizable scenes. We do not need the power of our imagination to understand these landscapes because they rely on reason, our understanding of a coniferous forest, a snowscape, a city skyline filled with skyscrapers, and field patterns we have seen from airplanes. While their heavily inscribed surfaces provide an introduction to our fairy tale, they do not, in and of themselves, elicit the sublime. The mind does not need to struggle to complete the representation.

The following four paintings, *Untitled*, *Twenty-Four Hours*, *Bear Forest*, and *Get Out Before Saturday*, however, clearly challenge our visual literacy, forcing our imagination to the limit of its power, and consequently creating a dissension with reason. Our understanding of scale is called into question, as bears and humanoid figures dominate the landscape, dwarfing homes and skyscrapers. We question the notion of weeping skies, toothy angels, and faceless human beings.

Figure 6.7 *Get Out Before Saturday*, 1999–2000. Artex, soot, burnt wood, acrylic on canvas, 72 × 72 inches

Yet as ridiculous as these elements may seem, they are placed in such a familiar context, among familiar elements that we have accepted in the first three paintings of the series, that we attempt to make some sense of the representation. We have seen red and yellow skies at sunset, the gray sky of a rainy day, and understand the image of a white arctic landscape, yet in these paintings, all these elements are strangely unfamiliar. Struggling to come to terms with these juxtapositions, between the form and the content of these paintings, a dissension occurs between imagination and reason, through our astonishment in the face of all that seems strange now being familiar. This is the sublime. Had the apocalypse been represented as a fantastical world, one that had no basis in what we understand as our reality, then it would not have engendered a conflict. There would be no sublime response. It seems that there is no better way to represent

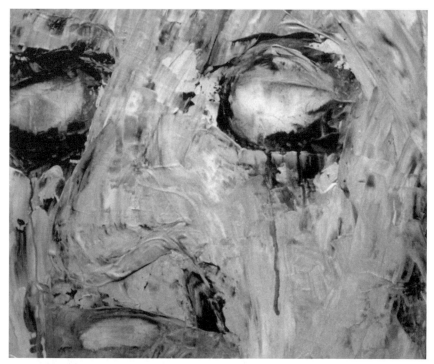

Figure 6.8   *Chocolate Boss of the WTO* (detail), 1999–2000. Artex, soot, burnt wood, acrylic on canvas, 72 × 72 inches

the unrepresentable than by using what we know and understand as a point of reference.

Similarly, as a group, the paintings elicit the sublime through the children's book format, through the telling of the fairy tale. Building on our preconceptions of children's illustrated books, we are welcomed into the story through the familiarity of the landscapes, only to be violently expelled from it through the catastrophic explosion at the end. The fairy tale is turned on its head, the gnomes and witches of our expectation are replaced by apocalyptic representations of mass destruction and monstrous figures of an extraordinary size. This is not a fantastical world of make-believe, but the one that we profess to know, run amok. The conflict between what is being imagined and what we understand as reasonable is created, and the dissension that emerges challenges our understanding of the fairy tale. The paintings elicit the sublime through their form as a children's book, and through the credible rendering of their apocalyptic content.

The warnings in the *Kid A* paintings are loud, they are not veiled as in the *OK Computer* works, they are not being hinted at or whispered in the shadows. They

Figure 6.9   *Bug Junction* (detail), 1999–2000. Artex, soot, burnt wood, acrylic on canvas, 72 × 72 inches

are clear and strong, and they are being screamed out frantically, 'Ice Age coming! / Ice Age coming!' ('Idioteque'). These ecological disasters may take place over an unfathomable period of time, but their prevention starts now. We are warned to stay alert to their inevitability in the face of our current inaction. We are warned of the real danger of nuclear weapons, and the people we elect that control those weapons.

Chocolate Boss of the WTO (Figure 6.8) and *Bug Junction* (Figure 6.9) are the last two paintings in the book. They are not landscapes, and stray to some degree from the fairy tale, but they complement the previous seven paintings as concrete materializations of the warnings. *Chocolate Boss of the WTO* is a wax-like melted human face, whose vacant eyes and thick and dripping features act as sponsors to the destruction: 'This apocalypse was brought to you courtesy of the WTO.' *Bug Junction*, the most blatantly warlike image of the series, shows red stealth bomber-like shapes, flying above the resulting explosion. This is the brave new world we have allowed.

The *Amnesiac* Special Edition book contains a series of ephemeral images, sketches, x-rays, cryptic bits of text and images, layered and pasted together.[3] This series has a close formal affinity with the *OK Computer* images in the works' sketchiness and lack of clarity. In some instances the works appear unfocused, carrying the dusty yellow colour palette of old newspapers and archival material. The cities are now completely empty, the weeping Minotaur dominates this new fantastical world, trees are hollowed out, skeletal faces adorn a seemingly endless series of gravestones. Our toothy bear appears in a few instances, as an angel, and as a crazed primitive creature. The human figures remaining are a few mad, seemingly political figures; in one instance two men embrace, overjoyed by the turn of events or their survival, in another the figure looks maniacal and is accompanied by a fantastical beast. The only other human figure is of a single man, eyes and mouth sewn shut. Donwood explains:

> With *Amnesiac* it was going in very close. Too close. So close you can only see a wall – graffitied, scratched, clawed at – in front of you. This is the home of the Minotaur … They were sections of wall in some horrible labyrinth under the burning cities … The *Amnesiac* book is designed to be left for decades in a drawer, in an old cupboard, in a dusty attic, in an abandoned house, and found after I am dead. (Donwood, October 8 2003)

This series, representing the remains after the apocalypse in *Kid A*, is desperate, desolate, depressing, and horrific. Total destruction has occurred, and all that remains is a vast labyrinth inhabited by crazed survivors. While the lyrics in 'Like Spinning Plates' echo the sentiment – 'While you make pretty speeches / I'm being cut to shreds / You feed me to the lions / a delicate balance' ('Like Spinning Plates') – 'Pyramid Song' finally offers relief from the constant anxiety, the aftermath bringing a bittersweet glimmer of hope:

> Jumped in the river, what did I see?
> Black-eyed angels swam with me
> A moonful of stars and astral cars
> And all the figures I used to see
> All my lovers were there with me
> All my past and futures
> And we all went to heaven in a little row boat
> There was nothing to fear and nothing to doubt

Pacific Coast (Figure 6.10), the cover image on *Hail to the Thief*, is the next chapter in the *Kid A* series. Gone is the grayness of the nuclear winter, the sky has returned to its familiar blue. People are still absent, and the bears, pyramids, and field patterns have disappeared. The words are no longer veiled and cryptic as in *OK Computer* and *Kid A*, they are no longer scratched and erased, but are now bold and graphic, loud and clear. But what do they mean? Can we finally find some comfort? Can we feel a little less anxious now?

In the opening track, '2+2=5,' Thom Yorke repeatedly shouts, 'It is too late now / Because / YOU HAVE NOT BEEN PAYING ATTENTION.' It may seem like a dire pronouncement, but it's not as though Radiohead and Donwood haven't been sounding the alarm for some time. So what does this final image

Figure 6.10 *Pacific Coast*, 2002. Acrylic, polytex polyripple, blackboard paint on canvas, 60 × 60 inches

mean? We've been distracted, and we haven't been paying attention, everything is gone. No more pyramids or bears, all that's left is the detritus that we thought was so important, all that survives after the apocalypse is the stuff. The 'bacon,' 'popcorn,' and 'cocktails' we consumed while watching 'videos' on our 'tv,' or chatting on the 'internet.'

A fairy tale is told to children so they learn about the consequences of their actions, or inaction. Donwood's fairy tale is inscribed in the paintings for us to read. Donwood and Radiohead have been sounding warning bells since *The Bends*, their desire to effect change a prominent concern. By providing representations of the apocalypse, they have forced us to imagine the unimaginable, and to struggle with our reasoned understanding of destruction, and its concrete representation. Whether an actual apocalypse would look like these paintings is not the point. It is that we recognize its possibility. Through the dissension between the imagination and reason, through the sublime, we are given some distance from the literal, and consequently accept as credible the threat of the apocalypse. How, then, can we recognize the possibility of the apocalypse without waking up and taking action?

Notes

1. I would like to thank Stanley Donwood for his invaluable assistance in the writing of this essay. He generously shared his time and insight, and kindly supplied reproductions of the artwork.
2. Since the terrorist events of September 11 2001, representations of skyscrapers aflame have become a gruesome reality. I will not be addressing these events, as they deserve to be discussed within a broader socio-political context than the theoretical and esthetic parameters of this essay.
3. Although not relevant to this discussion, it is worth noting that Stanley Donwood and Tchocky won the 2001 Grammy Award for Best Recording Package for the *Amnesiac* Special Edition book.

Chapter 7

Radiohead's Antivideos: Works of Art in the Age of Electronic Reproduction[1]

Joseph Tate

Introduction: test specimens

The icon you see on this page (Figure 7.1) is called a 'test specimen.' Wide-eyed bears with murderous grins, drawn alternately as symmetrical, disembodied heads or frantically sketched stiff-limbed figures, they punctuate the art of the music group Radiohead, from CD packaging and packing slips, to website images and promotional stickers.

Figure 7.1 Website image

Although directly analogous to the easily recognizable character-mascots used to establish a product's unique brand identity, the bears function like painter Philip Guston's hooded men, with a difference: while Guston's figures, versions of Ku Klux Klansmen, gave a disturbingly organic shape to American civil unrest and racial injustice in the late 1960s and early '70s, Radiohead's test specimens are protagonists in a self-referential pastiche that estheticizes the band's commodification and the operation of capital at large.[2]

In what follows, I explore the bears' appearances in QuickTime computer-animated music video shorts released concurrently with *Kid A*, the band's critically anticipated fourth album.[3] Titled 'antivideos,' or 'blips,' the short videos (10–30 seconds in duration) were released only on the internet, a virtually inexhaustible distribution channel. Via this medium, the antivideos provide a useful plateau from which to consider popular art's current state and future potential in the age of electronic reproduction.

Commodified culture, culturalized commodification

In *The Fragile Absolute, or Why is the Christian Legacy Worth Fighting For?*, Slavoj Žižek observes that 'today's artistic scene' consists of two opposed movements. The first is the 'much-deplored commodification of culture (art objects produced for the market),' while the second, and 'less noted but perhaps more crucial *opposite* movement,' is 'the growing *"culturalization" of the market economy itself*.' He elaborates:

> With the shift towards the tertiary economy (services, cultural goods), culture is less and less a specific sphere exempted from the market, and more and more not just one of the spheres of the market, but its central component (from the software amusement industry to other media productions). (Žižek 2000: 25)[4]

We can add to this list the music industry. The paired phenomena of commodified culture and a culturalized market is as evidently pervasive in few other markets, and it is these movements of commodification and culturalization that Radiohead's antivideos thematize.

Originally released on the band's website several weeks before the October 2 2000 release of *Kid A*, the antivideos jettison the standard hierarchy between song and music video as elaborated by media critic Jody Berland. According to Berland, 'the 3-minute musical single' is a music video's

> unalterable foundation, its one unconditional ingredient. A single can exist (technically, at least) without the video, but the reverse is not the case. As if in evidence of this, music videos, almost without exception, do not make so much as a single incision in the sound or structure of the song. However bizarre or disruptive videos appear, they never challenge or emancipate themselves from their musical foundation, without which their charismatic indulgences would never reach our eyes. (Berland 1993: 25)

As if in direct response to Berland's phonocentrism the antivideos do exactly what music videos do not and/or should not: make radical incisions and changes to the sound and structure of the songs they promote.

The website's title introduces the antivideos bluntly as 'Brief films used as promotional material.'[5] Immediately, visitors are alerted to the antivideo's situation within a matrix of capitalist exchange, an unusual acknowledgement in an industry that regularly denounces any discernible trace of commercialization. As music critic Lawrence Grossberg has noted, 'Rock fans have always constructed a difference between authentic and co-opted rock. And it is this which is often interpreted as rock's inextricable tie to resistance, refusal, alienation, marginality, etc.' (Grossberg 1993: 202). Authentic rock has as its ideal a 'collective, spontaneous creativity,' in the words of Kalefa Sanneh, critic for the *New York Times*, that is unfettered by the crass demands of capital. Co-opted rock, however, is an example of what Žižek calls the 'much-deplored commodification of culture (art objects produced for the market);' co-opted rock is commercially successful music with an international distribution that fails to hide adequately its commodification, thus opening itself up for censure. Radiohead's music, videos, cover art, and packaging, however, expose its commodification and culturalize it.

As one example, the CD packaging for *Kid A* foregrounds its own commodification. A limited number of CDs contained a supplementary text hidden beneath the jewel case's polystyrene tray. The untitled booklet by Stanley Donwood, the band's artist, and Tchock, a pseudonym for Thom Yorke, the band's lead singer, comprises fragmentary phrases juxtaposed against images of test specimens posed as either cartoonishly violent corporate sycophants or traumatized victims of surveillance. Rarely are listeners asked to disassemble the object that distills a performer's presence for uniform portable consumption, only to find a text that decries consumption. Radiohead's antivideos work similarly as agents of disassembly, leading consumers into a labyrinthine network of hyperbolic images that pastiche commodification.

Flying bears

The first antivideo on the Radiohead site is titled 'Flying Bears,' a 19-second movie that imagines limitless reproduction with a twist of surreal horror. The scene opens on two figures, both of whom stare up in horror at a murky sky crowded with flying test-specimen bears (see Figure 7.2). The movie then fades into an exclusive focus on the flying bears, the brand icons for Radiohead, while

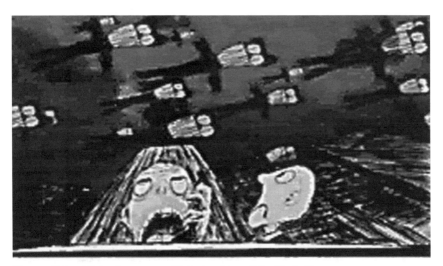

Figure 7.2 'flyingbears.mov.' Music video. Dir. Chris Bran

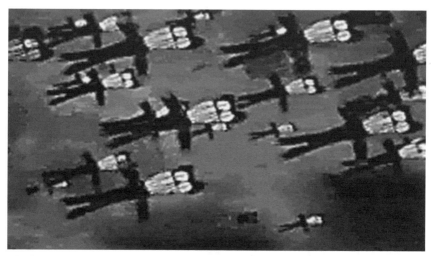

Figure 7.3   'flyingbears.mov.' Music video. Dir. Chris Bran

the antivideo's soundtrack plays an excerpt from the song 'In Limbo.' Yorke's voice unhurriedly croons the refrain, 'You're living in a fantasy / You're living in a fantasy' (see Figure 7.3). Finally, our view shifts to a close-up of a frightened onlooker, eyes fixed upward and mouth opened in muted fear. Furiously, he clutches a mobile phone – a device that may be his last connection to the world: a connection enabled and mediated by an electronic communication network (see Figure 7.4).

Figure 7.4   'flyingbears.mov.' Music video. Dir. Chris Bran

The fantasy, then, of which the lyrics speak and that the onlookers inhabit is not a pleasant one, as the alarmed facial expressions evince. Instead, it is the ultimate fantasy of the capitalist/communist dyad: 'unbridled productivity' (Žižek 2000: 18). As Žižek notes, it is no accident that the rise of capitalism and communism are historically simultaneous: 'Marx's notion of Communist society is itself the inherent capitalist fantasy – a fantasmatic scenario for resolving the capitalist antagonism he so aptly described' (Žižek 2000: 19). The bears metaphorize the boundless commodification that modern technologies facilitate. Radiohead's symbols threaten to overcome the onlooker. In this way, the antivideo critiques its own medium – the internet, a technology that allows endless and nearly effortless production. Once an antivideo reaches the internet, it can be accessed indefinitely by multiple viewers simultaneously.

The limitless reproducibility of visual and aural art objects that the internet enables is the apogee of simulation, as it is defined by Jean Baudrillard. Via digital technologies, 'The real is produced from miniaturized cells, matrices, and memory banks, models of control – it can be reproduced an indefinite number of times from these' (Baudrillard 1994: 2). The real or the authentic cease to matter, an inevitability that Radiohead's music and art incorporates.

Nevertheless, the real is what audiences, music critics, and fans alike, desire. Critic David Fricke commented in *Rolling Stone* that despite the experimental sounds of Radiohead's electronic music what you actually hear is 'real rock singing and chops, altered beyond easy recognition' (Fricke 2001a: 48). What Fricke fails to grasp is that Radiohead's esthetic undermines the real he attempts to recover on the band's behalf. Fricke's and others' misreading of Radiohead's music has a venerable antecedent: Walter Benjamin's 'The Work of Art in the Age of Mechanical Reproduction.'

Fricke would agree with Benjamin that mass reproduction corrupts the art object's authenticity, an essential, if intangible, element of art: 'that which withers in the age of mechanical reproduction is the aura of the work of art' (Benjamin 1968: 221). But, unlike Benjamin, Fricke and the sum of music industry rhetoric stops there. Benjamin's anxiety increases as he considers the possibility that the real may cease to exist at all. As he explains in the case of photography, the question of authenticity 'makes no sense' when one can make innumerable prints from a photographic negative (Benjamin 1968: 224). Similarly, the internet acts as a spectral production line: an immense factory open to all comers, which has transcended production's physical limitations.

A fear that authenticity will lose significance animates Benjamin's essay but does not explain Fricke's naive praise for a hidden, real rock music underlying Radiohead's experimentation. The band's music, I argue, is not a distortion of 'real rock,' but an uncovering of its absence, its phantasmic structure. Fricke assumes that the real continues to bloom, when, as Baudrillard told us, and as Benjamin knew would happen, it has long since been a desert.

Benjamin's anxiety is the emotion that animates the onlookers' faces in 'Flying

Bears.' The antivideo's countless test specimens are the epitomic image of electronic reproduction, specifically, the internet's realization of the fundamental capitalist fantasy of unimpeded production. But, here the capitalist dream is refigured as a nightmarish scenario of flying bears looming over frightened mobile phone users. However, the precession of simulation, to use Baudrillard's phrase, that capital desires is its own undoing, as I argue in the following section.

'I'm not here / This isn't happening'

The fourth song on *Kid A* is titled 'How to Disappear Completely.' The lyrics, while supposedly based on a dream, eerily narrate the singer's subject position as experienced by the listener: 'I'm not here / This isn't happening.' The point is so simple as to go unnoticed: when I hear Radiohead's music the band is not here, where I am at the moment of listening, and the performance is not happening, and may have, in fact, never happened. Like Miles Davis's *Bitches Brew*, an achievement not of instrumental virtuosity but of production technique ahead of its time, *Kid A* is the record of a performance never performed. Instead, the album is an electronically constructed collage of disparate studio recordings, found sounds, drum loops, samples, and other forms of noise.

While *Kid A* challenges authenticity, the antivideo 'Screaming Bears' is a pastiche of it. 'Screaming Bears' casts the test specimens as performers furnishing what spectators crave – an authentic performance. Gradually, five agitated bears (notably, Radiohead has five band members) appear from stage left on a flat, desolate landscape (see Figure 7.5) populated randomly by pyramids

Figure 7.5   'screamingbears.mov.' Music video. Dir. Chris Bran

that resembles Cy Twombly's *Anabasis*. The performance is blatantly pointless: the bears enter, the bears leave.

Nevertheless, the bears' performance is more compelling than what is offered by the performers from Radiohead. In 'Morning Bell,' Thom Yorke plays a piano, face averted from the camera and downcast, in a lonely, possibly domestic, setting. We are given an authentic band member, but the authentic person, compared to the screaming and dancing test specimens, is far less thrilling. It is the simulation that captures our attention, not the authentic. The intimate, if artificially staged, mood of 'Morning Bell,' intimated by the black-and-white film and overhead perspective, the common position of surveillance cameras, is more akin to voyeurism than spectatorship (see Figure 7.6). Whatever authenticity 'Morning Bell' may have laid claim to is dissolved by 'Yeti,' another antivideo that calls attention to the band's status as object and role as victim of surveillance, or rather of an institutionalized gaze so well embodied by David Fricke above.

To return to Fricke's assessment, Radiohead's music is 'real rock singing and chops' (2001a: 48). This desire to establish the band's music as real rock is a near-death symptom of capitalism. Capitalism, especially its embodiment in the music industry, frequently reminds us of 'its foundations in real people and their relations' (Žižek 2000: 16). Underneath the mysterious celebrity-identity there is a real person, which the hunched-over Yorke of 'Morning Bell' perfectly signifies. Another example proves instructive: on August 8 2001, fans had the chance to chat online with Jonny Greenwood, the band's lead guitarist and keyboardist. An event hosted by the Yahoo! website, such a promotional move is not unlike another that Žižek describes: 'Visitors to the London Stock Exchange are given a free leaflet which explains to them that the stock market is not about some

Figure 7.6   'morningbell.mov.' Music video. Dir. Chris Bran

mysterious fluctuations, but about real people and their products – this is ideology at its purest' (2000: 16). Being able to chat with Jonny Greenwood in real time: this, too, is ideology at its purest.[6]

But this reassertion of the real, Baudrillard argues, is capital's attempt to calm its characteristic powers of 'abstraction, disconnection, deterritorialization' (1994: 22), the very powers that now threaten it. To confront the oceanic elision of difference it inaugurated, capital re-injects the real, but to no avail:

> as soon as [capital] wishes to combat this disastrous spiral by secreting a last glimmer of reality, on which to establish a last glimmer of power, it does nothing but multiply the signs and accelerate the play of simulation. (Baudrillard 1994: 22)

It is this reassertion of the real that 'Yeti,' the next antivideo, forms into a pastiche.

In 'Yeti,' a test-specimen bear is caught on camera, much in the same way the appearances of supposedly mystical monsters – e.g. Bigfoot and the Loch Ness Monster – are captured on videotape. To reinforce the antivideo's relation to surveillance footage, the movie begins with and is interrupted by moments of static (see Figure 7.7). Most often a nuisance, the camera's disruption of images, its intrusion as creator of artifice into a reality that would ideally otherwise remain unaltered, here signals reality. Between these staged disruptions, the camera slowly pans across an empty snow field (see Figure 7.8) and eventually locates a test specimen (see Figure 7.9), who flees upon realizing he has been discovered. Like Sartre at the keyhole, hearing footsteps approaching from behind, the test specimen turns in shock: 'Someone is looking at me!' (Sartre 1992: 349).[7] Presumably, the test specimen escapes into the forest; the antivideo

Figure 7.7   'yeti.mov.' Music video. Dir. Chris Bran

Figure 7.8 'yeti.mov.' Music video. Dir. Chris Bran

ends before the bear is captured. We are left with a noisy image of the bear running away (see Figure 7.10). Surveillance video, the electronic gaze with which authorities establish incontrovertible fact, is used frivolously: to follow a cartoon bear. Comparatively, this antivideo renders the ostensibly authentic scene of 'Morning Bell' artificial and thus simultaneously lampoons authenticity more generally, exposing capital's covert insistence that commodified celebrities are real people.

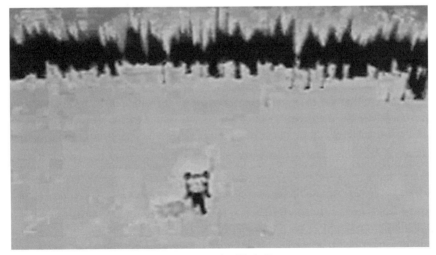

Figure 7.9 'yeti.mov.' Music video. Dir. Chris Bran

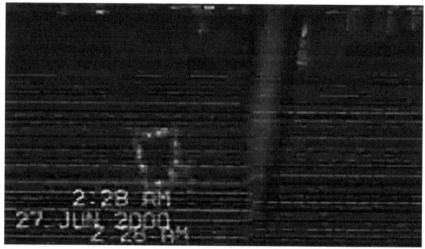

Figure 7.10   'yeti.mov.' Music video. Dir. Chris Bran

Is a music video without music a music video?

Slavoj Žižek tells an interesting personal story in *The Fragile Absolute* worth quoting at length. During a trip to Berlin he noticed

> along and above all the main streets numerous large blue tubes and pipes, as if the intricate cobweb of water, phone, electricity, and so on, was no longer hidden beneath the earth, but displayed in public. My reaction was, of course, that this was probably another of those postmodern art performances whose aim was, this time, to reveal the intestines of the town, its hidden inner machinery, in a kind of equivalent to displaying on the video the palpitation of our stomach or lungs – I was soon proved wrong, however, when friends pointed out to me that what I saw was merely part of the standard maintenance and repair of the city's underground service network. (Žižek 2000: 162, n.13)

Before recounting the story of what he terms a blunder, Žižek contextualizes his confusion, citing the example of a recent art performance in Potzdamerplatz in Berlin, where the movements of several gigantic cranes were orchestrated for an art performance. A similar performance, he fails to note, happened in Helsinki in the early 1980s.

In this context, Žižek's confusion in Berlin is understandable, and, I argue, symptomatic of the postmodern era. What begins to emerge is that postmodernism can not be regarded merely as a set of objective attributes for which objects can be tested, but might instead be considered a perspective, a condition of the subject as well as objects. Not a radical thesis, by any means, but an important one that marks the difference between Jean-François Lyotard and Frederic Jameson: the former promoting distrust of meta-narratives, a subjective state, as distinctive of postmodernism (Lyotard 1984: xxiv), the latter elaborating a stylistic description with architecture serving as the 'privileged esthetic language' (Jameson 1991: 37).

Another example of confusion symptomatic of postmodernism is my own; 13 of 16 antivideos released in June 2001 in support of the band's fifth album, *Amnesiac*, are musicless. These latest antivideos, to reuse Jody Berland's vocabulary quoted above, emancipate themselves from their musical foundation, so much so, in fact, that the musical foundation is shunned altogether. My initial response to these musicless antivideos was to declare myself in the presence of a postmodern pastiche of John Cage's revolutionary *4'33"*.

At 8:15 pm on August 29 1952, an audience gathered at the Maverick Concert Hall in Woodstock, New York, to hear the pianist David Tudor perform John Cage's latest composition. They heard nothing, a nothing entitled *4'33"*. Inspired by Robert Rauschenberg's three-paneled *White Painting* of 1951, Cage's handwritten score indicated a silence of three movements. Music without music: is it still music? Cage, of course, thought it was. Cage's modernist aesthetic was heavily influenced by eastern philosophy. The point of the performance of *4'33"* was to force the listener to listen closely, to close-read his or her immediate sonic environment. *4'33"* is often mistakenly referred to as 'the silent piece,' given that Cage maintained that silence of any kind did not exist (Cage 8).[8]

Radiohead's aesthetic, then, in this instance, was Cage's impulse turned against the commercialization of music through the relentless promotion of music videos. Music videos are promotional materials but, without music, what can they promote? Nothing, and promoting nothing they become advertising simply for advertising's sake. Further, the resulting effect isn't modernist shock (what have I endured!?), but what Jameson termed the postmodern sublime: a panic-boredom (I have to endure this for how long!?) (Jameson 1991: 37–8).[9]

My theorization of the antivideos along these lines was disturbed, however, by information I received from the primary artist responsible for Radiohead's antivideos, Chris Bran, one of the self-titled Vapour Brothers. In July of 2001 I interviewed Bran via e-mail. Responding to a question regarding how and when the *Amnesiac* antivideos were created, Bran wrote that they were, 'just out takes, left overs, works in progress. they were all created for the current radiohead project I am doing. we just decided to put these online and try to build up a gallery of video ideas' [*sic*]. When asked specifically why a majority of the shorts do not use music, Bran responded with reference to the earlier response, 'as i said these are all works in progress, unfinished ideas or out takes.' The last comment Bran added was, 'check out radiohead.com in the next few weeks.' What was to come was the release of 'I Might Be Wrong,' an internet-only, traditional music video constructed from the various musicless antivideos and created entirely on a laptop computer.

What Bran's comments required of me was to erase the earlier response, or at least to rewrite that response, in this way: the soundless antivideos are not the postmodern descendants of John Cage's famous silence, they are, instead, waste, leftovers, in other words, excrement. While Bran's words frustrate the genealogical connection to John Cage, his comments open up a new set of theoretical problems. Waste, in its various forms, is now routinely handled by critical theory and theorists.

Žižek, leaning on the work of his former mentor and analyst Jacques-Alain Miller (the son-in-law of Jacques Lacan), offers a compelling description of what material condition is historically particular to postmodernism: waste. Late capitalism, Žižek writes (2002), has introduced 'a breathtaking dynamics of obsolescence' (40) that generates massive mounds of waste. I quote Žižek quoting Miller:

> The main production of the modern and postmodern capitalist industry is precisely waste. We are postmodern beings because we realize that all our aesthetically appealing consumption artifacts will eventually end as leftover, to the point that it will transform the earth into a vast waste land. (quoted in Žižek 2000: 40)

Along these lines Žižek notes that,

> in today's art, the gap that separates the sacred space of sublime beauty from the excremental space of trash (leftover) is gradually narrowing, up to the paradoxical identity of opposites: are not modern art objects more and more excremental objects, trash (often in a quite literal sense: faeces, rotting corpses …) displayed in – made to occupy, to fill in – the sacred *place* of the Thing? (Žižek 2000: 26)

Perhaps the most famous example of this is Chris Ofili's 1996 painting 'The Holy Virgin Mary,' a portrait of the religious icon as a black woman decorated with elephant dung. The painting was featured in the 1999 Brooklyn Museum of Art show 'Sensation: Young British Artists from the Saatchi Collection,' an exhibit former Mayor of New York Rudolph Giuliani called 'sick stuff.'[10]

Back in Berlin, the esthetic wonder Žižek felt at seeing the innards of the city exposed need not necessarily be considered a blunder. The actual circumstances of any situation, the ultimately phantasmic Real, is, as Lacan instructs us, only a fantasy that has yet to be unveiled. Instead, what we witness in Žižek's confusion (which was, interestingly, submerged in a footnote – the exposed innards of the book, the book's waste products) and my own is the epitome of the postmodern condition – the subject thrust into a state of perpetual awareness, never knowing where art will come from next.

In place of a conclusion: a myth

With the release in June 2001 of *Amnesiac*, the band's fifth album, the test-specimen bears of *Kid A* have been replaced by crying Minotaurs. While the bears were adaptable to various situations, the Minotaurs are unambiguously and consistently modeled as victims. In one interactive portion of the Radiohead *Kid A*-era website visitors could participate in 'Experiment #6: Torturing the Minotaur,' where they have a chance to inflict pain upon a crying Minotaur using a small trident. The game, if it can rightly be called a game, is in the tradition of Stanley Milgram's psychological experiments conducted from 1961–62. A somewhat milder version of the same experiment was available at Capitol Records' Radiohead site, a separate site not directly maintained by the band. At the top of the main page, one click would cause a Minotaur to weep while a continuously depressed mouse button intensified the Minotaur's sorrow, prompting him to rub his tearful eyes ruefully as he shakes his head.

Unlike Milgram's experiments, however, these opportunities to torture a Minotaur test not our willingness to obey, but the limits of curiosity – our desire for knowledge. However, like Milgram's experiments, and more significantly, 'Experiment #6' is a simulation. We torture nothing. We instead simulate a torture, a process far more dangerous, according to Baudrillard. Comparing a simulated and a real hold-up, he writes:

> the latter does nothing but disturb the order of things, the right to property, whereas the former attacks the reality principle itself. Transgression and violence are less serious because they only contest the *distribution* of the real. Simulation is infinitely more dangerous because it always leaves open the supposition that, above and beyond its object, *law and order themselves might be nothing but simulation.* (Baudrillard 1994: 20)

Capital attempts to stabilize its power via the maintenance of reality. This, to reiterate Žižek, 'is ideology at its purest' (2000: 16). Simulation resists this stabilizing influence.

However, the band's reflexive esthetic effectively disrupts naive consumption, confronting the listener with music and art that adheres to opacity versus authenticity as a guiding principle. As the novelist Nick Hornby wrote in a *New Yorker* review deriding Radiohead:

> You have to work at albums like *Kid A*. You have to sit at home night after night and give yourself over to its paranoid millennial atmosphere as you try to decipher elliptical snatches of lyrics and puzzle out how the titles ('Treefingers,' 'The National Anthem,' and so on) might refer to the songs. … *Kid A* demands the patience of the devoted … (quoted in Dettmar 2001)

That a listener would be given pause by a mass-produced art object troubles Hornby, who prefers not to enter Radiohead's maze of possible meaning.

Thus, explicitly evoking the myth of the Minotaur with *Amnesiac*, Radiohead has found an icon more fitting than the test specimens. A limited-edition CD of the album is packaged in a cloth-bound book. Inside we find the following disclaimers: 'This book is to be hidden. Labyrinthine structures are entered at the reader's own risk. Nosuch Library and Lending Service cannot be held responsible for Misuse.' Radiohead's music and art is, finally, as Hornby acknowledges, a labyrinthine structure that, once entered, baffles with its mesmerizing difficulty.

While Radiohead's music and art together sustain a significant critique of capitalist ideology, the band has no pretension to saving the world single-handed. Instead, its website at http://www.radiohead.com/00.html recommends links to alternative news and information sites with similarly worthy, if unattainable, goals: to revise the relationship between consumer and commodity. The goal of both *Kid A* and *Amnesiac*, however, is far more modest: to revise our relationship to popular music and forms of popular culture more generally, a goal that Radiohead, I argue, achieves.

Notes

1. A version of this essay originally appeared in the May 2002 issue of *Postmodern Culture*. An even earlier version was presented at the *Seeing Things* conference in Tours, France, sponsored by the British Council. I would like to thank the members of my seminar for their comments. The essay benefited along the way from various readers: Lisa Hogan, Cody Walker, Conseula Francis, Jeremy Arnold, Steven Aldridge, and others.

2. I follow Frederic Jameson's assertion that, in postmodernism, pastiche eclipses parody. His definition is useful: 'Pastiche is, like parody, the imitation of a peculiar or unique style, the wearing of a stylistic mask, speech in a dead language: but it is a neutral practice of such mimicry, without parody's ulterior motive, without the satirical impulse, without laughter, without that still latent feeling that there exists something *normal* compared with which what is being imitated is rather comic' (*Cultural Turn*, 5).

3. *Kid A*, which received a Grammy award for Best Alternative Album in 2000, was keenly anticipated due to the success of *OK Computer*, the band's 1997 album, which was among the top-ten highest-selling albums in Great Britain. In 1998, *OK Computer* received a Grammy award for Best Alternative Album (Hale 1999: 127) and the band was nominated for four MTV awards (Hale 1999: 133). Comprehensive indexes of the band's album reviews and awards are available in both Jonathan Hale's *Radiohead: From a Great Height* (ECW Press, 1999) and Martin Clarke's *Radiohead: Hysterical and Useless* (Plexus, 2000).

4. This echoes Jameson's claim that 'aesthetic production today has become integrated into commodity production generally' (*Postmodernism*, 4).

5. The antivideos, in this way, epitomize Nam June Paik's words. The experimental video artist wrote the following about television commercials generally:

> Plato through the word, or the conceptual, expresses the deepest thing.
> St. Augustine thought the sound, or the audible, expresses the deepest thing.
> Spinoza through the vision, or visible, expresses the deepest thing.
> This argument is settled for good.
> TV commercials have all three. (Paik, in Hanhardt 2000: 223)

6. Discussants' questions remained superficial throughout the chat. At one point, Greenwood comments: 'Apparently 90% of your questions are about hair.'

7. As Paul Virilio notes, '"Surveillance and punishment" go hand in hand, Michel Foucault once wrote' (1994: 65). In this instance, the shame of being caught in a voyeuristic act functions as a form of non-corporal punishment.
8. A now famous anecdote tells of Cage visiting NASA's soundproof room at Harvard University. Expecting absolute silence, he instead heard two sounds: 'one high and one low' (1973: 8). The first, he was told, was his nervous system, the second his circulatory system. Even silence could not be silent.
9. One antivideo, 'minotauralley,' makes an excellent case for Jameson's postmodern sublime. For 46 seconds the viewer watches a cartoon Minotaur weeping with inexplicable calm in a deserted, wet alleyway.
10. Thanks to Steven Aldridge for correcting this from MoMA to BMA.

Chapter 8

Deforming Rock: Radiohead's Plunge into the Sonic Continuum

Mark B.N. Hansen

... it's here that non-musicians, despite their lack of competence, can most easily have encounters with musicians. Music is not solely an affair of musicians, to the extent that it renders sonorous those forces which are non sonorous, forces that can be more or less revolutionary, more or less conformist, for example, the organization of time.

Gilles Deleuze

'Yesterday I woke up sucking a lemon.' So begins Radiohead's 'Everything in its Right Place,' the opening track on the band's fourth studio album, *Kid A* (2000). Vehemently rejecting insinuations that the song is gibberish, Radiohead singer and leader Thom Yorke links it directly to the 'primal trauma' that might well be partly, if not largely, responsible for the band's marked shift in direction away from the comfortable post-rock formula it had perfected with its third album *OK Computer* (1997). As Yorke explains, the expression 'sucking a lemon' refers to the 'face you pull because a lemon is so tart,' and the song it begins refers more generally to Yorke's breakdown seven months in to the year-long European and American tour for *OK Computer*: 'It's totally about that,' Yorke insists. Not insignificantly, the most prominent symptom of Yorke's breakdown was his utter inability to speak. As he recounts,

> I came off at the end of that show, sat in the dressing room and couldn't speak. I actually couldn't speak. People were saying, 'You all right?' I knew people were speaking to me. But I couldn't hear them. And I couldn't talk. I'd just had enough. And I was bored with saying I'd had enough. I was beyond that. (Fricke 2001a)

With the benefit of hindsight, we can now see just how this literal muteness played the role of trigger for Radiohead's plunge into the sonic continuum – if, that is, we can view the silencing of the voice as the necessary precondition for the complex deterritorializations to which Radiohead submitted the voice and its instrumental avatar, the guitar, on *Kid A* and *Amnesiac*.

In this essay, I propose to evaluate Radiohead's plunge into the sonic continuum in relation to several issues more or less directly bound up with the music-sound-noise complex. Perhaps most prominent among these are claims – both critical and laudatory – that this plunge amounts to a radical interruption of the band's trajectory, the advent of a wholly new direction in its musical production. By showing that such claims are too simple – that there is indeed a deep continuity between the first three and the final two studio albums – I shall position Radiohead's experiment with sonic deterritorialization in a way that both does justice to the band's concrete function as a linkage point between rock and indie music (or avant rock)[1] *and* distinguishes the value of its experimentation from arguably more radical contemporary experimentation, both theoretical and practical, that seeks to overcome what music historian Douglas Kahn has glossed as the 'modernist strategy for musical rejuvenation' (Kahn 1999: 71). As a rock (or, in current terminology, a 'post-rock') band, Radiohead does not share – and thus cannot be evaluated in terms of – the program(s) motivating contemporary art music and sound installation artwork. That said, the parallel with experimental art music will prove to be illuminating up to a point, since it helps to expose the specificity of Radiohead's own experimentation with a machine-based aesthetic in which the elementary unit of sound is no longer dictated by the rhythm of the breath but is the single, molecular, and potentially imperceptible sound particle. Whereas the motivating aim of the radical sound artist – at least as Kahn sees it – is to compose at the molecular level, with instruments 'constructed … at the constellated semiotic dislocations invoked by the sound' (Kahn 1999: 77), Radiohead's encounter with and appropriation of techno rhythm and digital composition aims to catalyze a co-becoming of the human and the machine, of breath and machinic beat, the ultimate payoff of which is nothing more nor less than an expansion in the domain of rock music. That is why, for example, Radiohead employs techniques of digital distortion 'live,' in the process of recording, and not afterwards, in remixing; 'if you're going to do something weird with a track,' Yorke explains, 'you make it weird there and then, rather than doing it in the mix afterwards, because the effect changes the way people play. They'll play to it. And that's really inspiring, because its like having a new instrument' (Reynolds 2001: 32). It is also why the predominately techno rhythms of the studio recordings are easily converted into more traditionally rock-based rhythms in live performance; on this score, Radiohead's recent album release of live recordings from the *Kid A/Amnesiac* material (*I Might Be Wrong*) lends concrete weight to Colin Greenwood's observation that 'it's really nice to be in a situation where something is that digital and to convert it to analog in a performance' (Turenne 2001: 4). In precisely this sense, Radiohead should be celebrated for its ability to mix together categories normally opposed – analog and digital, rock and techno, breath-based and machine beat – in ways that expose ever deeper sonic affinities between noise and music, and deploy them to expand rock itself.

Machine

Yorke has described *Kid A*/*Amnesiac* as being about 'bearing witness' to the world's becoming paradoxically both overcontrolled and out of control (Reynolds 2001: 30). Concretized in musical terms, the notion of bearing witness can be fruitfully contrasted with the allegorical mode of *OK Computer*, where Yorke sang of the instability of the information age and of the younger generation's uncertain yet unavoidable commitment to it. As Alex Ross notes in his *New Yorker* piece on the band, 'Yorke's lyrics [on *OK Computer*] seem a mixture of overheard conversations, techno-speak, and fragments of a harsh diary. … The songs offered images of riot police at political rallies, anguished lives in pretty suburbs, yuppies freaking out, sympathetic aliens hovering overhead' (Ross 2001: 115). Covertly signaled by Ross's decision to focus on the lyrics, the allegorical mode of *OK Computer* is, in short, the mode of the referential – music as a way of speaking *about* the world. What a contrast with the 'symbolic' mode of *Kid A*/*Amnesiac*, which finds Yorke, as Reynolds aptly puts it, 'literally voicing (rather than articulating) contemporary feelings of dislocation, dispossession, numbness, impotence, paralysis' (Reynolds 2001: 30). In songs like 'You and Whose Army,' Yorke paradoxically uses his voice – the physical expressiveness or 'grain' of his voice (Roland Barthes) – as an *instrument* particularly well suited to expressing the defiant resignation characteristic of the globalized information age.

I want to take this difference literally and ask what exactly the shift from a referential-allegorical to an expressive-symbolic mode has to do with Radiohead's experimentation with techno music techniques like sampling and digital sound processing. For there is more to Radiohead's shift than the simple exposure to techno music. While we know that Yorke purchased the entire Warp Records catalog after the 1997 breakdown and that he found inspiration in the work of outfits like Aphex Twin, Autechre and Squarepusher, we also know that he had been actively listening to techno since before the release of Radiohead's first album in 1993. Accordingly, the important question to ask is how exactly the newfound obsession with techno combined with a properly 'hermeneutic' swerve to yield the curious and inspiring experimentation that became *Kid A* and *Amnesiac*. If, that is, Radiohead's shift betrays a retreat from detached observation to resigned inclusion within a thoroughly technologized socius, how might this be bound up with the band's willingness to deterritorialize its rock sound by adopting techniques from what one recent commentator has aptly dubbed 'intelligent techno' (Pinhas 2001: 4)? The answer, of course, will have everything to do with the voice, and specifically with the deterritorialization of the voice from its privileged status as something over and against instrumental music (that is, as the bearer of a linguistic message). But before we explore this deterritorialization, and in order to do so, we will need to gain an understanding of the specificity of techno music as a technico-cultural stage in the development of musical recording technology and the recording industry.

As both Douglas Kahn and Friedrich Kittler have argued, phonography holds a crucial role in the history of sound, and more generally in the recent history of technology, because it marks the moment when self-hearing is exteriorized and the voice is severed from the body.[2] Yet whereas Kittler celebrates phonography for its capacity directly to inscribe the real (and thus to do away with the mediation of the symbolic), Kahn sees phonography as a watershed moment in the 'breakup of naturalization' that began with the rise of communications technologies in the nineteenth century. For Kahn, that is, phonography symbolizes the 'sociality of sound,' which comprises the fundamental achievement of technical mediation:

> Phonography played a crucial role [in the breakup of naturalization], for with it came the unique ability to return the subject's voice to his or her own ears; previously this return had been limited to mandibular and cranial resonance along the throat on up through the head. The voice as the privileged site of union between audition and utterance (perhaps the most common privatized act performed in the company of others) was 'deboned' as vocal presence was wrenched from the throat and phonographically inscribed. This served to represent and technologically manifest the severance of speech from the speaker, the voice from the body, the voice from the soul, and the voice from the literary voice. The mix of utterance and audition moved from experience to representation, a representation bereft of the resonating chamber of the skull or the reflective landscapes of the echo; but it could move back toward experience, simulating it, in moments of dislocation, composition, relocation, dispersal, and so forth. (Kahn 1999: 72)

As the very emblem of the socialization of sound, phonography thus gave sustenance to a trajectory that has culminated in contemporary digital processing of sound and the graphic model of sound recording technically facilitated by digital audio recording workstations which, to follow Kahn's metaphor, confer the capacity to 'word process' with sound. In a certain sense, then, there is a straight line that runs from phonography to contemporary techno music and that finds a perfect symbol in scratch sampling techniques (characteristic of rap music), which might best be understood as transformations of the linear inscription of the musical gramophone record into a randomly accessible, repeatable, and infinitely recombinable database of separate, quasi-autonomous sounds. Following the migration of sound from the record to the computer (analog to digital), the operative principle of such repetition and recombination sheds even its lingering connection to the hand (and body) of the DJ, being concentrated instead in the digital action of the finger and mouse.

In his remarks on techno music, Pierre Lévy lends some internal differentiation to this seemingly unified trajectory. Contending that techno demarcates a fundamental shift in the materiality of sound itself, Lévy differentiates 'digitization' [*numérisation*] from notation and recording as a third model for the inscription of sound. Rather than yielding a convergence of sound with writing, the advent of digitization materializes the flux of sonorous matter as a 'universality without totality':

> In techno, each actor in the collectivity of creation rises out of the sonorous material flux circulating within a vast technosocial network. This matter is mixed, arranged, transformed, then reinjected in the form of an 'original' piece into the flow of digitized music in circulation. Thus each musician or group of musicians functions as an operator on a flux in permanent transformation in a cyclic network of co-operators. (Lévy 1997: 169–70)

One important consequence of this shift is the intimacy it brings to the contact between individual creators; as Lévy puts it, the link between them is now 'traced by the circulation of musical and sonorous material itself, and not only by hearing, imitation or interpretation' (Lévy 1997: 170). In principle, these remarks would extend to all of sonorous matter, which means, though Lévy does not make the point directly, to the human voice itself. Within the techno aesthetic system Lévy is describing, that is, the voice has the very same material status as any other sound: it comprises a part of the flux of digitized sonorous material that is materially akin to the rest of that flux. Whereas the phono-graphing of the voice made it available for analog techniques of sampling that only indirectly, i.e. mediately, contest its differentiation from sound, the digitization of the voice renders it immediately samplable and manipulable following processes identical to those of all other digitized sounds. In this sense, Lévy's insistence on the priority, within the techno aesthetic, of 'making an event happen' over adding an item to the archives of music could equally well characterize Colin Greenwood's above-documented excitement at the possibilities for re-analogizing the digital during performance: performance – which means first and foremost *vocal* performance, that is, performance as the mode of self-presence or auto-affection – operates a certain punctuation of the constantly evolving digital flux of sound, a punctuation that, not insignificantly, underscores the continued role of embodiment in the 'event' of musical sound.

For the same reason, Lévy's account lends a curious twist to Kahn's vision of a molecular compositional process stemming from 'the capacity to join sonic and phonic events at the level of the signifier and move to and from larger events and to fields between and among them' (Kahn, 1999: 76). Whereas Kahn's commitment to a radical program for liberating sound from music renders him contemptuous of the urge to anchor the unanchorable auditive signifier in physicality, utterance, nature, and music, for Lévy there is (or can be) a deep continuity between the molecular materiality of sound and its molar anchoring in music and the voice. In this sense, Lévy's position resonates with the compositional process followed by Karlheinz Stockhausen in *Gesang der Jünglinge* (1955–56), where, as Robin Maconie observes, 'For each sound component of spoken language there exists a synthesized equivalent. ... Thus a continuum between electronic sound and vocal sound is established at every point between the extremes of tone and voice' (quoted in Connor 2001: 476). One can add to this the fact that, with the digitization of electronic sound and voice, the continuum need no longer be merely typographic, but exists at the molecular level of sonorous materiality itself. Or, to follow the logic of contemporary composer Trevor Wishart, that the very distinction between the physicality of the voice and the abstractness of sound breaks down in the age of digitization: 'In the real physical world,' Wishart notes,

> we are able to say quite clearly that the sound of a metal bar falling to the ground is not an utterance, whereas a sound produced by a being is. In the virtual space of loudspeakers this sort of distinction may be difficult to make. ... We may, in fact, play with the utterances of a sound-object. (quoted in Connor 2001: 481)

Contextualized against this indifferentiation of voice and sound, Radiohead's experimentations with techno music techniques and digital processing would appear to yield a certain indifferentiation of the very binary – rock versus techno – with which critics and fans alike have tended to saddle them. Moreover, we can now see that what distinguishes Radiohead's contribution at the sonic threshold is its capacity to move back and forth between the worlds of analog performance and digital composition – or, more specifically, its willingness, on the one hand, to deterritorialize its rock sound (by undoing the distinction between voice and sound) in a process that yields an expansion in the sonic terrain of its music, and its effort, on the other hand, to bring this expanded terrain back to bear on the performance-oriented model of rock itself (by, for example, employing atypical instruments like the ondes martenot capable of 'simulating,' to borrow Kahn's term, the molecular continuum of digital processing in a live environment).

Voice

Music historians have been aware, at least since John Cage's legendary experiments with the anechoic chamber, that there is no such thing as silence. Shutting out noise from the environment simply brings to the fore the insistent hum of the blood circulating and the busy firing of neural synapses. To this idealized picture of the body as source of natural noise, William Burroughs' conception of language as virus adds yet another type of noise, a socialized counterpart, as Kahn has noted: 'Try halting your sub-vocal speech,' Burroughs challenges, 'Try to achieve even ten seconds of inner silence. You will encounter a resisting organism that *forces you to talk*' (quoted in Kahn 1989–90: 55). Not only does the 'inner voice' interfere with the audition of Cagean bodily sounds, but it also filters the entire perception of the aural world, metamorphosizing this latter, always already, through a seemingly ineliminable anthropomorphic calculus. This is why Kahn proposes the radical, speculative remedy of new instruments that would tap into the legacy of phonography as an alternative to embodied sound. 'The sound of a phonographic instrument lies elsewhere,' he says. 'The sound is not fully generated at the site of the instrument's physical location but instead plays out along a materiality of signification related ultimately to its phenomenal or imaginary source. The new idea of instrument simply starts at the source ...' (Kahn 1989–90: 57).

Taking account of the complex impossibility of silence, what are we to make of Yorke's allegedly catalytic experience of deafness and dumbness? If nothing can truly silence the inner voice, what contribution can his traumatic paralysis be said to have made to Radiohead's shift in direction? Did Yorke's experience somehow compel him to reconfigure his inner voice such that rather than forcing him to talk, it forced him to make noise? And, if so, how exactly did this passage from orality to aurality take place, and how did its taking place necessitate a detour through the inscriptional – or, better, numeric (digitized) – materiality of the contemporary aural world?

Yorke himself cites his disgust with the sound of his own voice – magnified by the host of imitators cropping up in the wake of Radiohead's success – as nothing less than the instigating factor behind the leveling of the voice-instrumentation hierarchy so central to *Kid A*/*Amnesiac*: 'Melodies became an embarrassment to me,' he recounts; 'It did my head in that whatever I did with my voice, it had that particular set of associations. And there were lots of similar bands coming out at the time, and that made it even worse. I couldn't stand the sound of me even more' (quoted in Reynolds 2001: 28). It was as if Yorke's voice expanded both outwardly and inwardly, swallowing up the entirety of the aural world while at the same time putting a stranglehold on 'the sound of me': both in the guise of other rock bands and in his own sonic self-affection, Yorke experienced the horror of vocalic indifferentiation, the becoming-voice of all the world's (and body's) sounds. Given their function as extensions of the differential program of phonography, it is not surprising that Yorke would turn to the rhythms of techno music and the techniques of digital composition in search of an antidote for this stultifying indifferentiation. What better way indeed to reintroduce difference, to rediscover the other, the world of sound, than to submit the voice to a digitized sonic babelization, to fracture its unitary form by filtering it through processes that transmit sounds originating in multiple and complex sources?

Nothing less is at stake in what Yorke refers to as the 'instrumentalization' of his voice; as he recounts, he 'got really into the idea of my voice being another one of the instruments, rather than this precious, focus thing all the time' (quoted in Reynolds 2001: 28). To accomplish this, Yorke took pains to interface his voice with technology, submitting it to digital processing, filtering it through other instruments, or treating it with sonic toys, in the process developing what he has called 'a grammar of noises' (quoted in Reynolds 2001: 32). Let us return to 'Everything in its Right Place,' the first track on *Kid A* and thus the literal as well as symbolic site of Yorke's re-emergence as a (now irrevocably – and indeed originarily – technical) voice: beginning with a simple keyboard melody overlaid with multiple repetitive, indecipherable, and fragmentary bits of voice, the song clearly announces the band's departure from the authoritative mode of vocalic assertion characteristic of *OK Computer*. When Yorke's voice finally enters in the proper mode of 'voice,' it is to deliver a repetitive series of four enunciations of 'Everything,' followed by four enunciations of 'in its Right Place,' all against the background of overlaid fragmentary vocalic bits. Only then does he intone the line so central to the symbolism of his traumatic paralysis: 'Yesterday I woke up sucking a lemon.' In a quite literal sense, the sub-vocalic build-up to this enunciation has the effect of deprivileging its referential status, transforming what might otherwise look like a prolongation of *OK Computer*'s allegorical mode into one element in a larger digital ecology of sound. The song continues to develop through a repetition of these three distinct vocalic modalities, offering a fragmentation of the voice designed to thwart any simple, unitary listening mode, including the heroic mode characteristic of traditional rock. Precisely by submitting the voice, from the very start, to a host of digital transformations, 'Everything in its Right Place' (which, not insignificantly, exists as a complete sentence only as a title, that is, in written form) challenges its status as a pregiven unified source capable of over-coding all other sources of sound, no matter how complex: what we are given instead is an inversion of this relation, such that the instrumentalization of the voice makes it simply one among many sounds. Yorke himself sees this dethroning of the voice as a means of disappointing expectations of authenticity and identity: 'By using other voices, I guess it was a way of saying, "obviously it isn't me"' (quoted in Reynolds 2001: 32). Still, it is necessary to resist the implication of intentional control, at least to some extent, since what falls under the category of voices here is not other 'voices' proper to Yorke, but rather all imaginable cyborg varieties of machine-voice, all possible technical 'otherizings' of the voice, to appropriate Simon Reynolds' felicitous term.

The technical fracturing of the pure self-affection of the voice is put to even more striking use in the second and title track to *Kid A* where Yorke's voice is vocodered through Jonny Greenwood's ondes martenot (an early electronic instrument made famous by French composer Olivier Messiaen). The effect is an unsettling, indeed downright eerie, leveling of the affective dimension of Yorke's voice that is in some ways reminiscent of *OK Computer*'s 'Electioneering,' except for the crucial fact that there the voice is purely and simply that of the computer, whereas here what is at stake is an indifferentiation of vocalic and machinic sound. Oddly enough, the result is a curious, if empowering inversion or de-differentiation of the ordinary association of human voice with expression and computer with simulation: while the computer voice on 'Electioneering' functions to preserve enunciative comprehension, the vocodering on 'Kid A' obscures all but a few words, transforming the voice into a sonic texture, a predominantly instrumental mode of expression. 'Kid A' begins with a spiraling, at first barely audible, arrival of sharply pulsed noise, overlaid and then replaced by a serial repetition of jagged, thin and icy keyboard sounds not unlike those made famous by Bernard Hermann's score for Hitchcock's *Psycho*. On to – or rather 'underneath' – this high-pitched sound is layered a fuller, lower-pitched melodic line from the ondes martenot, doubled by a drum beat, that will subsequently give a place of abode, indeed a source, for the voice. Roughly one and a half minutes into the song, drums proper are introduced as the rhythm accelerates and the sonic layering becomes more complex, only subsequently to flatten out leaving only the lingering beats of the drum machine … Then, in a reprise of the song's beginning (though now overlaid on top of the drum machine), the jagged, icy keyboard sounds resume, followed by the vocodered voice, the return of drums, with the whole sonic *mélange* finally culminating in an oddly calm and de-energized electronic scream tapering off into digital hum. Again, Yorke's tendency is to assess the significance of this vocalic transformation against the backdrop of rock expectations: processing his voice through the ondes martenot allowed him to 'sing things I wouldn't normally sing,' or in other words, to evade the responsibility of intentionality and meaning imposed by rock's ethos of authenticity. 'On *Kid A*,' he specifies, 'the lyrics are absolutely brutal and horrible and I wouldn't be able to sing them straight. But talking them and having them vocodered through Jonny's ondes martenot, so that I wasn't even responsible for the melody … that was great, it felt like you're not answerable to this thing' (quoted in Reynolds 2001: 32). Here, more clearly than in the case of 'Everything,' we can see how the technical otherizing of the voice has the effect of de-differentiating voice and sound, not only making the enunciation of the song's verbal message secondary to the expressivity of its sonic texture, but making the 'live' (that is, not pre-recorded) voice an expressive extension of an instrument, an effectuator of aural sound.

Yet another, perhaps less inherently deterritorializing modification of the voice comes by way of the Autotuner, a device for producing perfect pitch used extensively in contemporary R&B. Deployed on 'Packt Like Sardines in a Crushd Tin Box,' the opening track on *Amnesiac*, the Autotuner lends a slightly nasal flavor to Yorke's voice, at once de-personalizing it and bringing it sonically closer to the low-pitched electronic melody driving the song. Whereas here, in contrast to 'Kid A,' the vocal track is clearly distinct from and overlaid upon the electronic melody, it continues to operate a convergence of voice and sound, a convergence that becomes more insistent as the rhythmic intensity mounts (largely due to the increasing frenzy of the drum machine). Similarly to 'Everything,' 'Packt' tapers off into a swirl of instrumental dissonance, only to begin again in a reprise of the becoming-indifferent of voice and melody. Indeed, just as 'Everything' set the tone for what was to follow on *Kid A*, 'Packt' trumpets the intentions of *Amnesiac* (and begins to explain the rationale of its demarcation from *Kid A* despite its having been compiled from the same recording sessions): 'Packt' gives us a feeling for the dominant movement of the album, a movement that, through the preservation of a certain autonomy of both voice and instrumentation, will begin a perhaps more complex process of reterritorialization, in which the voice returns toward a post-rock mode now more confident because extended through its experience of sonic deterritorialization, and in which sound returns toward a post-rock confidence similarly linked to its liberation from the 'vocalic' continuum of the guitar line. (The fruit, but also the test, of this reading comes by way of *I Might Be Wrong*, the collection of live recordings from the *Kid A/Amnesiac* material, where this dual return is literally at stake.)

This interpretation holds even in the case of 'Pulk/Pull Revolving Doors,' easily the most radical of the songs on *Amnesiac* from the standpoint of vocalic deterritorialization. Indeed, the deployment of vocalic synthesis here would appear to work in some sense at cross-purposes to the above examples from *Kid A*, since the technical mediation – namely the use of the Autotuner to generate music from speech – does not so much blur the voice and sound as bring them together into a productive relationship while continuing to preserve their separation. Not insignificantly, traces of this slight shift can be discerned in Yorke's own description of the deformational 'trick' made possible by the Autotuner, where the binary between speech and music remains prominent and, as it were, undeconstructed. As Yorke explains, 'you give the machine a key and then you just talk into it. It desperately tries to search for the music in your speech, and produces notes at random. If you've assigned it a key, you've got music' (Reynolds 2001: 32). Far from operating a becoming-indifferent of voice and sound, this co-functioning of speech and technology to generate music utilizes a process of coding which, no matter how randomized, serves to mediate between speech as the dominant modality of voice, on the one hand, and music as what Kahn would gloss as the traditional form of self-containment of sound, on the other. One index of this shift to a model of co-functioning is the comprehensibility of the vocals on 'Pulk': despite the transformational process, the verbal message of the song retains precisely that kind of autonomy specifically targeted and undermined by the more radical convergence operative in 'Kid A.'

'Pulk' begins with four distorted drum-machine beats, followed by some faint, tinny electronic noises, punctutated with a dissonant guitar chord, and then reprised in two slightly modified cycles encompassing this entire beginning, at which point Yorke's 'autotuned' voice enters, speaking the barely, but still audible lines, 'There are barn doors. ... And there are revolving doors.' The song develops as a repetition of this pattern with the insistent distorted drum-machine beats setting the pace and the always lingering electronic noises operating four different punctuations as they crescendo into harmonic interludes of vastly varied length and intensity, always again followed by the return of the insistent drum beats and the variously distorted spoken voice (except in the last case, at which point the song ends). The effect of this compositional overlaying of voice on drum-machine background with harmonic interludes is a kind of tolerant co-existence of voice and sound, where occasionally one crosses over to the other's proper domain. The autotuning of the voice can thus be seen as a kind of mirror of the harmonic interludes: while these latter operate a momentary becoming voice of the sonic texture, the vocalic distortions function to simulate noise *within* the voice. Still, what we confront here is dissimilar in one important respect from the becoming-indiscernible of voice and sound on 'Kid A': here, that is, the respective autonomy of instrumental sound and of the voice is retained even as each term discovers its own proper modes for producing the effects of the other. It is as if the potential for deterritorialization at issue in the experimentation of *Kid A* – a deterritorialization operated by the becoming-indifferent of voice and sound – were here being established as a potential proper to *both* the voice and instrumental sound by themselves. This is perhaps most striking in the case of Yorke's vocals, which take a far more traditional form than they did anywhere on *Kid A*. Far from the fragmentation the voice underwent on 'Kid A,' here the voice is made to perform its most characteristic, most articulated function: speaking complete sentences. And whatever distortion the Autotuner introduces is itself put in the service of a signifying, even referential function: producing vocalic effects that mimic the content of the utterances.[3] Thus, beyond giving the effect of voice coming in and going out of the range of discernibility or articulation, the modulation of the autotuned voice (via the use of various decoding 'keys') restores a compatibility between expression and referentiality that functions to displace the earlier (i.e. *Kid A*) correlation of vocal expression with autonomous sound. Thus Yorke's speaking the line 'There are sliding doors' culminates in a whooshing, sliding noise, and his intoning 'There are secret doors,' in a hollow noise. When, subsequently, this reconciliation of expression and referentiality moves beyond the effects of the Autotuner to be supported directly by the instrumentation, we brush up against what we might call the strong program of *Amnesiac*. For as Yorke's line 'There are trap doors' gives way to a punctuation of an instrumentally generated machine whirr, only to resume with the conclusion 'that you can't come back from,' the invagination of voice and instrumental sound gives way to a more traditional division between speech and sound, a division markedly reminiscent of the allegorical mode of *OK Computer*. Still, less than signaling a sell-out or a return to the earlier formula for success, what this progression would seem to express is a newfound confidence and an expanded range of voice and instrumental sound as co-agents in the production of music. It is as if, having found sound *within* the voice and voice *within* sound, Radiohead could go forward by revisiting its origin, and indeed by repeating its rock roots with a difference: the difference that arises out of the deeper indifference of sound and voice, digital and analog, techno and rock.

It is precisely this payoff – namely, Radiohead's newfound confidence and ability to repeat its rock origin with a difference – that is expressed in Colin's above-cited celebration of the continuum between the digital and the analog. Not surprisingly, this payoff is strikingly displayed in the live performance of

'Everything in its Right Place' from *I Might Be Wrong*. Like the other performances of songs originally produced with technological gadgetry and digital sampling techniques (e.g. 'Idioteque' and 'The National Anthem'), 'Everything' effectuates a simulation to a second degree, as it were, reproducing through the analog technologies of voice and traditional rock instrumentation (guitars, drums, etc.) the effect of the studio simulation – the digital fragmentation, molecularization, and multi-sourcing – of Yorke's voice and the band's instrumentals. Indeed, the performance of 'Everywhere' comprises something like a primer on how to effectuate such a second-order simulation. It begins with Yorke tuning his voice through a digital processor that will permit effects of distortion and delay. Not surprisingly, this tuning is explicitly anchored in the breath, as Yorke exhales three times prior to his first intonation of the test line, 'Here comes the flood.' As the song develops, the delayed echo and distortion will simulate the sampling that was so central to the studio recording of the song (and also, as we saw, to the 'solution' of Yorke's inhibiting traumatic muteness). The effect of this solution is the restoration of sorts of what we might call the rock voice: that is, the voice as anchored in the body of the singer, though now coupled with machinery which can bring into it possibilities for fragmentation hitherto foreign to the rock voice. Without being treated as an autonomous, digitized sound particle, as it was on the studio release, the processing of Yorke's voice is able to simulate the effect of this technique, thus opening a new range within vocalic performance itself. That this processing culminates in swirling oscillations between the ever more artificial repetitions of 'There are two colours in my head' and Yorke's 'natural' intoning of the same line suggests the continuum that flows from one pole to the other, from the artificial embodiment of the digitized sound particle to the natural origin of the voice in the phenomenological body. Still, the fact that the 'natural' voice remains the ultimate source for the whole performance testifies to the constraints the rock model places on experimentation, even in its most expanded form.

A similar pattern – opening of a continuum coupled with a recognition of the 'natural' voice as privileged – animates the other live performances of songs from *Kid A*. Thus, in 'The National Anthem,' the tripartite division between the rock (bass and drum) line, the free play with electronic sounds, and the voice is *per force* simplified into a duality, with the instruments and, more surprisingly, the voice playing the role of both vocalic signifier and instrumental sound source. Thus the split between traditional rock sounds (here the distorted guitar line and the drum beat) and electronic noises is itself anchored in a more primordial continuum of sound, whose principle is precisely the range of the instruments themselves: in addition to intoning the driving guitar line, guitars (with the aid of keyboards, the ondes martenot, and who knows what else) produce simulations of electronic noises. Similarly, the voice assumes a more prominent role than in the studio version: not only does it first enter – in the form of muted grunts – as a kind of doubling of the drum rhythm, but it singularizes itself through quavering and steadily intensifies as it attempts to simulate the sound of the ondes martenot to which it is coupled (itself a simulation of the – strikingly absent – trumpet work of the studio version). Accordingly, whereas the *Kid A* version of 'The National Anthem' operated a kind of dissolution of the voice in the midst of complex layering of sonic textures (a layering driven by the dissonance of the trumpet as a usurper of the voice), what we get in the live version is something like a becoming-instrumental of the voice – with the vocalic chant and the ondes martenot echoing one another – in which the privilege of the voice as origin remains intact.

Similarly, in the live performance of 'Idioteque' – of all the songs on *Kid A*//*Amnesiac* at once the most 'techno' in its sound and traditional in its vocals – this pattern plays itself out once again. Gone from the live performance is the leisurely pace of the studio recording and, with it, the separation of the various sonic components of the song – drum-machine beat, ondes martenot line, vocals. Instead, from the first drum beat to the percussive crescendo, the song rushes headlong, with all elements sped up and transformed – the eerie ondes martenot line into the equivalent of a guitar chorus, the drum-machine beats into a driving expanse of noise, and the once detached voice into plaintive and quavering plea that functions to drive the headlong pursuit of the song through a long stretch with just drum accompaniment, only to culminate in the song's amazing (and crowd-pleasing) climax in the wash of percussive noises of cymbals and bells, tapering off into the final ondes martenot chorus and vocal repetition. Here it is as if the elements that were held apart so carefully in the studio original were subjected to a furious intertwining that once again testifies to the continuum of the sonic elements as well as their vocalic origins.

One final comparison – of the two versions of 'Morning Bell' – will serve to symbolize the programmatic differences distinguishing *Kid A* and *Amnesiac*, and to expose the empowering effects of Radiohead's experimentation with techno sounds. Whereas the *Kid A* 'Morning Bell' is a tour de force in vocalic doubling and complex fusion of fragmented voice with machinic instrumentals, the not insignificantly titled 'Morning Bell/Amnesiac' invests in the harmonic interchangeability of voice and instrumental sound (including, prominently, guitar sounds). Here it is as if the band has simply lost its fear of vocalic imperialism with the result sounding – contra Simon Reynolds – something very like Radiohead unplugged.[4] In the largely acoustic 'Morning Bell/Amnesiac,' voice and instrumentals (guitar melody) begin simultaneously, the traces of the hand manipulating the guitar's frets and strings are given a prominent place, and Yorke's voice is pitched to resonate with the instrumentals. What a difference from the earlier 'Morning Bell,'[5] where the voice is subordinated to the instrumentals that begin the song and where its initial efforts at a plaintive self-assertion (partially undercut by digital distortion) follow the increasing pace of the instrumentals and finally, toward the song's end, culminate in a fundamental reconfiguration in which the voice is fragmented and complexified as it is 'rebuilt' from within the bounds of the instrumental rhythms. Here what we are given to experience is something like an aesthetic education – or, more exactly, an industrial drilling – of the voice, as it gradually loses its supposed autonomy and devolves into low-pitched rhythmic noises passing over into repeated words and short phrases, all doubled by a vocalic melody, and ultimately dying away as the instrumental pitches play out to the song's end. In this sense, *Kid A*'s 'Morning Bell' can be said to symbolize the deterritorializing movement of an album that has itself been characterized by at least one band member as 'one single song,' and that not surprisingly yielded no singles or music videos.

This deterritorializing movement opened the terrain for Radiohead's further work by underscoring something like a sonic bottom line. As expressed, for example, by the fluid sonic transitions between songs (e.g. from 'Kid A' to 'National Anthem' or from 'Idioteque' to 'Morning Bell'), *Kid A* performed the function of disarticulating the voice by de-differentiating it from the sound – here sound in its instrumental mode – which can never be silenced. That this de-differentiation yielded a new confidence and an expanded range of 'rock' expression becomes strikingly apparent in the live performance of 'Morning Bell' where something like the effect of balance achieved via the acoustic mode of 'Morning Bell/Amnesiac' is wrought through second-order simulation. Even while retaining the original sonic complexity of the *Kid A* version, this performance collapses the distinction between rock instrumentals and electronics, utilizing swirling guitars to produce the sonic textures of the original's electronic experimentation. And here, too, the plaintive and quavering tones of Yorke's voice lend it a bodily expressiveness absent from the more purified vocal lines of the *Kid A* 'Morning Bell.' As an index of Radiohead's reterritorializing of its rock sound *after* its experimentation with techno, this live performance of 'Morning Bell' shows just how much the ineliminable fact of sound is bound up with its bodily origin.

Breath

In his *Wire* article, Simon Reynolds refers to Radiohead's plunge into the sonic continuum as a 'self-deconstruction.' By this, he explains, he means the way the band tampered with or discarded the 'two elements most celebrated by fans and critics alike: their guitar sound and Yorke's singing and lyrics' (Reynolds 2001: 26). Up to a point, this characterization is without doubt an apt one, since the *Kid A/Amnesiac* material, as we have now seen concretely, follows a line of flight into the domain of techno precisely in order to displace the music-noise economy characteristic of rock and with it the more or less unchallenged reign of voice and guitar. Yet in demonstrating how the borderline between music and noise – like that between rock and techno – is a fluid, constantly morphing one, Radiohead does more than simply displace a recalcitrant and constraining binary. Indeed,

Radiohead's deterritorializing and subsequent reterritorializing of rock music poses the very question that lies at the heart both of the modernist endgame culminating in Cage's all-sound aesthetic and of the reinvigorated avant-garde represented by Kahn's pleas for the radical liberation of sound: what is music? Whereas Cage answers by identifying music with sound as such, and Kahn by opposing sound to music, as a sonic space that would escape Cage's democratizing (and, as Kahn rightly points out, anthropomorphizing) gesture, Radiohead's work takes no explicit stand on the issue. None the less, the process we have just analyzed – Radiohead's plunge into the sonic continuum – implies an answer that contrasts markedly with both of these approaches: in effect, by simultaneously exposing the sonic continuum between rock and techno, 'music' and noise, breath-based and machine-based rhythm, and yet also conceding the privilege of the voice as the origin of (rock) sound, Radiohead returns the question (what is music?) to the domain of listening. If, in the wake of its experimentation, any sound (noise) can potentially become music, what makes a sound music has something fundamental to do with the body, with the process through which sound is embodied. What Radiohead learns, in a sense, is that music is the embodiment of sound.

Put another way, it learns that music is a temporal object. As theorized by Edmund Husserl in the *Lectures on the Phenomenology of Inner Time Consciousness* (1905), a temporal object is an object whose being coincides with its being perceived and is inconceivable without the perceptual process of inner time consciousness. Not insignificantly, Husserl's example of a temporal object is a musical melody. As corrected by Ricoeur, Derrida and, most recently, Bernard Stiegler,[6] Husserl's analysis of the time consciousness of a melody requires that individual sounds be experienced, always already, as musical notes (and not, hyletically, as individual sounds in isolation), since they are inseparable from the retentional horizon of the immediately preceding notes as well as the whole of the developing melody. Here what makes the notes music is not a codified economy independent of the experience of reception so much as the synthesizing activity of inner time consciousness, which is to say, the act of listening as listening (or, to speak like Heidegger, of listening as a form of understanding). Here, Barthes' duly famous emphasis on listening (as against hearing) acquires a properly onto-hermeneutic aesthetic function: listening quite literally produces music.[7]

This account of music as a temporal object whose origin is listening cuts through the tired set of oppositions Radiohead is said to deconstruct through its own self-deconstruction: rock versus techno, analog versus digital, authentic versus artificial music, music versus sound, breath-based versus machine-based rhythm, and so on. For if music comes into being through the embodied process of synthesizing a succession of notes, any sound whatsoever can potentially become a musical element provided that an embodied listener can be made to listen to it. One crucial consequence of this discovery is an indifferentiation of the opposition between sounds originating in the body and those generated synthetically: what makes them both into music is the process of listening – that is, the embodied synthesizing activity of an essentially temporal being (which means, following Derrida, Jean-Luc Nancy, and Stiegler, among others, a being endowed with 'retentional finitude'). And if this is the case, then the very privileging of technology that informs the sonic avant-garde from Luigi Russolo through Cage to contemporary experimenters, and that is exemplified in the phonographic break and its legacy (up to and including today's techno techniques) is, in a certain sense, deeply misguided. For, contra Kittler and Kahn, *it is not the phonograph that originarily introduces difference into the voice, but rather the difference intrinsic to the voice, the originary self-differing of the voice itself, that is extended and exteriorized in the phonograph (and its contemporary legacy).*

That this inversion will require an expanded account of listening – one that capitalizes on the flexibility of the self-differing body – is the burden of Portuguese philosopher José Gil's analysis of the voice. Extending Derrida's contamination of expression and indication in his critique of Husserl, Gil contends that just as the power of expression is rooted in a double translation of bodily indication, so too is the allegedly pure self-affection of the voice founded in the double sensation of the body, or in other words, in an infinitesimal interval of embodiment:

> ... one can see in the result of Husserl's analysis the very presence of what he wanted to exclude, the body. Obviously, the reduplication of *I*, the proximity of self to self, can be understood in this reduplication as the condition for the pure presence of the object to consciousness. The subject hears itself as mediated by the body, and it is in the infinitesimal interval separating the speaking and hearing subjects that this object places itself. But there is something else. Doesn't this reduplication of the subject itself reduplicate the fact that the body can think about itself and take itself as its own object? ... If this is the case, the reduction of the space and of the experience of the body itself in the phenomenon of 'listening to oneself speak' can be assimilated to an 'infoliation' of the space of the body. Its paths will follow, against the grain, the lineaments of the paths of exfoliation. This seems so true that 'listening to oneself speak' is not the 'pure' autoaffection Husserl talked about, but also an experience. There are multiple modalities of 'listening to oneself speak' that presuppose diverse infoliations. (Gil 1998: 192)

Added to the Husserlian conception of the temporal object, this analysis has the effect of *embodying* time consciousness in a manner particularly relevant for our analysis here: it is breath itself, on account of its primitive function as a 'permanent mediation, a modulating pathway, between the interior and the exterior of the body,' that gives the principle for temporal synthesis. 'Because it "hears itself speak" – that is, because the fact of "hearing oneself" reorganizes into a whole certain sounds (which form a whole in themselves) for the subject – the human body constitutes itself as a specific totality, which, in its own physiology, is not reduced to a single living material'; '... breath – and voice –

appears as that which makes up the body as an articulated totality in time' (Gil 1998: 193).

In this striking inversion of its onto-theological determination, we encounter a conceptualization of breath as the principle of the body's (and the voice's) constitutive self-differing. Not insignificantly, this conception goes far toward undermining Barthes' dismissal of the breath in favor of the 'grain of the voice'; the breath, says Barthes, 'is the *pneuma*, the soul swelling or breaking. ... The lung, a stupid organ (lights for cats!), swells but gets no erection; it is in the throat, place where the phonic metal hardens and is segmented, in the mask that *signifiance* explodes, bringing the soul but *jouissance*' (Barthes 1977: 183). Eschewing the very binary opposition operative in Barthes' theorization – disembodied, spiritual breath versus embodied, erectile voice – Gil cites the breath as the most primordial embodied function that none the less can serve neither as origin nor unity. Rather, the breath (and the voice founded on it) opens the interval constitutive of the bodily self-differing that, in the sonic dimension, opens the experience of listening by means of which a grouping of sounds – whether of 'internal' or 'external' provenance – is *reorganized* into meaning.[8] In this respect we can say that breath is the grain of the listening voice. Significantly, *this* role of the breath – to inaugurate the possibility of listening – does not aim to affix sound to a physicality, which would be its singular and unitary origin. On the contrary, by opening up a complexity within listening – 'multiple modalities' and 'diverse infoliations' of sonic (self-)affection – Gil's redemption of breath allows for sonic heterogeneity (e.g. purely synthetic sounds at the threshold of perceptibility) to be preserved while also being heard: far from impacting the materiality of sound itself, listening 'structurally couples' it with the embodied rhythms of human experience. In this way, the digitized sonic flux of techno – and, beyond it, the experimental exploitation of the 'semiotic dislocations invoked by sound' (Kahn 1999) – does indeed hold the potential to operate a sonic deterritorialization, an expansion of the range of embodied listening. If such potential falls short of opening a domain of sound outside music, it testifies eloquently to the bodily constraints built into listening (as the process of musicalizing) and, at the same time, to the promise of a convergence with sonic machines in which the creation of new sounds will play the role of triggering the internal self-reorganization of embodied listening. Needless to say, this promise has as much to do with the plasticity of the body as it does with the autonomy of digital sound synthesis. Indeed, that is precisely why the primordial function of breath is as necessary for the experience of listening to the machine-based rhythm of 'techno' as it is for that of listening to the breath-based rhythms of 'rock.' And it is also why there is a more primordial indifference of these alleged sonic opposites beneath their alleged technical opposition.

In this sense, Gil's demonstration that sound has meaning only via the body has the salutary effect of putting a reality check on some of the more ebullient claims advanced on behalf of techno music and the digital materialization of sound.

Correlatively, as a kind of application of this lesson within the domain of pop music, Radiohead's plunge into the sonic continuum furnishes a test of the limits of sonic experience itself. In this respect, the embodied aesthetic of Radiohead's post-rock experimentation serves to undermine the 'inhuman' aesthetic of infinite sonic flux that is often invoked in discussions of techno. We have seen something of this in the analysis of Pierre Lévy cited above and it appears with even more exuberance in Richard Pinhas's 'De Nietzsche à la Techno,' where the extraordinary claim is made that

> The interior simultaneity [*simultanéisme*] [of 'intelligent techno'] undoes the tripartition of the present, past and future in favor of an infinite production brought into evidence … in the machine technical connections [of 'intelligent techno']. … It is a technical apparatus [*dispositif*] where modulated repetition and the formation of true temporal blocks found a continuous putting-into-variation of sonic production, the variations and modulations of motifs, the correlation [*mise en boucles*] of sequences of silicon, musical conjunction, and eternal return in a literally unsensed [*inouïe*] vast innovation. The practitioners of the multiple open up to difference and to active repetitions; they affirm a world of possibles and a putting-into-act of incompossible, aerian and ethereal universes. They literally suspend musical units [*cellules*] in the capture of sonic forces hitherto unknown and inaudible which compose a purely acoustic cosmic environment (Deleuze, on the refrain). (Pinhas 2001: 4)

While Lévy, even at his most exuberant, manages to keep in sight the occasional need for a punctuation of the sonic flux with an event (rave), Pinhas abstracts away even this minimal concession to actualization and embodiment, celebrating instead something like a sonic equivalent to Friedrich Kittler's vision of digitized knowledge circulating in an infinite and endless loop.[9] Given Pinhas's theoretical alliance of 'intelligent techno' with an infinite, atemporal sonic flux, any such punctuation – including, first and foremost, the punctuation of embodied listening – can only constitute an all-too-human betrayal.

As the final parenthesis of Pinhas's passage indicates, the philosophical source for much of the exuberant machinism invoked in reference to techno is Deleuze himself. And indeed, though he himself does not address techno explicitly, there is a direct filiation between Deleuze's molecularization of the musical field and the inhuman syntheses invoked by the likes of Pinhas and Lévy. When, for example, Deleuze calls for a liberation of matter from life, isn't he calling for a radical deterritorialization of 'vital rhythms and durations' such that these would take their articulation not from spiritual forms, but from 'the outside, from molecular processes that traverse them' (Deleuze 1978)? And if this liberation of matter from life opens a new musical possibility – non-pulsed time – isn't this the time of the sonic flux itself, of the sonorous molecules of music, and not the time of listening, in however expanded a form? In the end, we must ask whether this 'becoming-molecular of music' manages to do away with the primacy Husserl places on listening or, in other words, whether matter can be perceived directly, beyond life, the interior life of the self-differing voice. Doesn't it rather remain the case that even a non-pulsed time – a time that 'puts us in the presence of a multiplicity of durations, heterochronous, qualitative, non-coincident, non-communicating' – can only be materialized in perception – that is, as identical with the time of its, now necessarily complexified and internally differentiated, listening?

By answering 'yes' to this question, we can rescue the concept of non-pulsed time as nothing less than the very basis for the synthesizing activity of embodied listening in its contemporary, post-rock and post-techno, form. For if what Deleuze's concept ultimately designates is the way that sound produces rhythm in the very process of its happening, then it can quite readily be applied to describe the way sound yields an embodied rhythm through listening. For this purpose, it is crucial to understand that the non-pulsed time of listening is neither breath-based nor machine-based, but rather precedes this division and diminishes its much overblown significance. In this respect, Pauline Oliveros's celebration of breath-based rhythm is no less one-sided than Deleuze's molecular machinism: neither breath nor machine have a lock on the 'innovation and new experience' furnished by the universe, or by matter once liberated from life (Oliveros 2001: 36). Indeed, as we have already learned from our discussion of the derived status of phonography, what is important is not technology as such, but the way technology is deployed to trigger the production of the non-pulsed, here understood as the bodily production of music (i.e. listening), on the basis of the body's own internal interval. Put another way, as an extension and exteriorization of the internal self-differing of the voice, technology can challenge the voice to complexify itself, to bring to life the perturbation of molecular matter, to embody rhythms hitherto unimaginable from the side of life, and thus to further the convergence of listening with the ever richer aurality of the technosphere.

Such is, ultimately, the lesson of Radiohead's plunge into the sonic continuum. By exposing the profound continuum linking breath-based and machine-based rhythm, and simultaneously accepting the priority of the voice as an internally complicated, differential 'origin' for listening, Radiohead gives one (perhaps paradoxical) recipe for overcoming the vococentrism of western music: do not fear the voice, for the voice is not opposed to sound, but is itself sound, the materialization of sound in listening – that is, the complex, self-differing condition upon which sound can become phenomenalized. To make music, process all sound through the body, through the voice, and simply listen to what results; your body will do the rest ...

Notes

1. Noting the apparent impropriety of *The Wire*'s devoting a cover story to a band of the stature of Radiohead, Simon Reynolds makes this function explicit, arguing that Radiohead has earned its place in the pantheon of mavericks and margin dwellers

championed by *The Wire*: 'What's fascinating, and unprecedented, is just how Radiohead pulled off this swerve from the path seemingly mapped out for them. Just when *OK Computer* had left them only a step away from becoming the biggest rock outfit on the planet, with *Kid A* first, and now *Amnesiac* they chose to operate as mainstream ambassadors for many of the musical innovators this magazine cherishes' (Simon Reynolds, 'Walking on Thin Ice,' *The Wire* 209 (July 2001): 26–33, here 26). Reynolds' position finds an echo in Bill Martin's recent comments on Radiohead in his book *Avant Rock*. As Martin sees it, claims about Radiohead as 'veritable messiahs of rock,' despite being much overblown, point to the fact that, as he puts it, 'at least one band matters.' What the phenomenon of Radiohead has done, Martin contends, is force listeners to come back to the music: 'Instead of following up their hit album, *OK Computer,* with "son of *OK Computer*," Radiohead changed direction, even while maintaining some continuity with the language they had begun to develop. (For one thing, for a band with three guitar players, there is very little that sounds like guitar on the two more recent albums.) So, even though I am not entirely convinced of the more messianic claims – nor has the group made these claims for itself – I say more power to Radiohead, and I hope that they keep making music the way they want to make it' (Bill Martin, *Avant Rock: Experimental Music from the Beatles to Björk*, Peru, Illinois: Open Court, 2002, 219).

2. See Kahn, 'Track Organology,' and *Noise, Water, Meat: A History of Sound in the Arts*, Cambridge: MIT Press, 1999, Chapter 5; Friedrich Kittler, *Gramophone, Film, Typewriter*, tr. G. Winthrop-Young and M. Wutz, Stanford: Stanford University Press, 1999.

3. Here one need only recall the function of onomatopoeia in the history of linguistics from Saussure to Benveniste and how, for Benveniste, onomatopoetic words served as one instance among many of the contamination of signification by reference.

4. 'In many ways, the "grunge ballad" sound of "Creep" and its lyrical stance ... made Radiohead into an English equivalent of Nirvana. ... But the crucial word here is "English." You can imagine Kurt Cobain, if he'd chosen to live, probably going the unplugged troubadour route, stripping down his sound to let his plaintive songs stand naked and alone, folky and forlorn. You could never imagine him doing a *Kid A*, plunging deeper into studio science. Therein lies the vast, enduring gulf between American and British ideas of rock' (Reynolds 2001: 28).

5. That is, earlier to be published. One can only speculate about the order of the recording, though it would seem that the *Amnesiac* version can only attain its true significance – as an example of Radiohead's newfound confidence in the original indifference of voice and sound – if it is heard and analyzed after and in light of the *Kid A* version. In this sense, Reynolds' too-categorical distinction might still hold the key to the band's singularity, if not to its singular Britishness.

6. See Paul Ricoeur, *Time and Narrative*, Volume 3, tr. K. McLaughlin and D. Pellauer (Chicago: University of Chicago Press, 1984); Jacques Derrida, *Speech and Phenomena, and Other Essays on Husserl's Theory of Signs*, tr. D. Allison (Evanston: Northwestern University Press, 1973); Bernard Stiegler, *Technique et Temps: La Désorientation* (Paris: Editions Galilée, 1996).

7. See Roland Barthes, 'Listening,' in Barthes, *The Responsibility of Forms: Critical Essays on Music, Art, and Representation*, tr. R. Howard (New York: Hill and Wang, 1985).

8. Here one could pursue the contrast with Barthes further, since Gil's redemption of the breath stems from physiological roots to encompass the symbolic in its widest scope, whereas Barthes' theorization of listening aims precisely to move away from the physiological to the symbolic as an autonomous dimension of the unconscious. See Barthes, 1985.

9. 'The general digitization of channels and information erases the differences among individual media. Sound and image, voice and text are reduced to surface effects, known to consumers as interface. ... Inside the computers themselves everything becomes a number: quantity without image, sound, or voice. And once optical fiber networks turn formerly distinct data flows into a standardized series of digitized numbers, any medium can be translated into any other. With numbers, everything goes. Modulation, transformation, synchronization; delay, storage, transposition; scrambling, scanning, mapping – a total media link on a digital base will erase the very concept of medium. Instead of wiring people and technologies, absolute knowledge will run as an endless loop' (Kittler 1999: 1–2).

Chapter 9
'Sounds Like Teen Spirit': Identifying Radiohead's Idiolect

Allan F. Moore and Anwar Ibrahim

I

OK Computer (1997) has been widely hailed as one of the landmark albums of rock's 50-year history,[1] gaining its 'age-defining' status through a combination of both musical and sonic exploration, with lyrics concerning the themes, simultaneously universal and personal, of alienation, information overload, and fear of an imminent new millennium. It is both a timely and a timeless record, unmistakably Radiohead but still managing to express sentiments shared by people in all walks of life.[2] With a newly enlarged fanbase, and the warm reception afforded *The Bends* replaced by gushing praise, Radiohead faced a dilemma: in the face of industry pressure to repeat such an unexpected critical and commercial success,[3] how could any band (let alone Radiohead) follow such an achievement? If fleeing rock music for the more experimental terrains of post-rock may, with hindsight, appear to have been a logical survival strategy,[4] the sense of shock felt by many upon the arrival of the techno-tinged, jazz-influenced, and classical-sampling *Kid A* (2000) should not be underestimated. That Radiohead's subsequent album, *Amnesiac* (2001), was even more extreme in places, through a similar replacement not only of instruments by mere sounds, but also of 'songs' by 'pieces', hinted at an increasingly experimental musical trajectory. In this context, *Hail to the Thief* (2003) is a problematic album, with its apparent refusal of musical and sonic progression, its partial recovery of guitars as sonic focus, and its re-employment of more conventional song structures all, perhaps, contributing to its predominantly muted critical reception. Opinion appears divided as to whether *Hail* is the 'real' successor to *OK Computer*, with the more extreme experimentation of the *Kid A/Amnesiac* sessions the work of a band fleeing the responsibility of writing a 'proper' follow-up, or that *Hail* is somehow the inevitable outcome of these albums, in the same way as Radiohead viewed *Kid A* as the only way forward from *OK Computer*.[5] Critics supporting the latter viewpoint cite the perceived emotional honesty of all the band's recordings as positioning each of its albums in logical progression, in the sense that they reflect accurately both the band members' collective state of mind and their relationship with the outer world at that particular point in time.[6]

Guitarist Ed O'Brien has suggested that *Hail* represents 'the end of an era,' adding that the band has taken 'this kind of music' as far as it can go.[7] Although O'Brien doesn't clarify whether he is referring to Radiohead's more experimental post-*OK Computer* output, or simply to its perceived attempts to push the boundaries of rock music with each subsequent release, this remains a tantalizing question. Does the assertion of *Hail* as the end of a single musical journey hint at the existence of an underlying logic to what, on the surface, appears to be a disparate collection of albums? Is there a (loosely) definable Radiohead idiolect that underpins all the apparent changes of style, genre, and musical complexity through which the band has moved? In other words, do we really hear the same Radiohead on *The Bends* (1995) as we do on *Kid A* (2000), or did the pressure of creating 'the most important record of its generation' in the interim force the band to reinvent itself and its music?[8]

Even if we disregard O'Brien's assertion, and also the close musical links between *Hail* and Radiohead's pre- and post-*Kid A* output, the fact that this album represents the completion of the recording contract the band signed with EMI in 1992 signals it as an intermediate full-stop to the band's career, and therefore a suitable vantage point from which to assess the band's peculiar take on rock music.[9]

II

Before moving any further, we should clarify what we mean by 'idiolect.' The everyday concept of musical *style* is a familiar one. In reasonably precise terminology, it 'refers to the manner of articulation of musical gestures ... [and it] operates at various hierarchical levels, from the global to the most local.'[10] In other words, it refers to a decision a band may make to play a song in, for instance, a 'rock' style rather than a 'country' style. *Idiolect* as a concept is frequently conceived[11] to be subsidiary to *style*. Thus, Glenn Miller's music is all couched within the style defined by the term 'swing.' Indeed, the term *style* is often used to cover not only the deeper hierarchical level, but also the more local one of simply Glenn Miller's music. In this chapter, we use the term *idiolect* to refer to the more local level. Thus, the idiolects of both Fats Domino and Chuck Berry carve out spaces within the *style* known as rock 'n' roll. They carve out different spaces, of course – that is why we recognize their work as their work individually, and do not confuse the two – but both singers' output is subsidiary to the style known as rock 'n' roll.

Much to the band's annoyance, some contemporary criticism insists on saddling Radiohead with the label 'progressive.'[12] One key feature of the first wave of progressive rock (broadly 1967–78) was that the *idiolect* associated with particular bands transgressed *style* boundaries. This can be heard most clearly in the incursions of 'free jazz' and 'sentimental song' in the music of King Crimson, 'folk' and 'synthesizer rock' in Jethro Tull, 'classical' in Genesis or Yes,[13] and 'medieval' styles in Gentle Giant. The key feature, though, is that progressive rock marked the realization that *idiolect* can operate without a fixed anchor in *style*. The fact that *Kid A* may seem at first encounter no longer to be 'rock' music does not mean that it hasn't been invented by a 'rock' band.

Radiohead's idiolect can only properly be approached through close attention to its recorded output. It cannot be defined rigorously – it tends only to be stereotypical idiolects that can be so specified – but it incorporates particular tendencies, the total of which summarizes what Radiohead 'sound like.' It is the nature of this apparent Radiohead 'idiolect' that is our sole concern here: is it best understood as singular, and loosely defined, reaching clearest representation in *OK Computer* but partially located in all their other albums (as hinted at by Jake Kennedy in *Record Collector* and the *Daily Telegraph*'s David Cheal), or is it more accurately represented as an accumulative process most clearly expounded in *Hail to the Thief* (as suggested by the earlier quote from Gareth Grundy's article for *Q* magazine)? Alternatively, perhaps Radiohead's idiolect is comprised of two loosely associated but ultimately separate strands that reach their most defined states in *OK Computer* and *Hail to the Thief* respectively (as believed by the *Daily Telegraph*'s Andrew Perry and also by all those who view the post-*OK Computer* material as inferior)? In the following discussion we will consider Radiohead's studio output[14] from various viewpoints, in an attempt to both answer this question and highlight some of the problems created by this contentious notion of 'idiolect.'[15] We shall focus on two constituent facets of this idiolect: intertextual reference and formal strategies. Others (harmony, melody, groove) will be treated much more lightly, partly for reasons of space, partly because we believe the patterns used in these domains to be less characteristic of what it is to sound like Radiohead.

III

> We don't sit down and say, 'Let's break barriers.'
> We just copy our favourite records. (Jonny Greenwood)[16]

An understanding of the cross-pollination that takes place between musics of different genres and artists is fundamental to any discussion of popular music. The notion of 'idiolect,' therefore, must be as preoccupied with derivation and idiosyncratic patterns of influence as it is with individuality. In spite of its groundbreaking status, Radiohead has never shied away from being influenced by other artists, nor from betraying these leanings in its recordings. *Pablo Honey* (1993) is the band's least individualistic album, and must be heard primarily as a response to the Seattle-based 'grunge' rock movement that crossed into the musical mainstream in late 1991. Indeed, the producer of *Pablo Honey* (Paul Q. Kolderie) had previously worked with Dinosaur Jr and engineered The Pixies' debut release, *Come on Pilgrim* (1986). Grunge's most identifiable musical characteristic was the soft verse (with clean guitar sound) and contrasting loud chorus (with heavily distorted rhythm guitar). This template appears on no fewer than five of *Pablo Honey*'s 12 tracks.[17] If the main philosophy of punk (grunge's clearest predecessor) was one of nihilism, grunge had an underlying theme of self-directed anger and self-hatred. Nirvana's Kurt Cobain wrote lyrics that were both cryptic and elusive. In comparison, those of *Pablo Honey*-era Thom Yorke, clearly influenced by both philosophies, were almost painfully direct, with such entirely self-explanatory lines as 'I'm better off dead' and 'I'm a creep, I'm a weirdo.'[18] Central to the perceived authenticity of these assertions, and the subject of continual debate, is Yorke's vocal delivery: because his voice is clearly untrained, many commentators have attributed to it a sense of emotional honesty and vulnerability.[19]

On *Pablo Honey*, specific references to pre-existing recordings are fleeting. Nirvana's *Nevermind* (1991) is *Pablo Honey*'s closest contemporary musical and lyrical counterpart, with a clear parallel between the chorus melody to Nirvana's 'Lithium' and the lead guitar riff of 'Anyone Can Play Guitar.' The Sex Pistols' *Never Mind the Bollocks* (1977) is another key influence, with the relentless distorted guitars, extreme brevity and Thom's largely atonal vocal delivery of the second verse of 'How Do You?' all highly reminiscent of The Sex Pistols' earlier 'Seventeen.' However, the biggest single influence on *Pablo Honey*, one noted by the band members themselves, comes from a group who came to prominence after the death of punk and before the birth of grunge: 'Reflecting on the light/dark dynamic and guitar solo in particular, Ed O'Brien said of ["Prove Yourself"]: "We were in hock to the Pixies and Dinosaur Jr up to our eyeballs."'[20]

The Pixies had a more significant effect on *Pablo Honey* than just the use of dynamic contrasts or string bends,[21] however: the first novel idea on the album is the added-note disrupting the otherwise 5/4 intro, which was most likely influenced by the equally striking added-bar idea employed in the chorus of The Pixies' 'Wave of Mutilation.'[22] Similarly, the atonal guitar squealing that preludes 'Anyone Can Play Guitar' bears a striking similarity to the introduction of 'Tame.'[23] That specific musical references to other recordings are almost entirely absent is not altogether surprising, considering that with their debut albums most artists attempt to define their own 'sound,' and clear references to other artists and their recordings will work against such intended individuality. Generalized references to the works of other artists, however, are abundant. As well as intimations of the introduction of Abba's 'SOS' (1975) and of José Feliciano's guitar style in the ambient opening of 'I Can't,' and the staccato rhythm guitar of 'Blow Out' respectively, the falsetto middle eight of 'Creep' owes a clear harmonic/melodic debt to The Hollies' 'The Air That I Breathe' (1974).[24] Similarly, the two-chord alternation and gradual build-up of 'Stop Whispering' has a clear parallel in U2's 'With or Without You' (1987). Perhaps the only truly striking moment on *Pablo Honey* comes right at its close, when for its final 90 seconds 'Blow Out' is engulfed by a cacophony of atonal guitar lines, ever increasing in pitch and intensity. Even this idea could have been borrowed, however, having been used (arguably to greater effect) by Radiohead's contemporary Suede at the climax of its 'Animal Lover' (1993).[25]

If *Pablo Honey* was the work of a band with a wide knowledge of music (as demonstrated through the range of influences portrayed) but one with a narrow stylistic vision, then *The Bends* (1995) is a more varied affair, with the generic complicity and pseudo-macho posturing of the former replaced with a more genuine sense of emotional fragility and a willingness to experiment stylistically. This is marked perhaps by a general fall in Thom Yorke's tessitura.[26] Whereas on *Pablo Honey* he would occasionally use his voice's highest register,[27] by 'Street Spirit' it had become very controlled and rather beautiful, and almost separated from the texture of the rest of the band, as if it were floating.[28] As a consequence of this shift, the influences of other artists and their recordings on *The Bends*, although clearly present, are harder to specify. While the opening four chords (and their accompanying rhythmic gesture) of 'Just' are an apparent transposition of those belonging to Nirvana's 'Smells Like Teen Spirit' (1991), this chord pattern also closely resembles the main riff of Magazine's debut single 'Shot By Both Sides' (1978).[29] And, although the opening two-bar guitar pattern of 'Black Star' is also clearly derivative,[30] few further references to other tracks are identifiable. Allusions are clear, however: 'Planet Telex' features a similar manner of rhythmic displacement to that so fêted in Beck's 'Loser' (1993),[31] while the guitars of the middle eight of 'Just,' double-tracked in parallel thirds, recall both Thin Lizzy and the more distant George Harrison. Similarly, the ringing guitar open E of the third verse of 'Bones' recalls that at the end of The Beatles' 'Strawberry Fields Forever' (1967).

Like *Pablo Honey*, many songs on *The Bends* are clearly indebted to both The Pixies and grunge, with six possessing the characteristic soft/loud dynamic shift in some form.[32] Also, the descending arpeggios that open 'My Iron Lung' bear more than a passing resemblance to those of Nirvana's 'Heart Shaped Box' (1993), and it does not take a leap of faith to compare the newly discordant guitar style of Jonny Greenwood (as found on 'My Iron Lung' and 'Just' in particular) with the characteristic atonal yet melodic style employed by The Pixies' guitarist and singer-songwriter Black Francis.[33] It is perhaps unsurprising, then, that references to *Pablo Honey* songs are also apparent: the guitar eruptions of 'Bones' and the opening chromatic descent of '(Nice Dream)' are both reminiscent of 'Ripcord,' while 'My Iron Lung' makes no quibbles about its similarity to 'Creep,' as demonstrated by the lyric 'this is our new song, just like the last one.' Furthermore, the characteristic double neighbor-note motion in the guitar used during the chorus of 'Bones' recalls not only that of the bridge of 'Vegetable' but also the Keith Richards staple employed on Rolling Stones songs like 'Gimme Shelter' (1969) and 'Brown Sugar' (1971). The main stylistic developments on *The Bends* occur through the increased employment of acoustic guitar, leading to the use of two genres previously unexplored by Radiohead, the ballad and the power ballad,[34] both of which are characteristic of heavy metal. Elsewhere, brief moments of dub-style bass appear in the bridge of 'The Bends' and at the end of 'Just,' the prominent vibrato keyboard chords of 'Planet Telex' are seemingly imported from a dance track, and the atmospheric use of electric guitar on 'Bulletproof ...' hints at the kind of extended guitar techniques usually reserved for avant-garde compositions.

If with *The Bends* Radiohead had begun to combat the almost overpowering twin influences of The Pixies and Nirvana, by *OK Computer* (1997), they appear to have been all but forgotten. In fact, so complete was the band's assimilation of influences that, where they can be found, they are altogether more subtle. For instance, while the title of 'Subterranean Homesick Alien' is a clear reference to Bob Dylan's 'Subterranean Homesick Blues' (1965), neither the musical nor lyrical content of the former bears any relation to the latter. Where references do occur, they are predominantly guitar related. The clean guitar arpeggios that open 'No Surprises' clearly evoke those of The Beach Boys' 'Wouldn't it be Nice' (1966) in both sound and content, and the clean, then rather crappy guitar sound with overdriven guitar in 'Electioneering' recalls Led Zeppelin's use of a similar juxtaposition on the change from 'Heartbreaker' to 'Livin' Lovin' Maid' (1970), with Thom Yorke's guitar riff clearly indebted to that of Elvis Costello's 'Tokyo Storm Warning' (1986).[35] 'The Tourist' references Fleetwood Mac pioneer Peter Green's mild guitar style, while 'Exit Music (for a film)' replays the 1970s topic of 'loner against the world,' which pitted a sole acoustic guitar against a full band,[36] here reinterpreted as lone voice against environmental sounds. On this album, the chromatic descending bass that has formed such a feature of Radiohead's output has reached some sort of fulfillment – refracted through 'Exit Music ...' can be heard Eric Clapton's sentimental 'Let it Grow' and, even more distantly, Richard Sherman's cloying *Chitty Chitty Bang Bang* lullaby 'Hushabye Mountain.' The production on 'Subterranean Homesick Alien' recalls Daniel Lanois' work with U2, while the fractured piano style and computer-generated noises of 'Fitter Happier' suggest Pierre Henry's *musique concrète* compositions. Even David Bowie's 'Space Oddity' (1969) and the cavernous production of Led Zeppelin drummer John Bonham's resonant kit[37] are both recalled on 'Climbing up the Walls.' Self-borrowing can also be posited: 'Exit Music ...' explodes with its final verse then ends with its quietest dynamic in much the same way as 'Fake Plastic Trees,' and the use of a brief chromatically descending guitar motif to mark the end of a section as found in 'Paranoid Android' previously occurred in 'My Iron Lung.' Similarly, 'Airbag' neatly revises the drone chord with suspended notes over a syncopated drum par so prominent on 'Planet Telex,' and its use of a dub-style bass line to signal a breakdown passage mirrors this feature's previous employment on both 'The Bends' and 'Just.'

OK Computer works as a coherent whole in a similar but superior way to *Pablo Honey*, mainly due to the similarly slow pace at which its songs unfold,[38] and the predominance of treated (but non-abrasive) electric guitar sounds. Stylistically, the songs featured on *OK Computer* defy easy classification through being multisectional,[39] multilayered in texture, and also through a lack of adherence to any existing stylistic conventions, creating for the first time the impression that, although references to the works of other artists are apparent, the music is very much Radiohead's own.

Where *OK Computer* featured 12 highly inventive and original takes on the concept of a rock song, *Kid A* (2000) saw Radiohead producing tracks that not only defied categorization as rock music but that, on occasion, also challenged perceived notions of 'song.' The latter's extreme exchange of guitar prominence for computerized sounds also signaled a further stylistic widening of influences. Yorke acquired the entire back catalog of the Sheffield-based electronica-oriented Warp label while writing and recording *Kid A*,[40] and the more abrasive end of the output of Aphex Twin (that label's most celebrated artist) has a clear influence on the beat-driven 'Idioteque.'[41] Similarly, the childlike simplicity and soft-focus treatment of the title track, and the abstract shapes and slow-paced atmospherics of 'Treefingers,' would not have been out of place on either Boards of Canada's *Music has the Right to Children* (1998) or Autechre's *LP5* (1998).[42] The influence of DJ Shadow's cut-up style on the drum track to *OK Computer*'s opener 'Airbag' has been noted by a number of critics,[43] and the first song on *Kid A* features a similar use of this style, this time involving treatment of Yorke's vocals. Elsewhere, musical influences stretch back further in time than on previous albums, encompassing both jazz and concert music. 'Motion Picture Soundtrack'[44] contains overlaid samples from an (uncredited) Alice Coltrane recording, while 'The National Anthem' contains a chaotic horn arrangement intended to sound like Charles Mingus.[45] 'The National Anthem' concludes with what appears to be a brief (again uncredited) sample from Elgar's Second Symphony, while the following track, 'How to Disappear Completely ...,' employs micro-tonal intervals in a style Jonny Greenwood credits to Penderecki.[46] The album's two credited samples, both featured on 'Idioteque,' straddle the electro-classical divide, being from electronic compositions by the classically trained composers Paul Lansky and Arthur Kreiger.

Comprising recordings taken from the same sessions that produced *Kid A*, *Amnesiac* (2001) is more a consolidation of Radiohead's new experimental direction than another stylistic leap. As opposed to the sense of a coherent whole created by both *OK Computer* and *Kid A*,[47] the album is more akin to *The Bends* through being more a collection of separate songs. The album's emphasis on juxtaposition between tracks underlies an even broader collection of influences: the minor/major 9th alternations involved in both the string arrangement for, and vocal melody of, 'Pyramid Song' hint at eastern modality, while the non-metric droning guitar solo that comprises 'Hunting Bears' is akin to modern-day ragga. 'Pulk/Pull Revolving Doors' suggests even more abrasive dance-related sources,[48] and is essentially a more extreme descendant of 'Fitter Happier,' similarly bereft of melody and harmony. Elsewhere, the jazz-flavored vocal harmonies on 'You and Whose Army' were modeled on those of the 1950s black American trio The Ink Spots,[49] while more traditional jazz influences appear again in both the piano style and arrangement of album closer 'Life in a Glasshouse.'[50]

With a five-album legacy of continually 'progressive' records, Radiohead has chosen to consolidate further rather than innovate with *Hail to the Thief* (2003). Most noticeable are the clear references back to previous Radiohead songs and styles: the additive rhythms of the homophonic piano idiom of 'Sail to the Moon' make it a clear descendant of 'Pyramid Song' and 'Everything in its Right Place,' while the heavy vibrato keyboards of 'Where I End and You Begin' create the same claustrophobic atmosphere first explored on 'Climbing up the Walls.' 'We Suck Young Blood' evokes the weary vocal delivery of 'Exit Music …,' with its brief interlude borrowing both the piano style and sound from the end section of *Amnesiac*'s 'You and Whose Army.' Similarly, 'I Will' manages to evoke both 'Exit Music …' and 'You and Whose Army,'[51] and contains vocal counterpoint similar to that of the mid-section of 'Paranoid Android.' External reference points are even more abundant: 'Sit Down, Stand Up' explodes at the three-minute mark into a Steve Reich-like profusion of percussive sounds, while the childlike simplicity of both the vocal melody and piano interlude, and the Bontempi-sounding keyboard blips of 'Backdrifts,' all recall Boards of Canada in a way similar to 'Kid A.' 'Go to Sleep' is built on a descending bass-driven guitar riff that recalls early Led Zeppelin in general, 'Riverwide' (1998) by Sheryl Crow and The Pixies' 'Tame' (1988) in particular, while 'Where I End and You Begin' features a Peter Hook-style bass line and guitar clips not uncommon in The Edge's guitar playing. Stylistically, the album does point in new directions, however: Yorke's speedy yet rhythmic vocal delivery on 'Wolf at the Door' betrays a hip-hop influence; the fuzzy keyboard sound on 'Myxomatosis' is commonly found in the synth-led 'industrial' rock/metal genre;[52] the riffs of 'Punch up at a Wedding' and 'Where I End and You Begin' pave the way for an (almost) funky groove; 'There There' commences to the sound of tribal drumming; and the final section of 'Sit Down, Stand Up' is as much drum 'n' bass as it is Steve Reich.

So, what conclusions can be drawn from this (by no means exhaustive) summary of the stylistic and artistic influences evident on Radiohead's recordings? It is perhaps their quality and increasing diversity that is most striking: almost every major popular genre is referred to at some point, and where specific references occur they invariably involve artists who either already exist within the rock 'canon' (The Beatles, The Pixies, Pink Floyd, Dylan, Bowie, etc.) or can be classed as either experimental (Alice Coltrane) or avant-garde (Paul Lansky, Autechre, Aphex Twin).

From the evidence of influences, then, Radiohead's 'idiolect' would appear to be 'progressive' in nature, with the above survey supporting and refuting both the theories presented earlier. Containing the fewest overt references to both the recordings of other artists and other Radiohead songs, *OK Computer* appears to be the most characteristically 'Radiohead' album, although the band's songwriting style has since progressed and expanded stylistically. We may assume that Radiohead's idiolect reaches its most developed state in *Hail*, as is suggested by the large number of references to previous Radiohead recordings it contains, but this becomes questionable when we realize that *Hail* also seems to contain the most direct references to works by other artists. Any conclusions must, however, be tempered by the knowledge that it is the influences that are almost undetectable that may prove the most important, as the following two quotes from Jonny Greenwood demonstrate. When asked about the fractured composition of 'Airbag,' he declares the track as 'a classic example of Colin and Phil saying, Let's make it sound like DJ Shadow, but unfortunately – or fortunately – it doesn't.'[53] Similarly, while noting an influence on 'There There' Jonny provides a valuable insight into his views on songwriting: 'It's got that Pixies thing that I love, which is a huge build-up of tension and release. Which is really important in music – it's not thinking of things being good in an instant way, but good thinking in terms of five minutes.'[54]

In our attempts to define Radiohead's idiolect, we must therefore sink from surface to structure, and consider if it is the form of a Radiohead song that gives it its 'Radioheadness.'

IV

Form is probably best thought of by analogy with the scenes of a film – a series of events or tableaux that happen in a particular order, sometimes sharing setting or characters, the order of which is crucial to the narrative of the film. Formal sections in a song encompass such things as verses, choruses, and other things not quite so easy to name. There are a number of different formal characteristics that are shared between the tracks on *Pablo Honey*. Most strikingly, every track on the album either repeats the introductory musical material, or develops it in the first verse. While the number of different formal sections varies between one and four, nine of the twelve songs feature a repeated section followed by a section of new material (a pattern we might symbolize as 'AAB'), and with five of these[55] having 'AABC' as an outline form. Of the remaining three, 'Creep' could be considered AAB according to its dynamic outline, while 'You' and 'Stop Whispering' proceed toward a final culmination.

Throughout the album, there is a predominance of open-ended, incessantly repeating harmonic patterns,[56] from the drone of 'Lurgee,' the two-chord alternation of 'Stop Whispering,' the insistent repetition of the codas to 'Anyone Can Play Guitar' and 'Ripcord,' to the more normal four-chord patterns of other songs. Although none of the patterns is striking as 'original' thought, at least that of 'Ripcord,' with its descending chromatic bass, sets it apart from much other contemporary 'indie' rock and looks forward to later obsessions. 'Stop Whispering' is an exercise in slow-building dynamics, echoed elsewhere.[57] Prior to this gradual crescendo, a 'breakdown' of sorts occurs. In fact, only four songs do not contain a breakdown section.[58] Similarly, only four songs do not have a discernible chorus, with three of the four involving a cumulative form to a certain extent: while 'You' is fully cumulative, both 'Lurgee' and 'Blow Out' degenerate in this way toward the end. Only 'Thinking About You' is the exception.

Perhaps surprisingly, *The Bends* is a more musically straightforward album than *Pablo Honey* in a number of ways. Most conspicuous is the near-absence of *Pablo Honey*'s extended playouts, although 'Fake Plastic Trees' and 'My Iron Lung' are both enhanced through a clever use of dynamic contrast. Similarly, recollections of such playouts through the repetition of a final section of new material, whether or not coupled with a slight dynamic increase,[59] are entirely absent on *The Bends*, songs now generally ending after a single repetition of the final musical section.[60] This second album also betrays a simpler approach to the presentation and development of musical material. Where eight of the twelve songs on *Pablo Honey* contain both a verse and a chorus, 'Fake Plastic Trees' is arguably the only song on *The Bends* that does not contain an obvious chorus. On *Pablo Honey*, musical development occurs through non-identical repetition of sections in all but three tracks.[61] On *The Bends*, however, only three tracks show any musical development, achieved in all three cases by the introduction of new material.[62] With the remaining songs, an increased simplicity of formal layout is displayed. 'Black Star' and 'My Iron Lung' contain four different musical sections (intro, A, B, and C), and 'Planet Telex' contains three, all the remainder featuring just two distinct musical sections.[63] This simplicity is also reflected in the formal layout of these songs, six[64] displaying variations on a repeated AAB form, and with the first half of 'Just' and all of 'Black Star' being AABC in form. On *The Bends* the role of the introduction becomes more complex, however: on only half of the album's tracks does it simply precede the first verse; with the introduction to 'The Bends' and 'Just' providing the chorus material; and those of three further songs[65] containing music found in neither the preceding verse nor chorus. Furthermore, three songs[66] contain a 'pre-intro' comprised of atmospherics. Only one song, 'Fake Plastic Trees,' does not contain an introduction. One clear similarity between the two albums occurs through the structural use of some form of 'breakdown' or instrumental dropout section, which occurs in seven songs on *Pablo Honey* and six on *The Bends*.[67]

The general impression of *The Bends*, as opposed to *Pablo Honey*, is of an album that has been subject to more careful and precise musical design. In 'Planet Telex,' the album's first track, greater attention to textural change is evident, while atmospheric textures are noticeable right from the song's introduction. The bridge to 'The Bends' also exemplifies this care, as the sustaining guitar strikingly drops from the texture. When we get to *OK Computer*, although the consistencies in the use of form and texture remain, the band appears to be considering its timbres even more judiciously, an approach that will continue through subsequent albums. Again, the first song signals the advance – the kit enters midway through the third of four introductory hearings of the opening riff of 'Airbag,' rather than being present right from the beginning.

Although the second half of 'Just' is a profusion of new musical ideas, and while 'Black Star' and 'My Iron Lung' explore differing phrase lengths and the dovetailing of sections respectively (and to striking effect),[68] these apparent idiosyncrasies are nothing compared to what occurs on *OK Computer*, and on 'Paranoid Android' in particular. With what is the band's most musically accomplished set of tracks, Radiohead explores the structural possibilities of the song form in a far more sophisticated way. Four of the tracks on *OK Computer* combine simple and compound time signatures within a single musical phrase,[69] while 'Fitter Happier' contains no pulse whatsoever. Only three songs on the album stick to the convention of 4, 6, 8, 12 or 16 bar-long phrases,[70] with five of the rest[71] employing odd-numbered phrase lengths. 'Paranoid Android' is the most complex song in terms of overall structure, appearing through-composed until the repeat of the break and guitar solo sections at its close.[72] Elsewhere, however, the formal layout of the tracks is on a par with *The Bends* in terms of simplicity, with only 'Fitter Happier' not formally based upon the AAB template.[73] Similarly, nine of the twelve tracks contain a recognizable verse and chorus.[74] The reliance on formal regularity means there is no room for the cumulative open-ended forms favored on *Pablo Honey*, with only 'Let Down' and the coda of 'Electioneering' showing any signs of such an approach.

So, the clearest sense of continuation and unity within the formal strategies presented on the first three Radiohead albums is threefold: the most prevalent structural template on these albums is that of AAB; development of material occurs most frequently through the varied repetition either of the template employed (through the addition or removal of bars) or of previously heard musical sections (either as part of a repeated template or as a continual repetition of a single section); and a 'breakdown' section is employed on approximately half of an album's recordings, and will usually be structurally significant.

To this point, even on *OK Computer*, Radiohead's idiolect has been characterized by a regular sense of meter. Indeed, this is such a normative feature that it partly serves as stylistically definitive of the whole of rock (excepting parts of progressive rock and thrash metal). Such regularity can no longer be assumed after *OK Computer*. *Kid A*'s most immediately striking characteristics all relate to its surface details, with the cut-up vocals of 'Everything in its Right Place,' the voice-less 'Treefingers,' and the techno beat of 'Idioteque' particularly noticeable. These features are accompanied by a high level of surface-level musical complexity: 'Everything …' may technically be in 4/4, but the continual syncopation and lack of rhythmic support (bass, drums) make it hard to follow. Similarly, 'In Limbo' alternates between 6/8 and 4/4 (verse and chorus respectively), while 'Treefingers' has no discernible pulse. Unusual phrase lengths and groupings can also be found, with both 'Everything ...' and 'Idioteque' containing seven-bar introductions, and with those of 'Optimistic' and 'In Limbo' beginning with ten-bar (8+2) and nine-bar ($4^1/_2$ and $4^1/_2$) sections respectively. Elsewhere, 'Idioteque' is comprised almost completely of five-bar phrases. This degree of irregularity is found very seldom on the first two albums.

In a way not dissimilar to its predecessor, *Kid A* counters the surface complexity (which in its case is predominantly rhythmic and textural) with a more straightforward musical content: all tracks except 'Treefingers' contain an introduction that prepares the verse material, and with 'The National Anthem' and 'Idioteque' the introduction provides the basic musical material for the entire track. All songs except the 'The National Anthem' and 'Treefingers' contain a discernible verse and chorus, with these two containing sections of an ambiguous nature. As in previous albums a breakdown section is employed on half the tracks,[75] although such sections now tend to occur more than once within a track, being both shorter in length and merely ornamental.[76] In terms of form, the album's closest relative is *Pablo Honey*: nine tracks end with a repeated section[77] (although the *Kid A* tracks dissolve instead of using the gradual build-up then cut-off technique of *Pablo Honey*). *Kid A* is the most formally complex of the first four Radiohead albums, with a clear AAB pattern apparent on only three tracks.[78]

With its tracks taken from the same recording sessions that produced *Kid A*, it is unsurprising to find that *Amnesiac* displays a similar degree of surface-level complexity, particularly the appearance of odd-length phrases on a number of tracks.[79] The alternating phrase-length idea, which first appeared in 'Morning Bell,' is reprised for its *Amnesiac* version (three bars then two), and also appears in 'Knives Out' and 'Life in a Glass House' (both four and five bars). Furthermore, the voice- and meter-less 'Hunting Bears' can be viewed as occupying the role taken by 'Treefingers' on *Kid A*, while six of the twelve *Amnesiac* tracks end with a repeated section (compared with nine of the twelve on *Pablo Honey* and six of the ten on *Kid A*). In a similar way to *Kid A*, the recordings contrast their busy surface with a relatively simple formal layout: four are centered on a single musical idea,[80] while none features more than three sections. This apparent harmonic simplicity is countered on both albums by the increased importance of melodic development, not only to provide surface interest but also to highlight formal divisions. In one key respect, however, *Amnesiac* is closer in character to *OK Computer* than its predecessor: seven of its tracks involve an AAB formal template, as did nine on *OK Computer*.

The main reason why commentators have problems assessing the position of *Hail to the Thief* in the Radiohead canon lies with its musical content, which reflects in turn each of the band's previous albums. Most noticeable is the prevalence of a bipartite song form, with sections replaced by an open-ended groove (extended playout) at the end of nine of the album's tracks.[81] This was the predominant formal layout on *Pablo Honey*, occurring on eight of its twelve tracks. An equal focus on melody and harmony was one of the main features of *The Bends*: it certainly occurs on four *Hail* tracks,[82] while on both albums all but two recordings contain both verse and chorus sections. Alternatively, the use of AAB formal structures on six tracks on *Hail to the Thief* links it with *OK Computer*,[83] with the level of surface complexity that accompanies the formal regularity also indicative of this album.

Hail to the Thief is most closely aligned to *Kid A* and *Amnesiac* through the consistently high level of musical intricacy of its tracks. Odd-length phrases occur in the chorus of '2+2=5' (both of five bars), while the seven- and nine-bar phrases of the introduction of 'Sit Down, Stand Up' contrast with the ten-bar phrases (5+5) of its verse material. Where 'Everything …' and 'Pyramid Song' were in such a heavily syncopated 4/4 as to obscure the meter, 'Sail to the Moon' is a yet more complex proposition. Up to the end of verse one, no two consecutive bars are of the same length, and it could be argued that although the verse section hints at 4/4, it has no real repeated meter. Harmonically, the album is very simplistic, with the indefinite key of 'Sail to the Moon' very much the exception to the rule: cyclic chord sequences form the majority of the musical material for ten of the album's fourteen recordings, with two-chord alternations forming the basis of two,[84] and with four of the remainder being based on a single musical idea.[85] The harmonic monotony of 'Backdrifts' and 'The Gloaming' are reminiscent of 'Pulk/Pull Revolving Doors,' although both are structurally more straightforward and also have greater harmonic content. This suggests that, although they break new ground stylistically for the band, they are also backward looking. Furthermore, while the use of breakdown sections on eight *Hail* tracks may provide another close link to *Pablo Honey*, their relative brevity and general lack of structural significance (except in 'Myxomatosis') is reminiscent only of *Kid A*.

V

So, does Radiohead have a discernible idiolect, and if so how does it relate to the 'progressive' tag most often leveled at the band? On an abstract level, there are elements in which Radiohead's albums are clearly similar, if by no means identical. There is a clear presence of AAB as a formal template, with later albums demonstrating a tendency toward contracting forms (i.e. following AAB with AB then a repeated C section). This has to be regarded as unusual within rock as a whole. Moreover, there is a strong tendency for a Radiohead song to feature a breakdown section. Perhaps unsurprisingly, given the psychical difficulty of truly breaking new ground, there is a clear tendency for any increase in musical complexity on a 'new' album to be counterbalanced with a decrease in formal complexity (and vice versa).

As for 'progressive,' it is clear that Radiohead's music has undertaken a stylistic journey from *Pablo Honey* to *Hail to the Thief*, a journey whose direction is more easily conceived as moving from 'simple' to 'more difficult/complex' than the other way round, and such a stylistic journey is often equated with 'progress.' In this sense, we may conceive Radiohead's idiolect in accumulative terms. However, this is a far cry from asserting a proper familial identity with any rock of the 1970s. There is no real stylistic amalgam here; the lyrics, while occasionally fanciful,[86] are thoroughly focused on relationships or their absence within the larger world,[87] and there are no extended musical structures. Stylistically, while Radiohead progresses, it is not 'progressive.' Moreover, when the musical content of the band's recordings is taken into consideration, Radiohead's career trajectory to date represents none of the models previously suggested, being more elliptical in nature: it appears that the band solved the problem of following *OK Computer* by gradually returning to its original musical ideals (open-ended structures, with songs based on a singular musical idea), with 'Paranoid Android' the apex of musical complexity and 'Pulk/Pull Revolving Doors' of simplicity, and with any differences between *Pablo Honey* and *Hail To The Thief* being more the result of the journey undertaken than of any conscious effort on the band's part either to backtrack or break new ground.[88] The key influence on Radiohead's recordings throughout has been The Pixies, with that band's employment of discordant guitar, use of unconventional song structures, reliance on guitar riffs and open-ended structures, and, most importantly, the thrilling unpredictability of its recordings, all present on its debut *Come on Pilgrim* (1986), and with these features also highlighting the key aspects of Radiohead's own recordings. In essence, while Radiohead as we know it today could easily have existed without its members ever being exposed to any Sex Pistols, Bob Dylan, or David Bowie recordings, it would be a very different proposition was it not aware of The Pixies' breakthrough album *Surfer Rosa* (1988).

Putting aside the similarities between Radiohead and The Pixies, a collection of features such as the one detailed above functions only partially as a description of Radiohead's idiolect: it is the unpredictability of the band's recordings that is arguably the only real constant, and that is also integral to its long-lasting appeal, with the resultant emphasis on difference and juxtaposition over similarity and unity greatly reducing the importance of any such assertions. It is in this respect that the music of Radiohead problematizes the specification of idiolect, for while its music has never been (or purported to be) in any sense original, the band has never hidden behind its influences, and its recordings have always been clearly and credibly its own.

We believe that the key track in this debate is the powerful 'Wolf at the Door,' the final song on *Hail to the Thief*. It is probably the album's least original track. Its descending chord sequence and arpeggiation are clearly modeled on the 'Iron Lung' b-side 'You Never Wash Up After Yourself.'[89] It opens with a timbral and textural reference to The Beatles' 'Because' (1969) before a series of three verses (with menacing, half-spoken vocals) and an overt chorus. The central section then intensifies the chromaticism, strongly redolent of the equivalent section of 'Paranoid Android,' and shortens the repeating length to five bars, the same length as the strongly similar pattern of The Beatles' 'I Want You (She's So Heavy)' (1969).[90] The textural shift from laid-back to tense marks the beginning of the second half of the song, which repeats the verses/chorus under a quasi-Neapolitan mandolin sound[91] as Thom Yorke fades from the foreground, becoming swamped by smooth, unfussy guitar lines. This also mimics 'I Want You,' where a gradual equalizing of the balance between noise and guitar at the end of the recording occurs.[92]

It is one of only four Radiohead songs to date where the music has not originated from Thom Yorke,[93] and yet it retains all of the rhythmic complexity, non-identical repetition and careful textural imagination that we would expect of a Radiohead song. With this recording Jonny Greenwood has effectively written a song template imitating the songwriting style of Thom Yorke, indicating that even if the precise details of a Radiohead idiolect are hard to quantify, the band members themselves clearly recognize that there is a Radiohead idiolect in existence.

Notes

1. The most recent polls in *Q* magazine for 'The 100 Greatest Albums Ever Made' have seen *OK Computer* occupying the top slot (*Q*, 137, February 1998), being named 'Best Album of *Q*'s lifetime' (*Q*, 182, October 2001) and coming second to Nirvana's *Nevermind* (*Q*, 197, January 2003).
2. The album, like the band's earlier single 'Creep' (1992/93), achieved both critical and commercial success in Canada, North America, the Middle East, Australia, and the Asian subcontinent, as well as in the United Kingdom.
3. By the time of release of *Kid A* the album had sold 4.5 million copies (David Cavanagh: *Q*, 169, October 2000: 98).
4. As opposed to the 'safe' solution, creating *OK Computer Mk II*.
5. Danny Eccleston notes a clear split: in his article on *The Bends* he views it as more of a flawed masterpiece than *OK Computer*, praising its lyrical introversion and subsequently greater emotional transparency, and expresses a desire that the band 'might deign to sound like this again' (*Q*, *Radiohead Special Edition*, EMAP Metro Limited: 34–5). Conversely, for Jake Kennedy, '*Kid A* ... represents a very logical progression from the previous three LPs' (*Record Collector*, November 2000: 33). Gareth Grundy concurs, arguing that '*Hail to the Thief* walks the line between *Kid A*'s elliptical electronic landscapes and *OK Computer*'s all-consuming swagger' (*Q*, *Radiohead Special Edition*, EMAP Metro Limited: 122). The *Daily Telegraph* devoted a whole page to this issue (June 5 2003: 21), with David Cheal supporting the former, and Andrew Perry the latter viewpoint.
6. Or more particularly those of the band's vocalist, lyricist, and main songwriter Thom Yorke. Of his songwriting style during the sessions for *OK Computer*, he has said: 'Writing as a witness. That was my ideal. A series of pictures, not even colouring them in really' (interview with Phil Sutcliffe, originally from *Q*, 133 (October 1997),

reprinted in *Q*, *Radiohead Special Edition*, EMAP Metro Limited: 69) and 'It's like the calm inside a Japanese bullet train, with the towns flashing by. The album was very much a journey outside, assuming the characters and voices of other people. It's like taking Polaroids of things happening at high speed in front of you' (Jim Irvin, *Q*, *Radiohead Special Edition*, EMAP Metro Limited: 59).

7. Chuck Klosterman, 'Meeting Thom is Easy,' *Spin* magazine, June 2003 (online at http://www.spin.com/modules.php?op=modload&name=News&file=article&sid= 80&mode=&order=&thold=).

8. James Oldman, *New Musical Express*, September 30 2000: 18. Similarly, Craig McLean described *OK Computer* as 'the greatest album, like, ever' (*The Face*, January 2002: 56) and Stephen Dalton as 'a coherent masterpiece' but 'one of the most hysterically praised releases in rock history' (*Uncut*, August 2001: 57–8).

9. One of the front-page articles in *Music Week*, June 20 2003, has the headline: 'Radiohead to stick with EMI after six-album deal expires.' This is clearly important news.

10. Allan F. Moore, 'Categorical conventions in Music Discourse: Style and Genre.' *Music and Letters*, 82/3, 2001: 441–2.

11. See Richard Middleton, *Studying Popular Music* (Open University Press, 1990: 174); Leonard B. Meyer, *Style and Music* (Pennsylvania University Press, 1989: 23–4). Meyer prefers the term 'idiom' to 'idiolect.'

12. David Cavanagh, review of *OK Computer* in *Q*, 130 (July 1997: 132–3) notes 'Greenwood's King Crimson-style guitar chords' on 'Airbag,' and that 'Yorke out-writes Roger Waters with heavy sarcasm' on 'No Surprises.' Concerning Pink Floyd in particular, Cavanagh directly compares *OK Computer* to *Dark Side of the Moon* (1997: 132). Commenting on such perceptions of Radiohead as 'the new Pink Floyd,' Simon Reynolds notes that 'The Pink Floyd analogy has dogged Radiohead since *The Bends*' ('Walking on Thin Ice', *The Wire*, 209 (July 2001): 28–33; 33). More recently, a writer for *Q* magazine noted that *OK Computer*'s 'cocktail of Open University experiment, Yorke's anguished lyrics and a cache of soaring melodies re-cast the band as a new Pink Floyd' (writer unknown, *Q*, 198 (January 2003): 82).

13. In the USA, this is the only incursion that is usually recognized as operative within the 'progressive' movement.

14. As the eight-track, mid-price live album *I Might Be Wrong: Live Recordings* contains only one previously unreleased track, entitled 'True Love Waits,' it will not be considered as an album proper for the purposes of this discussion.

15. Bearing in mind that the term *idiolect* relates to how individualistic traits are perceived ('read') rather than presented, a more proper term for our focus might be *idiogloss*. However, it is probably too late for a correction for the sake of etymological nicety.

16. In an interview with James Oldman, *New Musical Express*, September 30 2000: 20.

17. 'You,' 'Creep,' 'Ripcord,' 'Vegetable,' and 'Prove Yourself.' This influence is especially notable considering the contempt expressed by Thom Yorke toward the artists on Seattle's then pre-eminent record label, and in particular their over-reliance on distorted guitars: 'I'd love to be on Sub Pop. Wouldn't that be just great? I wouldn't have to write any songs, then, just get myself a couple of Marshall stacks and some pedals, and I'd be well away, eh?' (interview with Peter Paphides, *Melody Maker*, February 6 1993: 40).

18. These lines appear in 'Prove Yourself' and 'Creep' respectively. Coincidentally, these recordings were the band's first and second single releases respectively.

19. For instance, while expressing concern over the musical direction explored on *Amnesiac*, Sylvia Patterson finds Thom's vocal performances on 'Pyramid Song' and the 'stunningly emotive' 'Knives Out' appealing: 'Where Thom's voice is truly Back,

though, it remains the most soulful, elevational soundwave in rock'n'roll history' (*New Musical Express,* May 19 2001: 30). Considering Thom's vocal performances on *The Bends*, Gavin Edwards has written the following: 'Singer Thom Yorke explored the expressive power of moaning ... The lyrics are filled with Yorke's unhappiness rendered as health metaphors ... "Street Spirit (Fade Out)." Over chiming guitar arpeggios, Yorke sings a hymn to his own claustrophobia and insignificance, making them sound like exalted states of being' (review of *The Bends*, online at rollingstone.com/reviews/cd/review.asp?aid=57678&cf=).

20. Steve Lowe, 'What the Hell am I Doing Here?', *Q*, *Radiohead Special Edition*: 37.

21. The track 'River Euphrates' on the album *Surfer Rosa* (4AD, 1988) features a similar use of guitar bends, with the result of the same tone being played on consecutive strings.

22. Track three on *Doolittle* (4AD, 1989).

23. Track two on *Doolittle* (4AD, 1989).

24. As noted by Gary Mulholland, *This is Uncool: The 500 Greatest Singles Since Punk and Disco* (Cassell, 2002: 336).

25. This is again notable since Suede is a band whom Thom has professed on many occasions to dislike strongly. See Peter Paphides, 'P.O.P.R.I.P.?' *Melody Maker* (May 14 1993: 46): 'So, am I really supposed to be excited or even challenged by Suede ... There's more art in the Tango and Pot Noodle adverts than there is in 'Animal Nitrate.''

26. For example, the first evidence of the emotional capacity of Radiohead's music, and of Thom's vocal performances in particular, can be found on its debut release, the 'Drill' EP (1992): consisting solely of an electric guitar and a single-tracked vocal, the miniature 'Stupid Car' employs a quiet dynamic and low vocal tessitura until its brief end section (which features a noticeably louder dynamic and significantly higher vocal tessitura).

27. As at the end of 'Creep,' and the monotonal climax points of 'You' and 'Stop Whispering.'

28. Note the intensified close-mic'ing on 'Planet Telex.'

29. Coincidentally, Radiohead later covered this Magazine song while performing at the Rock Werchter Festival in Belgium on September 12 2000.

30. In this case of Mick Ronson's guitar playing on the introduction of David Bowie's 'Ziggy Stardust' (1972).

31. Both songs are in 4/4: 'Loser' de-emphasizes the fourth beat, while 'Planet Telex' displaces the fifth beat of a repeating two-bar pattern.

32. 'The Bends,' 'Bones,' 'Just,' 'My Iron Lung,' 'Black Star,' and 'Sulk.' 'Fake Plastic Trees' could also be included, with its sudden shift to a loud dynamic for its final verse.

33. In particular, Black Francis (or Frank Black) has a fondness for conjunct descending atonal melodies, as is clearly demonstrated on the introduction to 'Bone Machine' and the break sections of 'Break My Body' (tracks one and two on *Surfer Rosa*). The influence on Jonny's guitar style can be traced back to *Pablo Honey*, where similar techniques can be found at the end of 'I Can't' and 'Ripcord' respectively. On *The Bends*, comparisons with Black Francis can be drawn with regard to the use of solo electric guitar in the refrain of 'My Iron Lung' and the guitar outro to 'Just.'

34. 'Street Spirit' and 'Fake Plastic Trees' respectively.

35. Also notable is the fact that both songs feature descending melodies involving conjunct movement.

36. See Allan F. Moore, *Rock: The Primary Text* (Ashgate, 2001: 113).

37. As heard on 'When the Levee Breaks' (1971).

38.   With the notable exceptions of 'Paranoid Android' and 'Electioneering.'

39.   Particularly in the case of 'Airbag,' 'Paranoid Android,' and 'Karma Police.'

40.   David Cavanagh, 'I Can See Monsters,' *Q*, 169 (October 2000: 94–104, 100).

41.   For instance, 'To Cure a Weakling Child' on *Richard D. James* (1996), and 'Bucephalus Bouncing Ball' on the *Come to Daddy* EP (1997).

42.   'Kid A' bears a striking textural similarity to 'Rae' on *LP5*, while the brief synthesized xylophone ostinato of the Radiohead track and Autechre's 'Melve' (also on *LP5*) are both monophonic and rhythmically monotonous.

43.   For instance, see Stuart Bailie, 'Viva La Megabytes,' *New Musical Express*, June 21 1997: 42; 'Head New Music' (writer unknown), *New Musical Express*, June 17 2000: 3; and Jim Irvin, 'Mean Machine,' *Q*, *Radiohead Special Edition*: 58.

44.   Note that the title clearly references *OK Computer's* 'Exit Music (for a film).'

45.   When asked about the obvious electronica influences on *Kid A* in an interview with James Oldman, Jonny Greenwood said: 'If we're getting a kicking for doing this, we should also be getting a kicking for ripping off Mingus and Alice Coltrane, people who we are equally stealing from … No-one sat down and said, "How can you so shamelessly take the texture of Alice Coltrane's second album and put it on one of your songs?"' (*New Musical Express*, December 23/30 2000: 54).

46.   Jonny Greenwood: 'Well, we stole a lot of Polish composer Penderecki's ideas,' in conversation with Stuart Bailie, *New Musical Express*, June 21 1997: 42.

47.   Unity is achieved in *Kid A* through the use of linking passages, a technique that occurs four times on the album.

48.   Such as Autechre's *Tri Repetae* (1996).

49.   Ed O'Brien, online diary, December 7 1999: 'looked at "you and whose army" again from two weeks ago. tried this 'different' vocal idea that thom and jonny had been going on about … three part but with a very low bass harmony, kind of inkspots-esque' (archived at www.greenplastic.com/articles/edsdiary/index.html).

50.   Humphrey Lyttelton's small ensemble appear on both this recording and the alternative version found on the 'Knives Out' (2001) CD single.

51.   Through chord sequence and arrangement respectively.

52.   Trent Reznor's Nine Inch Nails are its most famous exponent.

53.   Steve Lowe, 'Back to Save the Universe', track-by-track guide to *OK Computer*, *Q*, *Radiohead Special Edition*: 95. Coincidentally, prior to the recording sessions for *OK Computer* DJ Shadow invited Thom to provide vocals on 'Rabbit in Your Headlights,' a track on his ill-fated collaboration album with James Lavelle, entitled *Psyence Fiction*, eventually released in 1998.

54.   John Robinson, track-by-track guide to *Hail to the Thief*, *New Musical Express*, May 10 2003: 35.

55.   'Anyone …,' 'Ripcord,' 'Prove Yourself,' 'I Can't,' and 'Lurgee.'

56.   A technique commonly found on recordings by The Pixies, occurring on all *Pablo Honey* tracks except 'How Do You?,' 'Thinking About You,' and 'Lurgee.'

57.   From the halfway point in 'You,' from the second verse to the end of the bridge in 'Creep,' from the bridge section to the end of 'Vegetable,' from the beginning of the outro to 'I Can't,' and the last 90 seconds of 'Blow Out.'

58.   'How Do You?,' 'Thinking About You,' 'Anyone …,' and 'Prove Yourself.'

59.   Which occurs on all tracks except 'Thinking About You' on *Pablo Honey*.

60.   Occurring on all tracks except '(Nice Dream),' 'Bullet Proof …,' and 'Sulk.'

61.   'Thinking About You,' 'Ripcord,' and 'Prove Yourself.' On all three tracks no real development is made.

62.   The title track, '(Nice Dream),' 'Just' (and arguably 'My Iron Lung').

63.   With the arguable exception of the cumulative 'High and Dry,' which by definition contains just one basic musical section.

64. 'Planet Telex,' 'Fake Plastic Trees,' 'Bones,' '(Nice Dream),' 'Sulk,' and 'Street Spirit (fade out).'
65. 'Planet Telex,' '(Nice Dream),' and 'Black Star.'
66. 'Planet Telex,' 'The Bends,' and 'Bullet Proof.'
67. The title track, 'High and Dry,' Fake Plastic Trees,' 'Just,' 'My Iron Lung,' and 'Black Star.'
68. Using eight-bar phrases elsewhere, the introduction to 'Black Star' is comprised of ten bars, its bridge eleven bars, and its three choruses thirteen, twelve and thirteen bars respectively. In 'My Iron Lung' the last phrase of the verse is dovetailed with the first of the chorus on two occasions.
69. The break sections of 'Paranoid Android' and 'Exit Music ...,' the verse of 'The Tourist,' and the introduction and chorus sections of 'Let Down.'
70. 'Subterranean Homesick Alien,' 'Karma Police,' and 'No Surprises.'
71. Six, if we include 'Fitter Happier.'
72. Early live performances of the song swapped this end section with cumulative repetitions of the three-chord bridge section, led by a Bach-style organ solo of increasing complexity. The presence of this end section makes this early version entirely through-composed (performance at Boston, MA, on August 8 1996: bootleg available at http://wezl.org/rhead/).
73. 'No Surprises' is the most loosely based of the recordings, having two and a half A sections for its first verse, and a half for its second and third verses.
74. All except 'Paranoid Android,' 'Exit Music ...,' and 'Fitter Happier.'
75. 'Kid A,' 'The National Anthem,' 'How to Disappear Completely ...,' 'Idioteque,' and 'Morning Bell.'
76. Again 'The National Anthem' is the sole exception, with its final breakdown signaling the disintegration of the song's structure.
77. All except 'Everything,' 'Treefingers,' and 'Motion Picture Soundtrack.'
78. 'Kid A,' 'How to Disappear Completely ...,' and 'Idioteque.'
79. Both 'Packt Like Sardines in a Crushd Tin Box' and 'Pulk/Pull Revolving Doors' contain an 11-bar phrase; 'I Might Be Wrong' uses both 7 and $3^1/_2$-bar phrases; 'Life in a Glasshouse' uses 5, $2^1/_2$ and $1^1/_2$-bar phrases.
80. 'Packt Like Sardines ...,' 'Pulk/Pull,' 'I Might be Wrong,' and 'Dollars and Cents.'
81. 'Sail to the Moon,' 'Backdrifts,' The Gloaming,' and 'Wolf at the Door' being the exceptions.
82. '2+2=5,' 'Sit Down, Stand Up,' 'There There,' and 'Scatterbrain.'
83. 'Backdrifts,' 'The Gloaming,' 'A Punch up at a Wedding,' 'Myxomatosis,' 'Scatterbrain,' and 'Wolf at the Door' all employ AAB structures to some extent.
84. 'Sit Down, Stand Up' and 'We Suck Young Blood.'
85. 'Backdrifts,' 'Go to Sleep,' 'The Gloaming,' and 'Myxomatosis.'
86. It seems to us that it was the ostensible content (both musical and lyrical) of 'Paranoid Android' that, as much as anything else, attracted this tag.
87. On BBC2 *Newsnight* (June 6 2003), in a discussion with Nitin Sawhney and Paul Morley, Bonnie Greer asserted of *Hail to the Thief*, 'I think this is an amazing, amazing album. What they have done is take a situation – as you both were saying – in the world. They very subtly commented upon it in their lyrics and the music. And at the same time you can take that sort of criticism and use it to talk about a boy/girl situation, anything else.'
88. As demonstrated by the Jonny Greenwood quote that opens the third section of this chapter, and the following from Thom Yorke regarding the *Kid A/Amnesiac* sessions: 'as far as we're concerned and this is absolutely true, we weren't being avant garde, I don't think it's avant garde at all' (interview with Sylvia Patterson, *New Musical Express*, May 19 2001: 29).

89. The pattern of 'You Never ...' is an eight-chord diatonic sequence, however, while that of 'Wolf ...' is six-chord and internally chromatic. The music for 'Wolf at the Door' was written almost entirely by Jonny Greenwood (see track-by-track guide to *Hail to the Thief*, *Q*, *Radiohead Special Edition*: 129), and that of 'You Never Wash Up After Yourself' by Thom Yorke.

90. Pink Floyd's 'Eclipse' (1972), and any number of descending bass lines, can also be heard echoing here. Coincidentally (?), all three of these share a key center of D.

91. The incomplete Neapolitan cadence at the end of each six-chord cycle in 'Wolf at the Door' has a clear ancestor in 'Exit Music ...,' heard in the latter at the words 'We hope your rules and wisdom choke you.'

92. When asked by Yoichiro Yamazaki about the influences on *Hail to the Thief*, Thom Yorke volunteered the following: 'The only thing that really made me think was listening to The Beatles ... There was this simplicity thing, and I thought, OK, I like that' ('Thom Yorke: The New Interview,' *Q*, *Radiohead Special Edition*: 132–9, 137).

93. 'Just,' 'The Tourist,' 'Idioteque,' and 'Wolf at the Door' all started from demos made by Jonny Greenwood.

Chapter 10

Public Schoolboy Music: Debating Radiohead

Dai Griffiths

Oxford, UK, August 2001. A decision must have been taken to put it about and get noticed. It's barely a year since Thom Yorke was on the cover of *Q* magazine in October 2000 as 'the only interview.' 'The only interview.' I don't think so. Since then the same again and again: Yorke on the cover and a big fat exclusive interview, exclusive simply not so, usually Yorke but also some of the others, on and in *Mojo*, *Uncut*, *NME*, *The Wire*, and another big splash without the cover for *Q*. BBC specials for Steve Lamacq on radio, Jools Holland on television. Two albums issued (*Kid A* and *Amnesiac*) and two singles, a little live album, concerts under a circus tent all around the world, and a mini-festival in Oxford. And this is just the stuff I know about: there was probably a similar glut in journals everywhere, for instance in the USA where in April 2001 *Spin* magazine had Radiohead top a list of the 40 'most important artists in the game right now.'

The story is familiar to everyone by now. Radiohead had produced two 'mighty rock' albums, *The Bends* and *OK Computer* (1995 and 1997), and seemingly contradicted expectation by issuing records that didn't closely follow the blueprint, a blueprint followed, it was argued, by bands such as Coldplay and Muse. The press was able exhaustively to supply context for Radiohead's maneuver – stacks of information as decoration to the features ensured instant authority: history, influences, opinions, arcana – but then simply moved on to the latest pop sensation. For music transparently critical there seemed to be no real critical perspective and certainly no follow-through, with rock journalism (or its more shady relative, broadsheet 'culture' commentary) now more than ever consigned to being little more than consumer guide. Marks out of ten, numbers of stars, charts; lifestyle options: buy a record, go to a concert; things to say, things to think; telephone numbers, websites, adverts. Radiohead, demonstrably opposed to the triumph of marketing, functioned splendidly within its tenacious reach. Bill Hicks, the band will know, has a great sketch where his request that people working in advertising and marketing commit suicide is interpreted as nothing other than an interesting marketing device on Hicks' part; similar circularities accompanied the devil in Marlowe and Milton: 'Why, this is hell, nor am I out of it.'

The best of these articles in my opinion was Sylvia Patterson's for the *NME*. The cover had the most disturbing portrait of Thom Yorke, with stubble like facial insects, and nastily and brutally blacked-out eyes, and another great picture inside of Yorke looking like a candidate for care in the community and weird beyond belief in a duffel coat with fake wooden toggles, on a housing estate. The article succeeded simply because, to evoke a familiar distinction, it worked (actively and as judgment) as a piece of writing rather than as the mere transcription of the views of the band – Nick Kent's *Mojo* article was a notable and surprising yawn-inducer in that respect – especially since, understandably as people who channel a lot of thought into music, what the band has to say is generally quite dull. Patterson went further in probing Yorke, leading to this interesting moment of seeming and seemingly genuine confession:

> Sometime last year, Thom remarked that 'guilt' was 'the most destructive force' driving him throughout his life. Four months ago, I asked what this guilt was over.
> 'I've had a very privileged upbringing,' he said, a man who studied Art and English at 'ultra-ultra competitive' Exeter University. 'I've had a very expensive education. And it took me years to come to terms with that. A long, long, long time.'

The fact that Radiohead all went to the same boys' public school seems to pass by with relatively little attention: mention yes, attention no. In the past I'd made up a genre of music based on the old grammar school, and the false continuity this essay affects has to do only with a similar feeling that school years matter a lot, especially from the ages of about 11 to 18 (though most public schools commence at 13). I'm driving hard the view, which I could well imagine finding fault with, that musical material derives directly from social circumstance, albeit in this case circumstances in the past. Social and psychological: if there is a sense in life that nothing changes, then this might have to do with a journey that everyone goes through *ab initio*, from relative ignorance to relative sophistication, and that happens mostly for a lot of us in school. No one is born having heard any music or read any books and, unless you're from a very knowledgeable or unusually artistic family, the role of the school and its teachers can be crucial, especially in giving out signals about what is acceptable and what isn't. As many as seven long years, 21 long terms, the peculiar intensity of those adolescent years, all mark secondary school as sediment that appears later in all sorts of things and situations, including, in this case, the material of songs and records.

Of course, there's more. What takes an extra long time to understand is that public schools in Britain are a quite special aspect of the social landscape. The public schools are really private schools, cash up front right now, but deeply historical and steeped in tradition, with an ability in some cases to adapt and survive that makes Nike and Pepsi look like new kids on the branding block. These schools involve not only, like the grammars, selection by merit but also, far more importantly, the payment of fees. Public-school parents presumably pay taxes for everybody else to go to school, and then spend some more on these special needs. Public school must be to a large extent a parent rather than a child thing; I can't remember asserting anything in particular at age 11 and would have piped up to make pertinent distinctions about educational provision least of all. Public schools themselves prefer the term 'independent schools,' but this surely doesn't do the job, and for a pop fan merely evokes the sense of being run from a room above a record shop.

We don't like to talk about public schools, do we? We could all have a damn good laugh at grammar schools: older readers could remember their racked and repressed products, and for younger people with no experience of the brutality of selection and failure at age 11 it was an entertaining idea or fiction. In fact grammar schools so-called are now often private schools themselves. Private schools are difficult to address, not least because the students we teach at colleges or universities will often include their products and one simply wouldn't dare to be open about this distinction. I don't think we know how to talk about all of this, possibly a very British blockage in that the thing is so palpably there. So let me ask: did *you* go to a public school? If so, how do you cope with that knowledge? The question is less Thom Yorke's 'what the hell am I doing here?', more Thom Eliot's 'after such knowledge, what forgiveness?' *Key Concepts in the Philosophy of Education* puts it thus:

> This lack of attention to private education as such might be the result of the distaste that many educationalists (and therefore many philosophers of education) feel for it. However, if so, the proper response to distaste may be attack rather than removing one's gaze. Or it may be the case that silence results from a deep feeling for the dilemma of parents who have to choose between what they think is good for society as a whole – an excellent state schooling system – and what they think is good for their own children – a place in a private school because the local state schools are less than excellent. Again, a proper discussion of the conflict, rather than turning away from it seems desirable.

Abingdon School, where the members of Radiohead went, is, let there be no doubt, *bloody* expensive: over £13,000 a year in fees according to *Whitaker's Almanack*, before you get started with the uniform and everything else. I don't even know how to express that as such, and find myself tempted into fake bonhomie: 'thirteen thousand quid for you, squire!' And poor Mr and Mrs Greenwood must have had two of them there *at the same time*. If you're earning anything under £30,000, probably lots more, and the average wage in Britain all told is around £20,000 to £21,000, presumably this amount sustained over five long years is out of the question. I'm only guessing here, since in truth the actual figures private education involves are just too far outside my comprehension even to contemplate. I've no doubt that there are scholarships and funds, distinctions between boarders and day pupils, and that parents *work really hard* to send and keep the kids there, and so on, but I'll leave it to others to debate and clarify and correct.

The simple things, you see, are all complicated. The questions I'm led to ask are whether the music of Radiohead reflects this background; in what way, if so; and whether the current conflict in the band's music continues and extends it. The most obvious way to get stuck in to Radiohead from this perspective is obviously over its stand on political issues globalization, logos, the nation state, surveillance, New Labour. Many of these issues could well be configured in a way that would refer to class, specifically to the class structure in Britain – low-wage service economies, an increasing gap between spectacular wealth and poverty, the abandonment of localities when global demand dries up – but presumably in Radiohead's case the particular discourse of class is not available since of course in educational terms the band members were pretty solid beneficiaries of the capitalist system. To put it far too bluntly far too abruptly, it's easy to have a go at sweatshop labour in Indonesia when just one year at their school costs way more than the minimum wage in Britain (about £8000). In fact when they went to school, in the years of the seemingly endless Thatcher government, a statutory minimum wage didn't exist. So what can a rich boy do? Join a rock 'n' roll band? Well, that's a deep question for public schoolboy music, the question of what the musical material refers to or means, where it comes from, and what the whole idea of being in music, let alone pop music, means or amounts to. The band could do a lot worse, we should safely and more kindly say, Radiohead surely being to *No Logo* what The Smiths were to vegetarianism, even though it has become a global brand itself, albeit of a strangely reflexive and critical kind. I think you have to push deeper to see the public school background really start to tell, less the external world of public issues, further into the heartland of the musical material. My guess is that, almost as a special consequence of the band members' schooling, they have a profound sense of being cut off from the rest of ordinary society, ordinary only to mean public-service-dependent, and that this was manifest as super-awareness, both in content and feeling, of late twentieth-century alienation. It may be that the desperate condition of actually being in a public school and, probably worse, subsequently understanding its peculiarity, made the band members more responsive to the solitary nature of computer-centered, screen-centered life. To put it another way, in order to be as alienated as Radiohead, going to a public school helps: anyone who has been to an English public school will always feel comparatively at home in prison. Sing along with Oasis and you're joining in a happy community, conscious of the band's limited purpose or precision; join in with Thom Yorke and you're quite consciously articulating the facts of his condition: anguished, racked, quite patently troubled. I remember being particularly struck once standing among hundreds of people singing a line from 'Paranoid Android': 'You will be first against a wall.' Your boyfriend? Mother? Everybody around? To be shot? To be flogged? This knowledge on Yorke's part will surely derive from an understanding of the present – that is to say: by staring at computers and TV screens, which, note, you might well be doing right now, we spend less time talking to each other – but also the way the present confirmed or continued similar currents in the past. 'Radiohead's merciless attention to the conditions of late-century alienation actually fed on what it was to have attended a traditional public school.' Discuss. The rather fresh feature of Radiohead to date, that it doesn't do love songs, may have more to do with being public school*boys* rather than *public school*boys – Lord knows what public schoolgirl music would be like, 'mighty rock' still being a bit of a boy zone – but this may again constitute the terrain: the 'you' of the Radiohead song tends to be a shady and fear-inducing man in a dark suit, wielding great and nonsensical amounts of power. While in a state school you might well imagine such a person a soldier or civil servant, you surely don't think of the teachers in that way, worn, conked-out, palpably overworked and underpaid as they are, but maybe in public schools all that's different. That the relatively small amount of human presence in these records sounds immediately and consistently like 'enemy' or 'threat' matters especially since what Radiohead has to say in the songs, in the words to the songs, especially on the recent records, is determined as much by a formal approach where the words don't necessarily develop from line to line, and there's little commitment to lyric, to rhymes, and the correspondence of melody and syllable. There's every chance that the sung line has become a rhythmic feature, so that a word is there as much for its rhythmic properties and its sound, rather than for its sense. Also, as we'll see, the lavish musical commitment to ostinato as structuring principle reflects a non-expressive and self-denying approach, especially in the instrumental support. When words are heard clearly, as is often, if not always the case, they're heard as statements, hard and short prose, for which visual correspondences can be found in the hidden insert of *Kid A*, arranged typographically as circus acts. This is a formal and even modern approach, and leads to the second extrapolation from public schoolboy background.

On the recent records especially, there is a confidence in responding openly to a wide range of musical influences, notably to music recognizably modernist, an awareness or openness that might have benefited, albeit paradoxically, from a thorough and traditional education. In this sense, too, I hear these records as the sound of public schoolboy music. All of the following are here in richly various ways.

Plenty of complicated rhythms, broadly defined. 'Horizontal' divisions of a standard beat into smaller groups are found in many songs: 'Everything in its Right Place' opens dividing ten beats (6+4) into groups 3-2-2-2-2-3-2-2-2. 'Morning Bell' in the *Kid A* version breaks its five beat into 3-3-2-2. 'Pyramid Song' is more complicated and sounds 'free,' at least until the drums enter to bring out the pattern 3-2-3, 3-2-3; within this pattern is a further pattern of piano chords: 2-1-2-2-1, 2-1-2-2-1. However and furthermore, the relation of rhythmic to harmonic phrasing is not straightforward. Some songs take this principle further by combining rhythmic asymmetries 'vertically' between instruments: 'How to Disappear Completely' starts as a simple 3 in the guitar, but the bass plays two beats to the three meter and the bass ostinato (F♯-A-B-E-C♯-A-B-E) then varies its collision with the harmonic pattern. 'In Limbo' is the most complex of these examples, but again ends up as a series of ostinatos – follow the bass again (6: D-A-Ex2-G-F). As though to underline the simplicity and system-driven nature of this procedure, starting the songs in concert Yorke with a tambourine will stand like a bored policeman at failed traffic lights and just rattle away, leaving the rest of the complexity to follow.

Sustained use of ostinato as organizing principle, often driven up from the bass: in addition to those mentioned above, 'The National Anthem,' 'I Might be Wrong,' 'Dollars and Cents' (*Abbey Road*'s 'Come Together' somewhere?), 'Worrywort.' Some songs, like 'Everything in its Right Place,' and ostinato songs like 'Packt Like Sardines in a Crushd Tin Box' or 'The Amazing Sounds of Orgy' also use the voice as rhythmic feature (reminding me of The Fall's 'Big New Prinz' of 1988).

Deliberately limited, quasi-modal harmony: 'Everything in its Right Place' and 'Pyramid Song' are a pair, with the second a varied transposition of the first from C to F sharp. The flat second gives them a particular harmonic character as does the contradiction between sharp third (on the first chord) and the minor third in the bass. 'Hunting Bears' is a simple electric guitar solo in a modal D minor.

Another more lambent harmony, which sounds late-nineteenth century by way of Satie and Messiaen: 'Morning Bell' has the juxtaposition of A minor and C♯ minor, with E common to both in the melody (and a nice B too), before circling through G to D – the contrast section is a simple transposition to E minor. Another common-note progression is found in the first section of 'Life in a Glasshouse' – A minor to C minor now in a jazz-harmonic context. 'Treefingers' and 'Idioteque' sound like Messiaen in parts: carefully spaced chords made of major seconds, perfect fourths and major sevenths (or, to use set theory, combinations of interval-class 2 and 5), so avoiding too clear a sense of major and minor, also the case by a different direction in 'Pulk/Pull Revolving Doors.'

A particular solution to electronic music, which reconciles both the earlier traditions of electronic and electro-acoustic music, largely housed in university music departments, with contemporary electronic dance music, especially the music of the Rephlex and Warp labels. 'Freeman, Hardy Willis Acid,' a track by Squarepusher and Aphex Twin on the Warp compilation *We Are Reasonable People* (1998), a brilliant 'instrumental' (without words) composition, is a germane background to these tracks. Tending towards electronic music as such: 'Kid A,' 'Treefingers,' 'Pulk/Pull Revolving Doors,' 'Like Spinning Plates,' 'Fast-track,' 'Kinetic' (Laurie Anderson's 'O Superman,' perhaps), and the surprisingly chirpy 'Worrywort.' Tending towards electronic dance music: 'Idioteque,' 'Packt like Sardines in a Crushd Tin Box.' These are clearly cases where 'song' gives way to 'piece,' 'composition,' 'track,' with the result that titles have to refer to something external to the material, although occasionally onomatopoeia acts as midpoint between sound and external reality: revolving doors, spinning plates, and, possibly, a wordless voice being someone running gradually faster around a track.

There's some evidence of an externally determined approach to form: at the end of 'Motion Picture Soundtrack,' in a 'hidden' track (at 4'18"), the notes D and A act as the signature of the record, the D and A of *Kid A*, before leading to the outer two notes of violin tuning. There may be some planning of, or a mind to, pitch and tonal continuity, especially on *Kid A*, *Amnesiac* seeming to center more haphazardly on recurring keys. So, the F of the riff of 'National Anthem' picks up the F that closes 'Kid A,' the D of 'In Limbo' emerges from the D of 'Optimistic,' and so on. 'In Limbo' again pushes the boundary – already harmonically dense, a floating D minor with added 7 and 9, in the contrast section settling on C minor with added notes, but third time as contrast going further again to E minor. 'Transatlantic Drawl' makes a very sharp cut between two very different kinds of music, the first with a foot in the bass-riff songs like 'The National Anthem.'

In fact, the tracks not mentioned can safely be assumed to be the ones like the 'mighty rock' songs on the previous albums: 'Optimistic' (hello Bono?), 'You and Whose Army?' (especially its last section), 'Knives Out,' 'Cuttooth,' 'Fog'... or evoking older, 'signifying' music – the surprise endings to both *Kid A* (Disney: 'Motion Picture Soundtrack') and *Amnesiac* (New Orleans/'Strange Fruit': 'Life in a Glasshouse'), and briefly ending 'The National Anthem' itself (sampled from Elgar?). Both the last tracks bring on walking bass, or slowly paced passing notes, for big effect and release. These are exceptions proving the rule of most of these tracks, in which the modern or revelatory maxim 'make it new' holds firm.

Making it new, no past or, as emblem of deracination, the 'no locality' of public school? I don't imagine for a moment that the actual music lessons at Abingdon contained much in the way of Squarepusher or, to date it more precisely, and use a bad pun, house music, but even negatively one comes out of that environment presumably with the sense that nothing artistic is going to be too big for you. There's no reason why it should, of course, but features of state education – among which are a sense of locality bordering on the parochial, community, warmth, growing up together, dullness, conformity, never getting the balance right between low expectation and forced ambition – can lead, again paradoxically, to conservatism. In fact, I imagine lessons at public school to be firmly traditional: never underestimate the conservatism of school teachers in general but notably, one would have thought, those who choose to teach in public schools. There's also in Radiohead an epic dimension, always able to conceive of vastness, because money is always somehow no object, or at least an object decisively, even derisively, to be overcome. Terrific and well-placed orchestrations adorn many of the tracks. We want an orchestra, we get one; a real orchestra, too, and not just models who happen to play violins, the current pop approach.

Is there such a thing as public schoolboy music? The track I kept playing over the last year, consciously as corollary to my listening to the challenging Radiohead material as it appeared, was 'I Know What I Like (In Your Wardrobe),' from *Selling England by the Pound* (1973) by progressive rock band Genesis. This was their classic line-up: Mike Rutherford, Tony Banks, Phil Collins (familiar as the successful Genesis of the 1980s), but also including Steve

Hackett and Peter Gabriel. Rutherford, Banks and Gabriel were also public schoolboys, educated at Charterhouse, an aspect described in a recent *Mojo* but captured better by Colin B. Morton and Chuck Death as 'The Genesis Story.' ('So they worked hard, got good A-level results, bought some Range Rovers and set out on "the road."') That 'I Know What I Like' was also a single, reaching number 18 in 1974, is as remarkable as 'Paranoid Android' reaching number 3 in 1997. It's a fantastic track, a foreshadowing or retrospective equivalent of Radiohead. Framed by electronic sound effects, it settles into a strange but distinctive groove with some hippy-eastern coding and, over steady but interesting beats, Gabriel's piercing vocal, the words, based on the painting by Betty Swanwick which was the album cover, evocative and full of character. The chorus is warmly and even pastorally English, beautifully dropping from the modal A major of the verse to a rich E minor 7, with D as soft landing, before a linking passage, straight out of the organ loft, mixes in D minor over A. A guitar solo opens with a fanfare (A-D-E-A), with Peter Gabriel's school-orchestra flute doodling towards the end. The 'Pythonesque' moment, the imitation of a yokel accent ('Me, I'm just a lawnmower') was always for us as teenagers the bit to imitate, and seems dead public school in retrospect – as, of course, does much of the Oxbridge-derived television comedy of the time. There's much to be said about this and surrounding Genesis records, and their relation to English identity at the time, and my guess is that in 30 years something of the same will be apparent retrospectively in Radiohead.

Deviating a little from the title of this chapter, my conception of the band's overall development – a thesis which I don't think is particularly sustainable – originates again in the classroom, and consists of the argument that what Radiohead has done is successfully to cross over from the art audience to the science audience, a jaded, British version of what it would be to achieve crossover among the genre charts in America. At least in my day, you had to choose surprisingly early in school between doing science or 'the arts,' and going for the latter put you very much *entre les filles*, the science stream an emblazered dump of scowling johnny. It's also worth noting that nearly all members of Radiohead have university degrees in the arts or politics, not, note, degrees called 'Being in a Band' or 'The Music Industry,' though also, unfortunately enough but maybe expressively so, not music degrees either. In fact, I should confess that Jonny Greenwood, the exception, did start a joint degree in Music and Psychology with us at the then Oxford Polytechnic, but the deal arrived from Parlophone and within three weeks he was gone. In those early years, captured on *Pablo Honey* (1993), in the very few times I've heard it but assuredly for the purpose of this argument, there's a sound somewhere in the art-school tradition, Roxy Music by way of The Smiths, say, the same lineage that gave rise to Suede and thence to Britpop itself. With *The Bends* Radiohead crosses over to the science crowd, shown primarily by a concern with technology, thematically and sonically, and ends up in the terms of 1973 (and why on earth those terms should matter is a fair question) sounding closer to progressive than glam rock. The science crowd is nothing if not tremendously loyal, and so both *Kid A* and *Amnesiac* have been dutifully received and bought; by art-school standards, over there with Jarvis and Brett and Justine, where you're only as good as your last haircut, your last fashion statement, those records would have been crucified. Make of this what you will; but there is clearly a dilemma for the public performance or presentation of the material on *Kid A* and *Amnesiac*, the songs without words suggesting a more static or contemplative form of reception, arty even, gallery or film perhaps, while concerts to thousands of people, confrontational, communal, may determine the selection only of 'mighty rock,' mostly from the past.

But let's get back to public schools. I feel for these people: Mr and Mrs O'Brien, Mr and Mrs Selway, Mr and Mrs Yorke (Thom liable to be have been bullied from an early age, one thinks), and Mr and Mrs Greenwood with their double invoice. They must all have thought one or two of the same things: that their local schools were rubbish, and that by sending the boys to a public school, they'd be giving them 'the best start' in life. But for what? What visions fire the fancies of these mums and dads, a bob or two to spare? The boys in suits, in nice spacious houses in the countryside, with healthy wives and kids? And would *your* picture be any different? And they look so sweet even now, on stage or on telly, twiddling away with their little gadgets, squatting down studiously like manual workers, devoting their lives to expressive and serious music, and Thom Yorke's voice swooping around, beauty of sound and intelligence of thought, Oxford's sweetness and light. The more miserable, tortuous side of him you could do without, you imagine the parents chatting to each other on the phone, massive dogs leaping playfully at the cord. But it's not so difficult, is it? The idea surely would be, and always has been, to make sure that all schools were good enough for people not even to think of needing to send children away. It certainly doesn't help that Britain now has a government with at least roots in socialism that simply doesn't turn its mind to such innocent virtues. But even if that were the case you still have to deal with the parental imaginary, the barmy dreams and visions, delusions and grandiloquences, the challenging of which just might be one of Radiohead's legacies. Somehow, though, I doubt it. The promises and claims, members of Radiohead insistently say, have turned out to be limitations at best, lies at worst. Dad, listen, it's easier for a camel to go through the eye of a needle than for a rich man to enter the Kingdom of God. And you know what they say, Mum: money can't buy you love. The purpose of public schoolboy music, if you see what I mean, is that we could all do without it.

Chapter 11

My Radiohead Adventure

Paul Lansky

It was a bright sunny Saturday morning in May 2000 when I opened my e-mail and saw a letter with the subject 'Message for Paul Lansky.' The letter began 'My name is Jonny Greenwood, and I play and write music as a member [of the] UK band Radiohead.' The letter went on to describe, quite apologetically, how a phrase from an ancient electronic piece of mine, *mild und leise,* had made its way into a song on the band's new CD. Jonny had come across an old LP of the piece in a used-record shop on the band's last tour of the USA and used it as source material during an improvisation session that subsequently filtered its way down to the song 'Idioteque.' He seemed quite anxious to assure me that they were not the sort to take things without asking, and went to some lengths to explain his musical interests and influences, which seemed to intersect in interesting ways with mine. He wondered how I would feel about the possible '... association with a [dread phrase] rock group. ... We are (I hope) as far from being a stereotypical rock group as it is possible to be. ... I didn't want us to remain an anonymous English group assuming they can sample your music and let someone else deal with it.' It was altogether a very charming, thoughtful, and serious letter.

I was aware of Radiohead, mainly through some of my graduate students who had become devoted fans, but my knowledge was limited to one hearing of *OK Computer.* I wrote back right away and assured him that our respective publishers could settle things easily enough. A few weeks later a delightful package arrived with several Radiohead CDs, another long letter from Jonny, including a picture of his analog synthesizers, a tape of the part of the improvisation session involving *mild und leise,* and 'Idioteque.' I sat down to listen with great interest.

mild und leise was my first computer piece. I wrote it in 1972–73 using Princeton University's only computer at that time, an IBM 360/91 that cost millions of dollars, had about one megabyte of memory, and required a staff to run it around the clock, including technicians from IBM. We communicated with the great beast using punch cards, and read the reports of our success or failure on wads of green-striped paper fed through noisy chain printers. Sounds were written in digital form on nine-track magnetic tapes, about an inch wide, with the diameter of an LP, and holding only about 16 megabytes of data, which then had to be taken to a separate facility for digital-to-analog conversion. I used a second-generation computer synthesis language, Music 360, written by Barry Vercoe specifically to take advantage of the capabilities of this machine. Even so, the process was slow and tedious, and the composition took the better part of a year.

It was not unusual for the machine to take an hour to compute a minute of sound, and this was working at a sampling rate of 14000 (as opposed to the standard rate today of 44100). At the time I thought I had really accomplished something important and, while I still am proud of it, I'd hoped that it would quietly disappear into my personal history. My work subsequently took a very different path and for me the piece is now more of biographical than musical interest. But this apparently was not to be. Jonny warned me that the piece would get lots of attention, and as a result of the Radiohead connection, it's probably my best-known work, alas.

My first reaction on listening to 'Idioteque' was that I felt as if I had participated in a musical time warp. I had recorded my part in the early 1970s when I was a bit younger than the members of Radiohead are now, and 28 years later the band came into the studio and did the rest. (Jonny reported to me that this had occurred to them as well.) This was really more than a reflection of ego, however, or of a subconscious desire of composers in my circle to be rock stars. It was, rather, a response to the seamless and ingenious way that Radiohead had woven a song around my chord sequence, using it repeatedly as the harmonic underpinning of 'Idioteque.' The piece puzzled me at first. I had never heard anything like it. Its profile was strange: sections were repeated many times, the tunes were relatively simple by Radiohead standards, and the textures were extremely unusual, with little deference to the slicker side of electronica. It took a number of hearings to begin to understand it, and eventually to genuinely like it. But almost immediately I was fascinated by what Radiohead had done and how it had done it.

The section of *mild und leise* that Radiohead uses consists of four different registral spacings of a four-note chord: [E flat, G, B flat, D] (a semitone higher in my piece, but transposed down in 'Idioteque' to accommodate Thom's tessitura; the band has, however, sometimes performed it at the original transposition). The top two voices move up from the middle register, [B flat, E flat], [D, G], [E flat, B flat], [G, D], while the lower two voices move down, [D, G], [B flat, E flat], [G, D], [E flat, B flat].

(Fs in parentheses are harmonics of low B flat)

mild und leise began as an exploration of Wagner's famous 'Tristan Chord,' which I thought of as a linking of the musical intervals of a minor third and a major third, by a minor third (E♯-G♯, B-D♯, linked by G♯-B). The title of the piece comes from the beginning of Isolde's famous aria at the end of the opera *Tristan und Isolde*. (There are more sophisticated and appropriate ways to think of how this harmony functions, but I was more concerned with interval networks at the time.) In the process of exploring this network of relations I combined two major thirds at the interval of a minor third, [E flat, G] and [B flat, D], to come up with this particular chord at this moment in the piece. I have a distinct memory of being quite pleased with the sound of the sequence. There were two fascinating things that immediately struck me about Radiohead's use of the sample: the way the band interpreted the implicit harmony in the chords and the process it used to write the song.

There are no real pitch-producing engines in 'Idioteque' aside from Thom's voice (with Ed's during the chorus, and sometimes during the verse) and the computer chords. The rest consists of an array of electronic and acoustic percussion sounds. (The evolution of the song through subsequent live performance since the release of *Kid A* has included an interesting proliferation of electronic effects. 'Idioteque' is unusual in that its initial form is in recording, followed by development through performance, rather than the other way around.) The choice of notes for the tune reveals a very sensitive and imaginative response to the color of the chords. During the verse Thom's tune rocks back and forth between a D and E flat, with an occasional dip down to B flat and C, and a few Fs. During the chorus Thom jumps to a high B flat while Ed takes over the D and E flat. While the chords all project a similar distinct color, since they all consist of different spacings of the same four notes, the choices of pitch in the tune reflect a subtle parsing of the chords into two overlapping triads (three-note chords), [E flat, G, B flat], an E flat major triad, and [G, B flat, D], a G minor triad. The last of the four chords in the sequence has E flat and B flat in the bass, and those who have suffered through traditional music theory classes will remember that this more forcefully projects an E flat major flavor than will other spacings. When this final chord arrives the notes of the tune move to E flat, while at other times D is more central. E flat and D are, of course, the two pitches that are not in the intersection of the E flat major and G minor triads. Thus the choice of notes for the tune, mainly using the pitches unique to the E flat major or G minor triads, pushes the song into a world where these triads oscillate and alternate. To make matters more interesting, at the end of the song on the CD, Thom remains on E flat throughout the chord sequence, thus effectively fusing the harmonies into a four-note chord again. (He doesn't always do this in live performance; I wish he would.) It's thus difficult to assert that the song is 'in' E flat major, or G minor. It's simply defined by the color of these two chords. Wonderful musicians that the members of Radiohead are, their choices reveal very sharp ears and an unusual sensitivity to the role that harmony plays in the band's music.

Radiohead's relation to harmony in general is sophisticated and unusual. It does not often rely on chord progressions that are typical in rock music, and has frequently used interesting chromatic harmonies, such as at the end of 'Paranoid Android.' Also, songs as early as 'Creep' reveal a keen sense of the way that melodies and harmonies interact. Thom's high suspended A over the return to G major in the refrain, though not unusual, is a powerful and effective use of a dissonant suspension. Many (perhaps most) Radiohead songs contain very interesting uses of minor and major modal mixture (combining minor and major scales). Again, this occurs as early as 'Creep,' where a C minor chord, borrowed from G minor, is used in a G major context (again, not unusual, but foreshadowing more extensive use of this technique later on). The harmonies and scale shifts in 'Just' and 'Permanent Daylight,' for example, are complex, pushing traditional tonal functional relations to the edge of a cliff. 'The Tourist' from *OK Computer* uses a fascinating and unusual chord progression. Beginning on a B major triad, it moves next to F♯ minor, then to A major, and then to G♯ major! Then in the chorus it goes from B major to F♯ minor and then to A minor (whose third, C natural, is enharmonically equivalent to the third, B♯, in the G♯ major chord). Statistically the piece would seem to be in some sort of world of E major (if only by virtue of the fact that most of the notes belong to the E major scale), but there is never an E major chord in the piece. Or perhaps it's in C♯ minor (the relative minor of E major), but again there is never a C♯ minor chord or cadence. The song floats, as many Radiohead songs do, in a modal harmonic world (B mixolydian?) where expectations are thwarted and the movement from one chord to the next is an interesting and often unusual event. But as in 'Idioteque,' it really doesn't matter what key the song is in, the harmonies forge their own syntactical unity.

While the harmonic vocabulary of *Kid A* seems almost an attempt to eschew some of the earlier luxuriance, the rich major/minor language of 'Everything In Its Right Place,' 'How to Disappear Completely,' and 'Optimistic,' among others, continues in the Radiohead tradition. Thom Yorke's reported interest in the electronic groups on Warp Records, such as Autechre, would logically lead to a view in which harmony is static rather than fluid. That is, chords are thought of as textures rather than aspects of progression, and the main focus of the moment is on the sonic qualities of the ensemble, using harmony as a kind of placeholder. One can certainly view 'Idioteque' in this light. The basic (and only) harmony is merely an overlapping E flat major and G minor triad, and there is no functional sense of progression or key. This continues in some of the songs on *Amnesiac*, 'Packt Like Sardines in a Crushd Tin Box,' for example. The static, yet persuasive harmonic language of pieces by P.J. Harvey such as 'We Float,' or, with Thom Yorke, 'The Mess We're In,' also displays some of the same qualities.

Since the harmonic language of most 'guitar-band' rock groups essentially uses regular chord changes as a way to create phrases and cadences, and the harmonies themselves basically recolor the text and tune, rather than create contrapuntal threads the way Radiohead's music often does, it too can be regarded as static, and not rich in implication or surprise. (The use of the guitar itself in the compositional process probably has something to do with this, while I suspect that keyboards play a larger role in Radiohead's workshop.) That is, one doesn't typically hear a harmonic progression as part of a story full of suspense and thwarted expectation the way one does in 'The Tourist,' or 'Paranoid Android,' for example. The success of 'guitar-band' songs, however, doesn't particularly hang on their harmonies (which, again, is not the case with Radiohead).

But this sense of stasis is not barking up the same tree as the one Radiohead is sniffing about in 'Idioteque.' For a view of this it's more useful to consider electronic groups like Autechre, Matmos, or Aphex Twin. In many of their tracks (a better term than 'songs' in this case) the focus is on a rich accumulation of electronic effects, and a single harmonic landscape will often be prolonged for ages without any significant change. The function of the static harmony is thus that it acts more like a placeholder, and a change in harmony is therefore more of a change in *place* than part of a complex grammar. Since a goal of much of this music is the elaborate and progressive design of a world made of rich and novel electronic sounds, it typically eschews noticeable harmonic progression. The listener is invited to contemplate the sounds for him- or herself, and elaborate harmonic changes might in fact prove distracting to that end. Radiohead's fascination (or at least Thom Yorke's) with electronic sounds is undoubtedly a factor in its interest in this sort of language. Part of the uniqueness of *Kid A* thus lies in its mixture of several worlds with orthogonally related designs.

The second thing that interested me is what I can glean of the process the band used to write this song. (My information is largely anecdotal, aside from the improvisation tape and a few conversations with Jonny Greenwood.) Apparently Jonny spent one afternoon throwing together a collage of sounds against his synthesizer's simulated drum track. These included *mild und leise,* music by Penderecki, Art Krieger (from the same LP as my piece), street noises, radio noises, and other sounds. He then gave the mix to Thom, who extracted the sequence from *mild und leise,* composing 'Idioteque' around it. I have no way to know whether this working method is typical for Radiohead, although I doubt that it is, since 'Idioteque' is so different from the band's earlier work and it seems that it was designed specifically to lead it in a new direction. Nevertheless, the notion that Radiohead would take an excursion into the domain of experimental music in composing 'Idioteque' is fascinating and significant.

Composition is not a methodical process, obviously. Different composers work in divergent ways and a composer will often use vastly varying methods for successive pieces. There are, nevertheless, two classical ways to think of the general relations between the product and the process. In songwriting, for example, some vague musical notion will often motivate a composition. A composer may invent an idea for a tune, or perhaps a chord progression, find some words to go with it, and then think about scoring and rhythm, developing the song in the process. These aspects may occur in different orders, and often in combination. (Paul McCartney is reported to have used the phrase 'scrambled eggs' as a verbal placeholder while he composed 'Yesterday.') In 'concert,' 'avant-garde,' or 'experimental' music – we'll bundle it all under 'concert music' from now on – similar processes take place. It's rare that a composition will emerge fully grown, and most often there is some particular musical motivation that initiates the process. (The collaborative compositional methods that rock bands often use probably follow the same pattern, though the interaction is bound to yield more unpredictable results.)

There is often, however, another aspect to the relation between product and process that may involve exterior, extra-musical factors. On a simple level we see John Cage consulting the *I Ching*, Bartòk using the Golden Section, Bach doting on the number 14 (the sum of the initials of his name), Berg on the number 23, Messiaen, Babbitt, Boulez, Stockhausen, and others mapping out parametric schemes to organize aspects of their music, Pauline Oliveros motivated to write music to enhance and create meditative states, and so on. The significant feature of most of these 'pre-compositional' activities, however, is that their ultimate manifestation is through musical objects, pitches, timbres, rhythms, whether or not these schemes subsequently emerge in obvious ways. Composers often use these techniques to keep their more fluid and knee-jerk intuitions at bay, to create some objective distance in the process, or as one of my colleagues once said 'to keep me from writing the same Miles Davis lick over and over again.'

But this perspective must now be extended by music's more recent evolution. Two developments during the past 50 years have exercised a powerful influence. First, conceptual models of what music is about have changed and evolved in significant ways. The influences of post-war serialism, Cage, Fluxus, electronic music, rock music (which met Fluxus when John met Yoko), and so on, have expanded the domain of the musically acceptable to include events and activities that were previously regarded as extraneous to the texture of music. It's only necessary to contemplate the now commonplace feel of the bleeps and bloops at various points during 'Idioteque,' for example, or of the electronic media noise at the seams of so many Radiohead songs (or to see Jonny Greenwood waving a portable radio around at concerts, tuning random sounds into the ongoing fabric) to see an instance in which noises in the sonic surface of a composition are no longer regarded as novel. Second, the use of technology in all its forms – reproductive, as in recording, and generative, as in the use of guitars, synthesizers, and computers – has shaped the way composers work. (Rock music has been much bolder in this respect than concert music, particularly in its orchestral and chamber music varieties, which still see technology as an external threat.) Radiohead's working method in 'Idioteque' reveals an adventurous attitude toward the compositional process, technology, and the musically acceptable. It is very interesting, at least in this case, to see the band visit the domain of experimental and avant-garde music. Its motivation for doing so is not common in the world of popular music, and is undoubtedly directly related to the artistic crisis that reportedly followed the success of *OK Computer*.

Among the reserves of invention that composers draw upon are resources to ensure that the same piece doesn't get written twice. Concert music composers, generally less susceptible to market pressures since the stakes are so much smaller, don't often feel the same need to continually repeat previous successes. In fact, the general attitude exerts pressure in the opposite direction, sometimes counterproductively. Market-driven popular music, on the other hand, is under enormous pressure to duplicate previous success, and discourages innovation and experimentation. The reception of *Kid A* seemed to rest more on its failure to recreate *OK Computer* than on its own merits as an artwork. What Radiohead seemed to be going through is the same familiar turmoil composers have always encountered when they realize that going forward often means eschewing aspects of their past. It's very easy to write the same piece again and again, and doing so has always been the signature of second-rate composers.

So, the tape Jonny Greenwood sent me, with all kinds of sounds mixed together, was very familiar as an attempt to create a kind of chaos out of which something new might arise, as well as an attempt to put the band in a position where it could avoid writing the same old Radiohead lick over and over again. Furthermore, it was specifically *pre-compositional*, had significant extra-musical components, and was certainly not typical in the world of songwriting. The band was intervening early in the compositional process with an arbitrary and experimental construction in order to come out in a new place. I interpret the freshness of 'Idioteque' to be a result of this highly experimental process. As a result, many features of Radiohead's music that struck me on listening to *OK Computer* are gone. 'Idioteque' eschews the luxurious harmonic language of 'Karma Police' or 'The Tourist.' It lacks the rhythmic and formal complexities of 'Paranoid Android.' *Kid A*, as was widely noticed, has little of the testosterone-driven guitars of earlier CDs. In their place is a simpler and more abstract harmonic and formal language, and a greater reliance on machine-made sounds. But, the working method that generated 'Idioteque,' and the motivation behind several of the other songs on the album, really maintains many of the virtues of the band's earlier music. The song is still clearly by Radiohead and retains several very important and meaningful features. (I wonder if the name 'Idioteque' has something to do with the novel process that led to its composition.)

A wonderful aspect of much of Radiohead's music lies in the way rhythm functions. This involves much more than the alternation of 3 and 4 in 'Paranoid Android,' or the use of 5/4 meter in 'Morning Bell.' One of Radiohead's great secrets, to my mind, is the inventive use of rhythmic levels, simultaneous projections of different metric layers. The opening of 'Paranoid Android,' for example, consists of an instrumental passage in which half-notes, quarter-notes, eighth-notes and sixteenths are projected in various timbrally distinct ways. The result is a rich texture that is made doubly fascinating when Thom's voice enters in syncopated quarter-notes (on the off-beat). The beat is thus a multivarious object that invites the listener to parse the music in different metric senses. The music doesn't grab one by the collar and assert that there is only one story line. Rather it provides a texture in which the ear can wander. (The verse/refrain difference in The Beatles' 'We Can Work It Out' is a classic example of the use of rhythmic layers, albeit successive rather than simultaneous.) 'Idioteque' begins with a relentless mechanical and machine-like rhythm projecting quarters on the off-beats with eighths and sixteenths mixed in. The computer chords then come in on the down-beat in half notes, creating a chilling and smooth contrast to the machine-like rhythm (although they are, ironically, also machine made). The voice enters with the approximate tactus of the drums and when it reaches the refrain moves to the pulse of the chords and adopts their lyrical quality. At the repeat of the verse ('Ice age coming') a new percussion instrument enters in 32nd notes, thus further subdividing the pulse in the opposite direction. Rhythmic levels are thus proliferating, and providing a new element of development and continuity.

Another aspect of Radiohead's music that struck me at first was the expansive and rich contours of its tunes. The opening few lines of 'Paranoid Android,' for example, span an octave and a third. Register plays a critical role in articulation. Melodies use different registers with great purpose and skill, again as early as 'Creep.' (I remember feeling the same way about early Beatles. 'All My Loving,' for example, is brilliant in the way that the wide contours are shaped and how critical moments coincide with changes in direction.) There is often careful attention paid to tunes that cover large registral spaces quickly, in combination with, and in contrast to, relatively flat melodies. The choral section in 'Paranoid Android' with its gently descending harmonies provides a stunning contrast to the quickly moving shape of the opening tune. Here, too, 'Idioteque,' despite its apparent differences from earlier work, uses these same ideas with great skill. The verse section is relatively flat, as mentioned earlier, oscillating gently between D and E flat. In the refrain things change when the voice leaps to a high B flat and the descending tune fills in the span of a perfect 5th, using a slower rhythmic pulse, matching that of the computer chords. The melodic and rhythmic relations and contrasts between verse and refrain are thus intensified and made more effective.

Of course Radiohead is '… as far from being a stereotypical rock group as it is possible to be.' There is nobody else like Radiohead, and the band's work is interesting to many who are not among the cohort of rock fans, although these form its largest audience. (At the band's Roseland concert in NYC after the release of *Kid A*, one young woman, noticing my thinning gray hair, said to me 'What are you doing here, are *you* a fan?' On the other hand, at the band's Madison Square Garden concert nearly a year later I saw George Plimpton, my senior by a significant number of years.) And just as The Beatles, using rock music of the 1950s as its initial language, vastly extended the meaning of the genre to a point where the band's music itself became iconic, so Radiohead, drawing on post-Vietnam rock, electronic and experimental music, has created a literature that rises above generic categories to become inimitable. Radiohead is not escaping rock as much as it is redefining it, which was the gift of The Beatles as well. To my ears the band is doing this through a lot of hard work, critical self-examination, extreme attention to detail, a refusal to recycle, and of course great musical talent. After Radiohead's Madison Square Garden concert I told Thom Yorke that one thing I liked so much about the band's music was that all the songs sounded so different from one another, to which he replied 'not to me.' I should have known better.

Chapter 12

Hail to the Thief:
A Rhizomatic Map in Fragments

Joseph Tate

Introduction: rhizomatics is pop analysis

In June 2003, Radiohead released its sixth studio album, 14 eccentric songs of electronica-influenced, guitar-driven pop entitled *Hail to the Thief (or, The Gloaming)*. What follows is a sort of index, or song-by-song guide, to the album, a map to the vast lyrical and visual terrain covered by the album's occasionally obscure and often allusive lyrics, CD cover art, and music videos. Some lines of inquiry lead into ponderous and unpaved culs-de-sac, while others trace wide spans of well-traveled roads. What emerges is not a single interpretation of the album, but a loosely connected and fragmented representation of the album's uncontainable and fragile heterogeneity of subject matter, a heterogeneity that points in the direction of Radiohead's past, present, and future. But why fragmented? The fragmented notes below are a necessary fiction, one that most accurately mirrors the radical incompleteness of any such project as this: way always leads on to way.[1]

The idea for such a mapping, an indexing of inter- and intra-relations, has two sources: first, the album's cover art and, second, Deleuze and Guattari's rhizomatics. First, the second source: rhizomatics is pop analysis (Deleuze and Guattari 1987: 24), a style of reading that, foremost, takes into account the principles of 'connection and heterogeneity: any point of a rhizome can be connected to anything other, and must be' (1987: 7). This way of thinking is 'very different,' they write, 'from the tree or root' way of conceiving things, a style of thought that 'plots a point, fixes an order' (1987: 7). In place of such strict tree-like cognizing, where there is a crown, trunk, and root, Deleuze and Guattari substitute rhizomatics: a way of thinking that 'operates by variation, expansion, conquest, capture, offshoots' (1987: 21). As they claim:

> A rhizome has no beginning or end; it is always in the middle, between things, interbeing, *intermezzo*. The tree is filiation, but the rhizome is alliance, uniquely alliance. The tree imposes the verb 'to be,' but the fabric of the rhizome is the conjunction, 'and ... and ... and ...' This conjunction carries enough force to shake and uproot the verb 'to be.' (1987: 25)

Following this notion, this essay, this map, this rhizomatic map of *Hail to the*

Thief is 'always detachable, connectable, reversible, modifiable, and has multiple entryways and exits and its own lines of flight' (1987: 21).

Second, the first source: the album's sleeve art is a series of maps. These maps, therefore, deserve a map.

Mapping maps

Eight maps comprise the artwork for *Hail to the Thief*. In an interview with the magazine *Bang*, artist Stanley Donwood explained that each painting was 'one and a half metres square … artex and acrylic and blackboard paint' (Morgan 71). When asked about the concept of the art, he says:

> well i nearly went badly wrong with that one. i had an idea about topiary and porn, and [combining] them. but then i went to LA and the colours of LA are red, green, blue, orange, and yellow. plus black and white. thats pretty much all the most advanced capitalist city used to advertise and sell stuff. its very loud. so i bought tubs of the most vivid colours and painted sort of real estate painting. as if each inch of the canvas was worth money. all the pictures for hail to the thief are of cities. i got the maps off the net. london, grozny, baghdad. 8 cities. santa monica, manhatten, kabul. i must have left a suspicious trail for the net police. ([*sic*], Morgan 71)

Donwood does not mention the name of the eighth city.

Donwood's abstracted and densely textual aerial maps resemble the work of French artist Jean Dubuffet, especially the 1961 painting 'Le Commerce Prospère.' Whether Donwood had this particular painting in mind when producing his *Hail* series is not nearly as important as is the overt critique of capitalism they share. Both Dubuffet and Donwood mimic capitalism's deployment of language by depicting spaces from above, spaces strictly delimited by words and phrases. Despite the clear visual similarities of how each painter renders a cityscape's jumble of commerce, their executions differ significantly in style and intent. Dubuffet's critique hyperbolizes capitalism's crudeness, creating satire through exaggeration, whereas Donwood's paintings are arguably devoid of humor, although occasional moments of black comedy do result from the surprising juxtaposition of unusual, decontextualized phrases – phrases largely taken from the notations of Thom Yorke.[2] The language of Dubuffet's painting is incendiary; he ironically reveals capitalism's subtexts:

> 'Cad and Company,' 'Shameless Riff-Raff,' 'Fake Weights,' 'Swindler,' and 'Rot-Gut' are among some of the milder epithets that Dubuffet employed as signage for the numerous colourful boutiques, buildings, and even for the bus. (Demetrion *et al.* 1993: 136)

Also, whereas Dubuffet constructs imagined signs for an imagined city, one crowded with nearly 50 figures, Donwood instead paints unfunny phrases on to maps of unpopulated but actual cities.

Donwood's paintings taken together depict the international cityscape dominated with a detached accuracy that intensifies their menace. Further, the cities, diversely ranging from Los Angeles to Grozny, are homogenized and heavily regimented via Donwood's reconception of capitalism's glaring visual presence: an oppressive sameness of style and color that mirrors globalization's reduction of difference. Both painters, despite divergent styles and separate historical conditions, have responded to their socio-historical moment with notably similar irony and acrimony. Donwood's canvases, however, have not been subjected to nearly as many questions of intent as has the album's controversial title.

The title: *Hail to the Thief (or, The Gloaming)*

In naming the album, the band followed the relatively traditional procedure of extracting a specific lyric from the album itself: the title is a line from the first song, '2+2=5.' What has interested reviewers and interviewers about the album title, however, is not how it foregrounds a particular song's thematic content or how it refracts the song's explicit allusive context, George Orwell's *Nineteen Eighty-Four*.[3] Instead, attention has constellated around a specific historical and political context of the phrase 'hail to the thief': the title is a now well-worn protest slogan that entered the popular idiom, at least in the United States, during the contentious presidential election of George W. Bush in 2000. Exactly who coined the expression or where it first appeared is uncertain, but it did feature prominently during inauguration protests on January 20 2001 in Washington, DC, as several news articles attest.[4]

This interpretation of the phrase has led to accusations of political extremism, accusations that Radiohead has spent significant time attempting to discredit. When *NME* published reader responses to the album title announcement, several readers were nothing less than spiteful.[5] Band members, however, have gone out of their way in interviews to deny that *Hail to the Thief* is a protest album. As Chuck Klosterman notes in *Spin*,

> Since April [of 2003], Radiohead have stressed that *Hail to the Thief* is not a political record and that the album's title is not a reference to George W. Bush's controversial victory over Al Gore in the 2000 presidential election (in fact, Yorke claims he heard the phrase during a radio program analyzing the election of 1888). (Klosterman, 'No More Knives,' 2003: 66)[6]

More explicitly, Thom Yorke himself told *Time* magazine that *Hail to the Thief* doesn't limitedly refer to problems in the United States. The album title is, he claimed, 'trying to express, without getting angry about it, the absurdity of *everything*. Not just a single Administration' ([*sic*], Tyrangiel 2003: 73). Again: '… with *Hail to the Thief*, the whole thing about it being political is a bit far-fetched. I keep reading stuff now about how this album is all about politics and anti-America … just because of the title and one or two quotes I gave. People overreact, read things into stuff, look for an angle…' (Kulkami and Morgan 2003: 64). And again:

> This record, to me, these new songs, they're not so much songs about politics as me desperately struggling to keep politics out. The past year … If I could have written about anything else, I would have. I tried really fucking hard. But how can any sensible person ignore what's been going on altogether? I couldn't, I really couldn't. Fuck, man, I would love to write lyrics free of politics! (Kulkami and Morgan 2003: 64).

Equivocating, Yorke here confirms the album's immediate historicity: it is firmly grounded in and derived from the political present. But why do Yorke and band members continually disavow this? The question is not answerable with any definitiveness.[7] Thom Yorke says, 'Someone gave me a tape a few years ago. It was an interview with John Coltrane, and he's saying, "I got into politics for a while and then I just decided to channel it down my horn because, ultimately, it was the best place for it to be. Everywhere else was ugly"' (Westenberg 2003: 86). In this quotation, Yorke deflects and redirects admission via Coltrane's words, but does here indirectly admit the album is indeed a result of the present political turmoil. Politics are channelled down Yorke's lyrical horn.[8]

Whatever context we apply to the album title, there's little doubt it gains its incisive satirical thrust by overtly rhyming with and subverting the American ceremonial tune 'Hail to the Chief.' Now also referred to as the 'Presidential March,' the song has a long and contorted history, well documented by Elise Kirk. The phrase itself comes directly from Sir Walter Scott's *The Lady of the Lake,* a long poem published in 1810.[9] Scott's poem was such a favorite, it was adapted for the musical stage the same year it was published. Two English playwrights, Thomas Dibdin and Edmund John Eyre, working separately, composed two different versions, but it is Eyre's version that traveled from England to America. The tune known as 'Hail to the Chief' was first heard in America in 1812 as part of Eyre's *The Lady of the Lake,* a play 'first staged at the New Theater in Philadelphia on January 1, 1812' and restaged numerous times over the next 50 years (Kirk 1997: 125). Not long after its theatrical debut, the song was used on February 22 1815 'to honor a president of the United States, though he was no longer living. With a new text and title, "Wreaths for the Chieftain," it was sung in the Stone Chapel, Boston, to celebrate both the birthday of George Washington and the peace with Great Britain' (Kirk 1997: 131). How this theatrical song came to be played at a political ceremony is not adequately explained by Kirk. The implication is that the song's popularity and subject matter made it a likely candidate for the occasion. Though Kirk adds that 'the theatrical and the patriotic traditions coexisted side by side for many years' (Kirk 1997: 131) before the political tradition came to dominate the song's usage, how the song acquired its political appeal remains unclear. Kirk argues that the song resonated uniquely with an America at war with England in 1812 (Kirk 1997: 128–9), but how an English song could become an American tradition at such a moment remains baffling.

Whatever the reason, the tune endured. 'The first living U.S. president to be honored with "Hail to the Chief" was Andrew Jackson. The popular march was played at a "celebration dinner in honor of the hero of New Orleans" on January 9, 1929' (Kirk 1997: 132). President John Tyler's first lady insisted on the song

> whenever the president made an official appearance. By the time of President James Knox Polk's inauguration in 1845, the piece was associated with the Commander-in-Chief in a ceremonious tribute that has embellished countless inaugurations right up to the present. (Kirk 1997: 133)

Today, the tune is played by the Marine Band, also known as the 'The President's Own,' more than 100 times per year.

Apart from the ramifications of this specific and controversial American political context for the album title, the phrase as it is used in the song '2+2=5' is satirical praise of a repressive leader.

2+2=5 (The Lukewarm.)

Politically, although containing the phrase 'hail to the thief,' the album's first song does not target a specific politician so much as it targets the potential fascism of all governments.[10] Its non-specificity is highlighted via its overt allusion to Orwell's *Nineteen Eighty-Four* (2003 [1949]), a book that targets no particular government, yet criticizes the very process of governing itself.[11] The lyrics, in part, read:

> Are you such a dreamer?
> To put the world to rights?
> I'll stay home forever
> Where two & two always
> makes up five
> I'll lay down the tracks
> Sandbag & hide
> January has April's showers
> And two & two always
> makes up five

This absurdist mathematical formula, two plus two equals five, is a recurring motif of Orwell's book, one that encapsulates the crucial lesson of *Nineteen Eighty-Four*: a reversal of the axiomatic notion so prevalent in popular culture that there is an unreachable, pure core of the self that those people in power can never affect.[12] Winston Smith, the book's central character, is told by Julia, his lover, that Big Brother, the people in power, 'can make you say anything – anything – but they can't make you believe it. They can't get inside you' (2003: 170). This, however, at least in *Nineteen Eighty-Four*, is not the case. As Thomas Pynchon comments in his Foreword to the book:

> The poor kid. You want to grab her and shake her. Because that is just what they do – they get inside, they put the whole question of the soul, of what we believe to be an inviolable inner core of the self, into harsh and terminal doubt. (in Orwell 2003: xxiii)

Winston himself thinks back on these words as he willfully traces the formula 2+2=5 on a tabletop: '"They can't get inside you," she had said. But they could get inside you' (300–1). Or in the words of 'The Gloaming. (Softly Open our Mouths in the Cold.),' a later song on *Hail to the Thief*: 'They will suck you down / To the otherside.' Or in the words of the pleading speaker of 'We suck Young Blood. (Your Time is up.),' 'We want the sweet meat.'

Note: the speaking voice of '2+2=5' shifts character position several times from a deadened and relatively unsympathetic Winston-like character, one happy to stay home 'where two & two always / makes up five,' to one more akin to O'Brien, *Nineteen Eighty-Four*'s antagonist, who admonishes repeatedly that we have not been 'paying attention.'

The song's 11th line reads: 'IT'S THE DEVIL'S WAY NOW.' Hell and the devil have not made an appearance in Radiohead's released work until this song.[13] The injection of the traditional Christian mythology of Satan at this point serves to highlight the song's focus on ideological struggle. Satan appears first in the biblical story of Job, but as 'the *satan*,' not a specific, continuous character. In all the varying stories of Satan's origin, there is a common thread: 'this greatest and most dangerous enemy did not originate, as one might expect, as an outsider, an alien, or a stranger. Satan is not the distant enemy but the intimate enemy – one's trusted colleague, close associate, brother' (Pagels 1995: 49). The mention of 'the devil's way' in '2+2=5' is the song's invocation of a religious apocalyptic vision, one not so intimate as abstract and extimate: 'This apocalyptic vision has taught even secular-minded people to interpret the history of Western culture as a moral history in which the forces of good contend against the forces of evil in the world' (Pagels 1955: 181). As Elaine Pagels accurately sums up:

> Many religious people who no longer believe in Satan, along with countless others who do not identify with any religious tradition, nevertheless are influenced by this cultural legacy whenever they perceive social and political conflict in terms of the forces of good contending against the forces of evil in the world. (Pagels 1995: 182)

Other songs on the album reinforce this thematic of struggle between forces of good and evil. The song's and the album's portrayal of this struggle is in near-

Manichean terms, a divided universe, one in which the devil appears more often than any version or even fleeting vision of a positive good.

Sit Down. Stand Up. (Snakes & Ladders)

Via the devil's way we walk into the jaws of hell. The devil's way into the jaws of hell is somewhat like playing at the children's game of snakes and ladders, the secondary title for 'Sit Down. Stand Up.' The game appears to have originated in second-century BC India as a way to teach children the difference between good and evil. The British appropriated the game and introduced it to England in the late 1800s. The American version, known as chutes and ladders, was first marketed in the United States in 1943.[14]

'Sit Down. Stand Up.' uses the imperative verb form throughout. From one perspective, this is almost a parody of the imperatives thrown at music audiences to 'get up' and dance. This song has that possible parody in common with R.E.M.'s song 'Get Up' on *Green,* a song about getting up, meaning waking up from both a figurative and non-figurative slumber, not just getting up to dance.

Radiohead's song not only commands us to sit down and then stand up, two contradictory, mutually exclusive actions, but also commands the listener to 'walk into the jaws of hell,' and the speaker lets the listener know that he and others (the first-person pronoun 'we' is used) 'can wipe you out anytime.' And God, the ultimate incarnation of authoritative power, wiped the earth clean, purified it, with a flood.

Sail to the Moon. (Brush the Cobwebs out of the Sky.)

This song contains what is perhaps the album's lone redemptive image. Given the struggle between good and evil established via overt and implicit references to the Christian version of the heaven and hell binary in earlier songs, this song continues in that vein by evoking the biblical story of Noah and the ark:

> Maybe you'll
> Be president
> But know right from wrong
> Or in the flood
> You'll build an Ark
> And sail us to the moon

Flood stories, like the one that spans Genesis 6:5 to 8:22, are 'so common to many peoples in different parts of the world between whom no kind of historical contact seems possible that the theme seems almost to be a universal feature of the human imagination' (Barton and Muddiman 2001: 46). In this song's imagination, then, the flood represents a future second chance (signaled by the future tense of 'You'll') after a present period of corruption.

Given this connection to the biblical Noah, the song takes on a lullaby quality when one takes into account that Thom Yorke's child is named Noah. The song thus, in biographical context, becomes addressed to a next generation in the same way that Orwell's *Nineteen Eighty-Four* may have been written indirectly for his son. Orwell's son was born the same year as the character Winston. Thomas Pynchon writes: 'It is not difficult to guess that Orwell, in *Nineteen Eighty-Four*, was imagining a future for his son's generation, a world he was not so much wishing upon them as warning against' (2003: xxv). In the same way, *Hail to the Thief* may not be imagining present ills so much as warning a next generation.

The song's subtitle may refer obliquely to Godfrey Reggio's 1983 film *Koyaanisqatsi*.[15] A Hopi prophecy sung in the film translates as follows: 'Near the Day of Purification, there will be cobwebs / Spun back and forth in the sky.' Likewise, the biblical flood referenced in the song was intended to purify: 'Now the earth was corrupt in God's sight, and the earth was filled with violence' (6:11). The purification was stringent and indiscriminate: God told Noah that He would 'bring a flood of waters on the earth, to destroy from under heaven all flesh in which is the breath of life; everything that is on the earth shall die' (6:17). God's people were backsliding, backdrifting, backtracking. They were rotten fruit, damaged goods.

Backdrifts. (Honeymoon is Over.)

Perhaps the earliest instance of the phrase 'backdrifting,' or the song's other phrasing, 'backsliding,' is in the King James Bible, Chapter 2, Verse 19:

> Thine own wickedness shall correct thee, and thy backslidings shall reprove thee: know therefore and see that *it is* an evil *thing* and bitter, that thou hast forsaken the LORD thy God, and that my fear *is* not in thee, saith the Lord God of hosts.

Notably, this book figures God's relationship to His people as an adulterous marriage, one in which, as the song's subtitle suggests, the honeymoon is over: 'Surely *as* a wife treacherously departeth from her husband, so have ye dealt treacherously with me, O house of Israel, saith the LORD' (3:20). In the face of such corruption, one can actively oppose it or passively accept it. Or go to sleep.

Go to Sleep. (Little Man being Erased.)

'Go to sleep' is often the first line of a lullaby and in such songs the verb 'go' most frequently stands in its imperative form. The command is that the child should 'go to sleep.' In this song, however, the speaker tells what he or she is planning to do: 'I'm gonna go to sleep / And let this wash all over me.' To what the relative pronoun 'this' refers is left ambiguous, but whatever 'this' is, the speaker is deciding to not confront it.[16] The song in this way echoes and enacts Žižek's estimation of the situation that what we do in the face of technological change is simply 'go to sleep' and let it wash all over us. The perfect response is to let the capitalist machinery go on without interruption. This is echoed in the disturbing video, where a computer-animated Yorke sings on a park bench while buildings explode around him and many oblivious passers-by. As Žižek writes:

> instead of trying to cope with the accelerating rhythm of technological progress and social changes, one should rather renounce the very endeavor to retain control over what goes on, rejecting it as the expression of the modern logic of domination – one should, instead, 'let oneself go,' drift along, while retaining an inner distance and indifference towards the mad dance of this accelerated process, a distance based on the insight that all this social and technological upheaval is ultimately just a non-substantial proliferation of semblances which do not really concern the innermost kernel of our being ... One is almost tempted to resuscitate here the old infamous Marxist cliché of religion as the 'opium of the people,' as the imaginary supplement of the terrestrial misery: the 'Western Buddhist' meditative stance is arguably the most efficient way, for us, to fully participate in the capitalist dynamic while retaining the appearance of mental sanity. (Žižek 2001: 12–13)

This distanced stance, Žižek writes,

> enables you to fully participate in the frantic pace of the capitalist game while sustaining the perception that you are not really in it, that you are well aware how worthless this spectacle is – what really matters to you is the peace of the inner Self to which you know you can always withdraw. (2001: 15)

The peaceful inner self cannot remain untouched, as *Hail to the Thief* attests, especially as its first song attests via reference to Orwell's work.

This withdrawal is figured in the song's computer-animated video in which a seated and minimally gesticulating and near-expressionless Thom Yorke (a digital reconstruction of him, he's not there and the video isn't happening) sings from a bench while well-dressed and busy businesspeople rush hurriedly by, all unaware of buildings exploding and then rebuilding themselves from their own rubble. Notably, when the buildings rebuild, their architectural style is radically different. Neo-classical structures are replaced by international-style buildings. The passers-by, though not literally asleep, are figuratively asleep: they take no notice of the drastic changes happening around them.

The song has various registers of lyrical allusion. The lullaby context suggested above is reinforced by the song's line: 'May pretty horses / Come to you / As you sleep.' These lines may derive from a common children's lullaby:

Hushabye, don't you cry,
Go to sleep little baby;
When you wake, you shall have cake
And all the pretty little horses.
Black and bay, dapple and gray,
Coach and six white horses. (Winn 1966: 22)[17]

Another source for the song's lyrics is Part One of Jonathan Swift's *Gulliver's Travels*, wherein the protagonist, Mr. Lemuel Gulliver, visits and is imprisoned in the country of Lilliput. After a shipwreck, Gulliver washes up on the shore of Lilliput and falls asleep. While he is sleeping, the inhabitants, who are 'not six inches high,' tie him down. The song's lyrics read:

We don't really want a monster taking over
Tiptoe around tie him down
We don't want the loonies taking over
Tiptoe around tie 'em down

Swift's satire in this tale targeted hostile responses to the unfamiliar but finally harmless: 'In Lilliput, the vices and trivialities of the little people are seen against the normal humanity and benevolence of Gulliver' (Mack 1964: 113). Tiptoeing round and tying Gulliver down is perhaps an overreaction, but the response is warranted at least insofar as the potential for violence, even if unintended, resides in what the Lilliputians experience as Gulliver's immense size, in the difference that resides between where the Lilliputians end and Gulliver begins.

Where I End and You Begin. (The Sky is Falling in.)

The first lines of this song read:

There's a gap in between
There's a gap where we meet
Where I end & you begin
And I'm sorry for us
The dinosaurs roam the earth
The sky turns green
Where I end & you begin

Dinosaur is the name given to

a group of reptiles, often very large, that first appeared in the Late Triassic Period about 215 million years ago and thrived worldwide for some 150 million years. Most died out by the end of the Cretaceous Period, about 65 million years ago, but many lines of evidence now show that one lineage evolved into birds about 150 million years ago. (Encyclopædia Britannica 2003)

The speaker is here clarifying via metaphor the radical strangeness that exists between himself and the addressee: to rephrase the lyrics, dinosaurs roam the earth and the sky turns green in the place where I end and you begin. The sky literally turns green as severe weather approaches. A researcher using a spectrophotometer to measure light wavelengths confirmed in 1995 that severe storm clouds do emanate the color green.[18]

Later lines of the song read:

Where I end & where you start
Where you, you left me alone
You left me alone.
X will mark the place
Like parting the waves
Like a house falling
Into the sea

The parting of the waves may refer to Moses' act in Exodus:

And Moses stretched out his hand over the sea; and the LORD caused the sea to go *back* by a strong east wind all that night, and made the sea dry *land*, and the waters were divided. (14:21)

Such a biblical reference would be in keeping with the album's patterns of allusion established thus far. Moses in this instance is leading the people of Israel out of a corrupt land. This gap between the waters is unlike the gap that separates me from you, as the song maintains. This supposed gap between 'Where I end & you begin' is traversed in the song's final lines: 'I will eat you alive / And there'll be no more lies.' These lines, 'I will eat you alive,' segue into the ensuing song, whose first line is 'Are you hungry?' – a rhetorical question. The speaker, we learn, is the one who is hungry.

We Suck Young Blood. (Your Time is Up.)

The first-person plural pronoun 'we' in the lyric 'we want young blood' is reinforced by the morose clapping, a sound that can only be made when one is not holding a musical instrument. The visual image becomes that of a group of people backing the singer-speaker with nothing else to do but wait and clap lethargically, a lethargy possibly intensified by their need for, as the song states, young blood.

The band first marketed the album with lyrics from this song posted as part of an advertising campaign. In Los Angeles, spoof talent-recruitment fliers were found posted in various places that read: 'Hungry? Sick? Begging for a break? Sweet? Fresh? Would you do anything? We suck young blood. We want sweet meats. We want young blood. 1-866-868-4433.' The phone number was a toll-free call in the United States and took callers to the *Hail to the Thief* hotline, a voicemail labyrinth in which callers can easily be lost but can also hear songs from the album.

The Gloaming. (Softly Open our Mouths in the Cold.)

The second opening line for this song reads, 'it is now the witching hour.' The 'witching hour' is traditionally considered to be midnight, and the phrase may derive from Shakespeare's *Hamlet*: ''Tis now the very witching time of night' (3.2.413). The song's title word, 'gloaming,' is an archaic poetic term that means the twilight or evening. The word was popularized by Sir Harry Lauder (1870–1950) in his song 'Roamin' in the Gloamin'.' According to the *New Grove Dictionary of Music and Musicians* (2000), Sir Harry Lauder was a 'Scottish baritone music-hall singer and composer' (2000: 543) whose 'stage personality was a stereotyped Scotsman, with a kilt and a generalized brogue' (2000: 543). His songs, including 'Roamin' in the Gloamin',' are internationally known. He published a memoir of his life in 1927 titled *Roamin' in the Gloamin'*.

In this song, however, the 'gloaming' is a euphemism for the present period of political problems. In a *Rolling Stone* interview, Yorke explains that the album's 'other possible title was *The Gloaming*. I wanted that because of the twilight that night in the car. But that title was too doom-y. And the record is not doom-y. Musically, the record is quite jubilant' (Fricke 2003: 54). The twilit night Yorke means:

> It was a formative moment – one evening on the radio, way before we were doing the record. The BBC was running stories about how the Florida vote had been rigged and how Bush was being called a thief. That line threw a switch in my head. I couldn't get away from it. And the light – I was driving that evening with the radio on – that was particularly weird. I had this tremendous feeling of foreboding, quite indescribable, really. To me, all the feelings on the record stem from that moment. (2003: 52–3).

The 'gloaming,' then, is upon us. From the Capitol Records website:

> The title of the record goes so much deeper than just being some anti-Bush propaganda. If we got into a situation where people start burning our records, then bring it on. That's the whole point. The gloaming has begun. We're in the darkness. This has happened before. Go read some history. ('Biography')

There There. (The Boney King of Nowhere.)

The phrase 'there, there' is often used as a quiet interjection of consolation. It is perhaps no coincidence that a song named with a phrase used to console children would spawn a fairy-tale video in which the main character's simple curiosity becomes an ugly and overpowering greed, a transition that ultimately ends with the character's transformation into a leafless and gnarled tree. The video's plot line is finally simple: one person taking what is not rightfully his. At twilight the protagonist, played by Thom Yorke, suspiciously darting eyes back and forth, enters the forest wary and cautious, a foreign place whose foreignness is highlighted by the unusual actions and activities the character espies: the character first sees a golden light, approaches it and comes across two squirrels dressed as men in vests and cravats, smoking in a small house by a fire; another golden light in the distance then draws him to a dinner party attended by a variety of small animals eating and drinking; he walks further on to discover a wedding; a final golden light tempts him on to find a gilded coat and shoes.[19] He puts on the coat and shoes, and dashes off upon realizing that the watching ravens disapprove. The chase leads through the tangled woods and he is swooped down upon and attacked by the ravens. The video ends as the magical shoes take over the character's body, making him run even faster, at which point the shoes slip off, making him stop, and rooting him to the ground.

Yorke's character is clearly an outsider, but not an outcast. When he finally arrives at the grotto containing a gold coat and shoes, the items are clearly meant for human wearing, but there is also no clear indication they are for the taking. Without asking, but also without knowing whom to ask, he takes them. He becomes, to borrow a word from the album's title, a thief, and is punished severely for his thievery.[20]

The visual style of the video is an allusion to the work of Oliver Postgate, as the following excerpt from an interview with *Q* magazine explains:

One day last summer, during a six-month hiatus from Radiohead, Thom Yorke decided to lavish treats on his son Noah. He bought the two year old some children's DVDs, among them *Bagpuss*, the 70s TV series featuring a ragged pink and white cat who lives in a shop with friends Prof Yaffle, a doll called Madeline, and a troupe of mice.

When presented with this archive classic, Noah got up and walked out of the room, but Thom found himself sitting through all 13 instalments. Episode 2 – The Owls of Athens – caught his eye and in particular, a song called the 'Bony King of Nowhere.'

'It's about this pipe-cleaner king with a bony arse who moans about the hardness and coldness of his throne,' says Yorke. 'So the mice scurry about trying to make him a comfy one.'

Naturally, you bite your lip as Thom tells you the story. But don't worry. He knows. In fact, the resonance with his own life was so strong he decided this would be the title of the new Radiohead album. What's more, he got on the phone to *Bagpuss* creator Oliver Postgate and asked if he'd make the video to the new single 'There There.'

Postgate is 78, retired, and therefore declined. In the end, the *Bony King of Nowhere* was deemed too 'prog' by the rest of the band and the more declamatory *Hail to the Thief* was preferred. Even so, the pre-eminent rock seer of his generation is undeterred.

I'm telling you, there's a lot in there. You could do a lot worse than get yourself the DVD of *Bagpuss*.'

Lines 10–13 of 'There There' read:

> There's always a siren
> Singing you to shipwreck
> Steer away from these rocks
> We'd be a walking disaster

The Sirens were 'sea-nymphs who had the power of charming by their song all who heard them' (Bulfinch 1978: 242). Odysseus and his men sail past the Sirens safely by filling the crew's ears with wax. Odysseus, however, had himself tightly bound to the ship's mast so he could hear the Sirens' song without succumbing to them. For as Circe warns Odysseus:

> Whoever, unaware, comes close and hears
> the Sirens' voice will nevermore draw near
> his wife, his home, his infants: he'll not share
> such joys again: the Sirens' lucid song
> will so enchant him as they lie along
> their meadow. Round about them lie heaped bones
> and shriveled skin of putrefying men.' (Bulfinch 1978: 244).

The Sirens and the rocks are separate dangers. Where the Sirens reside is most frequently translated into English as 'meadow.' Further, 'The Sirens,' Gabriel Germain writes, 'promise knowledge' (Germain 1962: 92). As the Sirens of *The Odyssey* tell Odysseus, listeners to their song leave having received 'delight and knowledge of so many things' (Homer 1990: 250). Even more tantalizing, they claim to know 'all things that come to pass on fruitful earth' (Homer 1990: 250).

I Will. (No Man's Land.)

This song was originally played backward to form the melodic foundation of *Amnesiac*'s 'Spinning Plates.' An excerpt from the August 2 2001 issue of *Rolling Stone*:

> *Amnesiac*'s 'Like Spinning Plates' is the track from another, unreleased song, 'I Will,' run in reverse. 'Thom learned to sing the backward melody forward,' says Colin. 'You can hear what the words are, but they sound like they're backward.'

There is no useful comparison between this song and The Beatles' 'I Will.' The same phrase, 'I will,' when used in different historical and musical contexts triggers a radical difference in thematic content.

A Punch-up at a Wedding. (No no no no no no no no.)

In a line of 'A Punch-up at a Wedding,' the song's addressee (positioned by the second-person, presumably singular, pronoun) is referred to as 'a bully in a china shop.' The common use of this phrase usually substitutes 'bull' for 'bully.' The phrase's entry in *Brewer's Dictionary of Phrase and Fable* reads: 'A maladroit hand interfering with a delicate business; one who produces reckless destruction.'

Two later lines from 'A Punch-up at a Wedding' read:

> the pointless snide remarks
> of hammerheaded sharks

The traditional phrasing is 'hammerhead shark' rather than 'hammerheaded.' The adjective 'hammer-headed' according to the *OED*, was first used in Arthur Golding's 1567 translation of Ovid's *Metamorphoses*, Book VII, line 74. Hammerhead sharks are often observed inshore dwelling in brackish water. The sharks are a unique combination of predator and scavenger. The *OED* claims the first reference to hammerhead shark occured in an 1861 book titled *British Fishes*.

The song's narrative, a wedding ruined by a belligerent guest, a social union interrupted, while not overtly political, does still fit with the album's general thematic concern with corrupted societal functioning.

Myxomatosis. (Judge, Jury & Executioner.)

Professor Frank Fenner received the Australian government's Prime Minister's Science Prize in 2002, in large part for work on the myxamo virus, or myxamatosis, a word also often also spelled 'myxomatosis.' Myxomatosis was originally a virus released by the Australian government meant to control the country's burgeoning rabbit population. The virus, however, spread uncontrollably through other countries around Europe in the 1950s, decimating over 90 percent of Europe's wild rabbit population.

Chuck Klosterman for *Spin* magazine writes: 'Myxomatosis is a virus that inadvertently devastated the British rabbit population after it was introduced in the 1950s, covering the countryside with bunny carcasses. The disease is not what the song is literally about' (in 'No More Knives,' 2003: 68). That the song is not literally about the disease is made clear in the lyrics; the speaker claims that he twitches and salivates 'like with myxomatosis.' The adverbial 'like' confirms that the speaker does not have the disease, but only acts as if he does. That humans cannot contract the virus was a fact confirmed by Frank Fenner publicly when he and two other scientists injected themselves with the myxamo virus to prove that it would not infect humans.

Yorke explains to Klosterman that,

> The song is actually about mind control. I'm sure you've experienced situations where you've had your ideas edited or rewritten when they didn't conveniently fit into somebody else's agenda. And then – when someone asks you about those ideas later – you can't even argue with them, because now your ideas exist in that edited form. (Klosterman in 'No More Knives,' 2003: 68–9)

Klosterman responds with a question: 'What does mind control have to do with a virus that kills rabbits?' He then claims 'The answer is "nothing"' ('No More Knives,' 2003: 69). Though it is unclear from the article whether Yorke actually responded 'nothing' (Klosterman may be employing inverted commas for emphasis rather than to indicate quotation here), if Yorke's response was 'nothing' it is not to be trusted: myxomatosis, as Yorke makes clear above, is the perfect analog for ideology, especially a government-sponsored ideology of repression and control that flouts national borders. The song's speaker eventually rejects the adverbial 'like' to claim:

> You should put me in a home or you should put me down
> I got myxomatosis
> I got myxomatosis

This confession of having contracted the disease is the speaker's confession to having succumbed to government-sponsored mind control. Yorke noted in another interview that during the 2003 war with Iraq, 'if you were opposed to the war, suddenly you were being accused of demoralising our troops. Everything seems to be based on fear and mind control' (Manning 2003: 48). Again, Yorke's hyperbolic 'everything' signals the pervasiveness of such control, a pervasiveness not unlike that imaged in Orwell's *Nineteen Eighty-Four*.

The notion that ideas can be transformed into an edited form, that their earlier existence would be unrecognizable, is foregrounded in the song's line 'I don't know why I feel so tongue-tied,' and also appears in the *Amnesiac* b-side 'Cuttooth.' The speaker feels so tongue-tied because the ideas he had as he 'sat in the cupboard / and wrote ... down real neat' have now been

> Edited, fucked up
> Strangled, beaten up
> Used as a photo in Time magazine
> Buried in a burning black hole in Devon

In other words, the speaker's words, even those presumably personal thoughts transcribed alone and away from the prying eyes of authority in a dark cupboard, are no longer his. As he reminds us, 'that wasn't my intention,' and he no longer knows how or why his intention has been morphed into a tongue-tied chaos of misused words.

Scatterbrain. (As Dead as Leaves.)

The first lines of 'Scatterbrain' read:

I'm walking out in a force ten gale
birds thrown around, bullets for hail
the roof is pulling off by its fingernails

The most common definition of gale is simply 'wind.' In the *OED*, the third definition reads:

1. a. A wind of considerable strength; in nautical language, the word chiefly 'implies what on shore is called a storm' (Adm Smyth), esp. in the phrases strong, *hard gale* (a *stiff gale* is less violent, a *fresh gale* still less so); in popular literary use, 'a wind not tempestuous, but stronger than a breeze' (J.). Also *gale of wind*. In restricted use, applied to a wind having a velocity within certain limits (see quots.).

Today, in stricter meteorological terms, a gale's force is measured on the Beaufort scale. A force-ten wind is often termed a 'storm' or a 'whole gale.' Generally, however, these and various other versions of the scale agree that a force-ten gale is a wind in which the sea turns white, trees can be uprooted and building damage occurs.

Historically, the definition of gale has shifted slightly as these entries in the *OED* indicate:

1923 N. SHAW *Forecasting Weather* (ed. 2) 456 As a result of the investigation of 1905 we now classify winds with velocity above 75 miles per hour as hurricane winds, those with velocity between 64 and 75 miles per hour as storm winds, and those between 39 and 63 as gales. 1963 *Meteorol. Gloss. (Met. Office)* 109 Gale, a wind of a speed between 34 and 40 knots (force 8 on the Beaufort scale of wind force, where it was originally described as 'fresh gale'), at a free exposure 10 metres (33 feet) above ground. Ibid., Statistics of gales refer to the attainment of mean speeds of 34 knots or over.

In the *OED*, the second definition of the word, now obsolete, has two entries; the first is subdivided: '1a. Singing, a song; merriment, mirth; 1b. said of the voice of an animal; and 2. Speech, talk.'

The song later mentions wind in reference to written, but not spoken, language: 'Yesterday's headlines blown by the wind.'

A Wolf at the Door. (It Girl. Rag Doll.)

The title of this song and its lyrics derive from and refer to several disparate sources. The idea of a wolf at the door, or the idea that one must 'keep the wolf from the door,' as the song claims, is at least as old as, if not far older than, line

1531 from John Skelton's 1522 poem 'Why Come Ye Not to Court': 'The wolf from the door.' The phrase also appears prominently in Charlotte Perkins Gilman's 1893 poem 'The Wolf at the Door':

> There's a whining at the threshold –
> There's a scratching at the floor –
> To work! To work! In Heaven's name!
> The wolf is at the door!

The song's subtitle phrase, 'It girl,' is used to denote a fashionable young woman. The idiom entered the popular imagination in 1927 with the movie *It*. Clara Bow, the movie's star, played salesperson Betty Lou Spence, who falls in love with a department store manager. After this role, Bow went on to become famous as a female sex symbol, or 'the It girl.' 'It' was a euphemism at this time for 'sex appeal.'

Other lyrics from 'A Wolf at the Door,' the last song on *Hail to the Thief*, read:

> get the flan in the face
> the flan in the face
> the flan in the face
> dance you fucker dance you fucker
> don't you dare
> don't you dare
> don't you flan in the face

In an interview with *Q* magazine, Thom Yorke mentions that 'a friend of his threw a flan in United Kingdom cabinet minister Clare Short's face.' The interviewer adds that 'Clare Short was hit by a custard pie at Bangor University in March 2001.' Clare Short is currently a Labour Party Member of Parliament representing the Birmingham Ladywood constituency in the United Kingdom.

No conclusion

Where do we go from here? Rather, where is the band headed? In an interview with Dutch magazine *OOR*, Thom Yorke claimed in reference to the sound of *Hail to the Thief*:

> This is *OK Computer 2*. What we will do from now on, should not be anything like we've done before. We will not go further back, like everyone expects. There won't be a second *The Bends*. There is not a single good reason for it. As a band, we have fully discussed this matter recently. Radiohead will be completely unrecognisable in two years. At least, I hope so. It's the only perspective of the future that I can live with. (quoted in 'Pop Will Soon be Dead')

If the band will be unrecognizable in 2005, then we are forced to consider this 2003 album an instance of Radiohead at its most recognizable.

Notes

1. This style is, in short, adopted directly from the website I have maintained since January 2001, *Pulk-Pull*: *An Ongoing Investigation of Radiohead's Music and Art*: (http://pulk-pull.org/).

2. In an interview with the *NME* (May 3 2003: 27) Thom Yorke explains how he composed the lyrics for *Hail to the Thief*: 'From the album title ... it's possible to get a first impression of "Hail To The Thief" as an overtly political album. It is, says Thom, not quite as cut and dried as that. "The point, which you chaps have failed to grasp, perhaps understandably," he says, "is that I was cutting these things out, and deliberately taking them out of context, so they're like wallpaper. Then, when I needed words for songs I'd be taking them out of this wallpaper, and they were out of any political context at all."'

    Yorke also spoke in a *Rolling Stone* interview concerning the composition of the new songs: 'When I started writing these new songs, I was listening to a lot of political programs on BBC Radio 4. I found myself ... writing down little nonsense phrases, those Orwellian euphemisms that our government and yours are so fond of. They became the background of the record. The emotional context of those words had been taken away. What I was doing was stealing it back' (Fricke 2003: 54). This method of composition mirrors that of Dadaist poet Tristan Tzara. Not surprisingly, Radiohead once posted on its website a version of Tzara's instructions on how to write a poem: 'Take a newspaper. Take some scissors. Pick out an article which is as long as you wish your poem to be. Cut out the article. Then cut out carefully each of the words in the article and put them in a bag. Shake gently. Then take out each piece one after the other. Copy them down conscientiously in the order in which they left the bag' (quoted in Peterson 1971: 35).

3. The band has a long-standing interest in Orwell's work. The *Kid A* song 'Optimistic' refers explicitly to Orwell's *Animal Farm*. In a strange twist, the band's merchandise website is titled W.A.S.T.E. after the underground postal system in Thomas Pynchon's *The Crying of Lot 49*. Forming a triangle of influence, Pynchon has recently written the introduction to a re-publication of Orwell's *Nineteen Eighty-Four*.

4. A January 20 2001 BBC news article by Nick Bryant features a photograph of a protester wielding a poster bearing the slogan: http://news.bbc.co.uk/1/hi/world/americas/1128324.stm. The phrase has also appeared as the subtitle to an e-book: *Mediaocracy 2000–Hail to the Thief* (West Hartford, CT: Electron Press, 2001), edited by Danny Schechter and Roland Schatz.

5. In a *NME* (April 5 2003) article written by Stephen Dalton, 'How Radiohead's LP Title is the Biggest Anti-War Statement Yet,' one respondent known as 'Kieran Evans' wrote: 'I believe in the US and I have faith in my president. I think it's sad this very talented band (perhaps the world's best) have gone from innovative lyrical and musical concepts to political protest. I don't need to get this CD. I think Jack White said it best: "I write songs about girls and being sad. Who am I to take a political stance?"'

    Another respondent: 'I'm a huge Radiohead fan but I'll be blacking out the title of the album when I buy it and ripping off the cover. I couldn't care less about their political beliefs. Celebrities are being mocked in America for screaming anti-war slogans because 70 per cent of the American people back the war.' — Ryan McGovern, Pennsylvania.

    Another anonymous reader wrote: 'Remember Thom, if it wasn't for us Americans and our "corrupt" government, you'd be speaking German right now!'

6. Jonny Greenwood writes on the Capitol Records website: 'We'd never name a record after one political event like Bush's election. The record's bigger than that. Hopefully it will last longer than Bush unless he's getting a whole dynasty together, which is always possible. One of the things Thom's singing about is whether or not you choose to deal with what's happening. There are a lot of lines about escaping and avoiding issues, about keeping your head down and waiting. Everybody feels like that from time to time as much as they feel frustration about things they can't change. It's a confusing time right now but that doesn't mean that we're issuing any kind of manifesto. It's more like we're summing up what it's like to be around in 2003.'

7. Contrast the band's supposedly apolitical art with this instance: at a concert in Bilbao, Spain, Alex Ross noted Thom Yorke dedicated the song 'No Surprises' to George W. Bush, a song containing the lines 'bring down the government / they don't speak for us' (Ross 2001: 116–17).

8. The album's political focus is demonstrated by these words, held up by Stanley Donwood during the band's December 18 2002 webcast. The words give a pointedly political cast to the album's title: 'If you're a proper fucking thief you can't be fucked with burgling properties in the middle of the fucking night because you got to fucking get up in the fucking morning to run the fucking country.' These words, among many others (for example, 'I am in hiding / I'm not coming out / until I'm ready / turn off the light / before you go' and 'Hello my name is / worm buffet') were held up to the camera.

9. The lines from the poem in question are from 'The Boat Song,' section XIX in Canto Two: 'Hail to the Chief who in triumph advances!' (Scott 1921: 46).

10. Authorizing this interpretation in an earlier interview, Yorke referenced the album's subtitle, *The Gloaming*, a title meant to convey a pervasive sense of decline, or as Yorke put it 'the absurdity of *everything*.' That everything is absurd is a calculated overstatement meant, in this situation, to suggest the perceived absurdity of the American and British political climate and the events born out of that climate.

11. Another possibility: *Nineteen Eighty Four* and *Hail to the Thief* are both oblique responses to what Deleuze and Guattari in *Anti-Oedipus* call 'the fundamental problem of political philosophy,' a problem they describe as follows: 'the astonishing thing is not that some people steal or that others occasionally go out on strike, but rather that all those who are starving do not steal as a regular practice, and all those who are exploited are not continually out on strike' (1983: 29). In other words, 'at a certain point, under a certain set of circumstances, they *wanted* fascism, and it is this perversion of the desire of the masses that needs to be accounted for' (1983: 29). The fundamental problem, then, is not so much the desire to repress but the desire for repression. The desire is for ease, the desire for being absented from work, the work that critical thinking and freedom requires, a constant and exhausting intellectual vigilance in which one is aware of one's surroundings at all times. So instead, one goes to sleep and lets it wash all over you, as the song 'Go to Sleep' on *Hail to the Thief* argues.

12. In this instance, both Stephen King's novella, 'Rita Hayworth and Shawshank Redemption,' and its subsequent movie adaptation are exemplary. In a passage from the book, Red, the narrator, says about the central character Andy Dufresne that Andy's persistence in the face of obstacles, 'was the part of me they could never lock up, the part of me that will rejoice when the gates finally open for me and I walk out in my cheap suit with my twenty dollars of mad-money in my pocket. That part of me will rejoice no matter how old and broken and scared the rest of me is' (King 1983: 100).

13. 'Hell' as a figurative slang word does appear in Radiohead's music. For instance, in 'Exit Music (for a film)' the singer-speaker tells the addressee he or she should pack,

get dressed, and escape before 'all hell breaks loose.' The 'Go to Sleep.' b-side song, a previously long unreleased track, 'I am a Wicked Child,' references the same heaven/hell binary as '2+2=5.' The singer-speaker here claims to be the 'devil's son.' Being born of the devil is a common theme of the blues genre, a genre alluded to via this song's feedback-laced harmonica.

14. This information is largely taken from Bruce Whitehill's *Games: American Boxed Games and Their Makers: 1822–1992*.

15. This connection was suggested to me by Dave Hartunian.

16. The song's ambiguous 'this' may be akin to Yorke's hyperbolic use of 'everything' in interviews (see above).

17. This connection was suggested to me by Anna Riechmann.

18. There is more on this phenomenon in the *USA Today* online article 'Green Sky and Severe Storms': http://www.usatoday.com/weather/resources/basics/wgreensky.htm. Frank Gallagher III, at the University of Oklahoma, has also performed extensive research on green thunderstorms. For instance, see his 1997 PhD dissertation on the topic.

19. The wedding scene mimics the work of Walter Potter, a Victorian era taxidermist who posed and photographed deceased animals in human clothing and situations.

20. Numerous characters in English literature have been punished by being trapped inside a tree. The most famous is Ariel in Shakespeare's *The Tempest*, who was imprisoned for 12 years in 'a cloven pine.' An earlier instance is Ovid's tale of Philemon and Baucis:

> Old Baucis look'd where old Philemon stood,
> And saw his lengthen'd arms a sprouting wood:
> New roots their fasten'd feet begin to bind,
> Their bodies stiffen in a rising rind:
> Then, ere the bark above their shoulders grew,
> They give, and take at once their last adieu.
> At once, Farewell, o faithful spouse, they said;
> At once th' incroaching rinds their closing lips invade.

Bibliography

Adorno, Theodor W. (1997) *Aesthetic Theory*. Gretel Adorno and Rolf Tiedemann (eds), Robert Hullot-Kentor (trans.). Minneapolis: University of Minnesota Press.

Albini, Steve (1997) 'The Problem With Music.' In Frank and Weiland, 164–76.

Anonymous (2000) 'Head New Music.' *New Musical Express* (June 17).

Anonymous (2001) 'Dear Superstar: Thom Yorke.' *Blender: The Ultimate Music Magazine* (June/July 2001, November 26 2001), at http://www.blender.com/articles/issue1/thomyorke.html.

Anonymous (2001) 'What is Aimster.' *Guardian Aimster* (December 18), at http://www.aimster.com/whatis.phtml.

Anonymous (2003) *Q*, 198 (January) [no title].

Attali, Jacques (1985) 'Noise: The Political Economy of Music.' Brian Massumi (trans.). *Theory and History of Literature*, 16. Minneapolis: University of Minnesota Press.

Bailie, Stuart (1997) 'Viva La Megabytes.' *New Musical Express* (June 21), 42.

Barthes, Roland (1977) 'The Death of the Author.' *Image, Music, Text*. Stephen Heath (trans.). New York: Hill and Wang.

Barthes, Roland (1977) 'The Grain of the Voice.' *Image, Music, Text*. Stephen Heath (trans.). New York: Hill and Wang.

Barthes, Roland (1985) 'Listening.' *The Responsibility of Forms: Critical Essays on Music, Art, and Representation*. Richard Howard (trans.). New York: Hill and Wang.

Barton, John and Muddiman, John (2001) 'The Story of the Flood.' The Oxford Bible Commentary. Oxford: Oxford University Press.

Baudrillard, Jean (1983) *Simulations*. Paul Foss, Paul Patton, and Philip Beitchman (trans.). New York: Semiotext(e).

Baudrillard, Jean (1994) *Simulacra and Simulation*. Sheila Faria Glaser (trans.). Ann Arbor: University of Michigan Press.

Baudrillard, Jean (2001) 'The System of Objects.' *Jean Baudrillard: Selected Writings* (2nd edn). Mark Poster (ed.). Stanford: Stanford University Press.

Bazin, Nancy Topping (1973) *Virginia Woolf and the Androgynous Vision*. New Brunswick: Rutgers University Press.

Bell-Metereau, Rebecca (1993) *Hollywood Androgyny*. New York: Columbia University Press.

Bem, Sandra L. (1976) 'Probing the Promise of Androgyny.' *Beyond Sex-Role Stereotypes*. Alexandra G. Kaplan and Joan P. Bean (eds). Boston: Little, Brown, 48–62.

Benjamin, Walter (1968) 'The Work of Art in the Age of Mechanical Reproduction.' *Illuminations*. Hannah Arendt (ed.), Harry Zohn (trans.). New York: Schocken Books, 217–51.

Benjamin, Walter (1986) 'Paris, Capital of the Nineteenth Century.' *Reflections: Essays, Aphorisms, Autobiographical Writings*. Peter Demetz (ed.), Edmund Jephcott (trans.). New York: Schocken Books, 146–62.

Berland, Jody (1993) 'Sound, Image and Social Space: Music Video and Media Reconstruction.' In Frith *et al.*, 25–43.

Bloomfield, T. (1993) 'Resisting Songs: Negative Dialectics in Pop. *Popular Music*, 12/1, 13–31.

Bornstein, Kate (1994) *Gender Outlaw*. New York: Routledge.

Borow, Zev (2000) 'The Difference Engine.' *Spin* (November), 111ff.

Bourdieu, Pierre (1992) *The Rules of Art: Genesis and Structure of the Literary Field*. Susan Emanuel (trans.). Stanford: Stanford University Press.

Bran, Chris (2001) 'Re: Questions.' E-mail to the author (July 15).

Bruzzi, Stella (1997) 'Mannish Girl: k.d. lang – From Cowpunk to Androgyny.' In Whiteley, 191–206.

Buchanan, Ian (2000) 'Deleuze and Popular Music.' *Deleuzism: A Metacommentary*. Edinburgh: Edinburgh University Press, 175–91.

Bulfinch, Thomas (1978) *Bulfinch's Mythology*. New York: Avenel Books.

Burke, Edmund (1971) *A Philosophical Enquiry into the Origin of Our Ideas of the Sublime and the Beautiful* (1757). New York: Garland Publishing, Inc.

Burke, S. (1992) *Death and Return of the Author: Criticism and Subjectivity in Barthes, Foucault and Derrida*. Edinburgh: Edinburgh University Press.

Burroughs, William S. (1985) *Queer*. New York: Penguin Books.

Butler, Judith (1998) 'Variations on Sex and Gender: Beauvoir, Wittig, and Foucault.' *Contemporary Literary Criticism* (4th edn). Robert Con Davis and Ronald Schleifer (eds). New York: Addison Wesley Longman, 611–23.

Cage, John (1973). *Silence: Lectures and Writings by John Cage*. Hanover, NH: Wesleyan University Press.

Carson, Paula and Walters, Helen (2000) 'Radiohead: Modified Organisms.' *Creative Review* (October).

Cavanagh, David (1997) 'Review of *OK Computer*.' *Q*, 130 (July).

Cavanagh, David (2000) 'I Can See the Monsters.' *Q*, 169 (October), 94–104.

Clark, Collis (2001), 'Genesis.' *Mojo* (March).

Clarke, Martin (2000) *Radiohead: Hysterical and Useless*. London: Plexus Publishing.

Connor, Steven (2001) 'The Decomposing Voice of Postmodern Music.' *New Literary History*, 32, 467–83.

Critical Art Ensemble (1994). *The Electronic Disturbance*. Brooklyn: Autonomedia.

Dalton, Stephen (2001) 'Anyone Can Play Guitar: Radiohead on Record.' *Uncut*, 51 (August).

Death, Chuck and Morton, Colin B. (1992) *Great Pop Things*. Harmondsworth: Penguin.

Deleuze, Gilles (1978) 'Conference Presentation on Musical Time.' IRCAM. T. Murphy (trans.), at http://www.webdeleuze.com/TXT/ENG/IRCAMeng.html.

Deleuze, Gilles (1984) *Kant's Critical Philosophy: The Doctrine of the Faculties*. Hugh Tomlinson and Barbara Habberjam (trans.). Minneapolis: University of Minnesota Press.

Deleuze, Gilles and Guattari, Félix (1983) *Anti-Oedipus: Capitalism and Schizophrenia*. Robert Hurley, Mark Seem, and Helen R. Lane (trans.). Minneapolis: University of Minnesota Press.

Deleuze, Gilles and Guattari, Félix (1987) *A Thousand Plateaus: Capitalism and Schizophrenia 2*. Brian Massumi (trans.). Minneapolis: University of Minnesota Press.

Demetrion, James *et al.* (1993) *Jean Dubuffet 1943–1963: Paintings, Sculpture, Assemblages*. Washington DC: Smithsonian Institute Press.

Derrida, Jacques (1973) *Speech and Phenomena, and Other Essays on Husserl's Theory of Signs*. D. Allison (trans.). Evanston: Northwestern University Press.

Dettmar, Kevin (2001) 'Is Rock 'n' Roll Dead? Only if You Aren't Listening.' *The Chronicle of Higher Education* (May 11), at http://chronicle.com/free/v47/i35/35b01001.htm.

Eccleston, Danny (2003) *Q, Radiohead Special Edition* (July). EMAP Metro Limited, 34–5.

Edwards, Gavin (n.d.) 'Review of *The Bends*,' online at rollingstone.com/reviews/cd/review.asp?aid =57678&cf.

Encyclopædia Britannica (2003) 'Dinosaur.' *Encyclopædia Britannica Online* (October 19), at http://www.search.eb.com/eb/article?eu=108935.

Entertainment Editors (2001) 'Capitol Records and Radiohead Create First Instant Message "Buddy" in Music History.' *Business Wire* (April 25), accessed via findarticles.com (December 10 2001) at http://www.findarticles.com/cf_0/m0EIN/2001_April_25/73641729/p1/article.jhtml?term=radiohead.

Entertainment Editors (2001) 'Capitol Records' Radiohead Extends Successful IM Marketing Program With GooglyMinotaur; Radiohead's Summer Tour Plays Through Instant Messaging.' *Business Wire* (November 19), accessed via findarticles.com (December 10 2001) at http://www.findarticles.com/cf_0/m0EIN/2001_Nov_19/80173819/print.jhtml.

Fornäs, J. (1995a) 'Listen to Your Voice!: Authenticity and Reflexivity in Karaoke, Rock, Rap and Techno Music.' *Popular Music – Style and Identity* (International Association for the Study of Popular Music, Seventh International Conference on Popular Music Studies). Will Straw, Stacey Johnston, Rebecca Sullivan, and Paul Friedlander (eds). Montreal: Centre for Research on Canadian Cultural Industries and Institutions.

Fornäs, J. (1995b) *Cultural Theory and Late Modernity*. London: Sage.

Foucault, Michel (1983) 'Preface.' *Anti-Oedipus: Capitalism and Schizophrenia*. Robert Hurley, Mark Seem, and Helen R. Lane (trans.). Minneapolis: University of Minnesota Press.

Frank, Thomas (1997) 'Alternative to What?' In Frank and Weiland, 145–61.

Frank, Thomas and Weiland, Matt (eds) (1997) *Commodify Your Dissent: Salvos from* The Baffler. New York: Norton.

Fricke, David (2001a) 'Radiohead: Making Music That Matters.' *Rolling Stone*, 874 (August 2), 42–8, 73.

Fricke, David (2001b) 'Radiohead Warm Up.' *Rolling Stone* (Australian edition), 589 (July).

Fricke, David (2003) Interview with Thom Yorke: 'Bitter Prophet.' *Rolling Stone*, 925 (June 26), 52–4.

Frith, Simon (1987) 'Towards an Aesthetic of Popular Music.' In Richard Leppert and Susan McClary (eds), *Music and Society: The Politics of Composition, Performance and Reception*. Cambridge: Cambridge University Press, 133–49, 145.

Frith, Simon and McRobbie, Angela (1990) 'Rock and Sexuality.' *On Record: Rock, Pop, and the Written Word*. Simon Frith and Andrew Goodwin (eds). New York: Pantheon.

Frith, Simon, Goodwin, Andrew, and Grossberg, Lawrence (eds) (1993) *Sound and Vision: The Music Video Reader*. London and New York: Routledge.

Gallagher, F.W. III (1997) *Green Thunderstorms*. PhD dissertation, University of Oklahoma, Norman, Oklahoma.

Germain, Gabriel (1962) 'The Sirens and the Temptation of Knowledge.' *Homer: A Collection of Critical Essays*. George Steiner and Robert Fagles (eds). Englewood Cliffs NJ: Prentice-Hall, Inc., 91–7.

Gil, José (1998) *Metamorphoses of the Body*. S. Muecke (trans.). Minneapolis: University of Minnesota Press.

Gingell, John and Winch, Christopher (1999) *Key Concepts in the Philosophy of Education*. London and New York: Routledge.

Gowing, Jonathan (1981) 'Turner and Literature.' *Times Literary Supplement* (July 10).

Gracyk, Theodore (1996) *Rhythm and Noise: An Aesthetics of Rock*. London: I.B. Tauris.

Green Plastic Radiohead, at http://www.greenplastic.com/lyrics/rh_songs/fakeplastictrees.php, accessed October 15 2003.

Greenwood, Colin (1999) 'W.A.S.T.E. EMAIL LETTER #1.' E-mail message (October 15 1999).

Greenwood, Jonny (2001) Online chat (August 8), at http://hollywoodandvine.com/radiohead/rha_primary_frame.html?chat.

Griffiths, Dai (2000) 'Genre: Grammar Schoolboy Music.' *Critical Musicology Newsletter*, 3 (1995), reprinted in Derek B. Scott (ed.), *Music, Culture, and Society: A Reader*. Oxford: Oxford University Press.

Grossberg, Andrew L. (1992) *We Gotta get out of this Place*. London: Routledge.

Grossberg, Lawrence (1993) 'The Media Economy of Rock Culture: Cinema, Post-Modernity and Authenticity.' In Frith *et al.* (eds), *Sound and Vision: The Music Video Reader*.

Grundy, Gareth (2003) *Q, Radiohead Special Edition* (July). EMAP Metro Limited, 122.

Guernsey, Lisa (2001) 'Advertising Invades Instant Messaging.' *New York Times* (June 28), accessed (December 13 2001) at http://www.nytimes.com/2001/06/28/technology/28INST.html.

Hale, Jonathan (1999) *Radiohead: From a Great Height*. Toronto: ECW Press.

Hanhardt, John G. (2000) *The Worlds of Nam June Paik*. New York: Guggenheim Museum.

Hardt, Michael and Negri, Antonio (2000) *Empire*. Cambridge, Mass.: Harvard University Press.

Hitchcock, H. Wiley and Sadie, Stanley (eds) *The New Grove Dictionary of American Music*, Vol. 10. London: Macmillan Press Ltd.

Homer (1990) *The Odyssey*. Allen Mandelbaum (trans.). Berkeley: University of California Press.

Irvin, Jim (2003) *Q, Radiohead Special Edition* (July). EMAP Metro Limited.

Irvin, Jim (2003) 'Mean Machine,' *Q, Radiohead Special Edition* (July). EMAP Metro Limited.

Jameson, Frederic (1991) *Postmodernism or, The Cultural Logic of Late Capitalism*. Durham: Duke University Press.

Jameson, Frederic (1998) *The Cultural Turn: Selected Writings on the Postmodern, 1983–1998*. New York: Verso.

Jay-Z (2001) 'Izzo (H.O.V.A).' *The Blueprint*. Roc-A-Fella Records.

Kahn, Douglas (1989–90) 'A Better Parasite.' *Art & Text*, 31 (December–February), 52–60.

Kahn, Douglas (1999) 'Track Organology.' *Noise, Water, Meat: A History of Sound in the Arts*. Cambridge, Mass.: MIT Press.

Kant, Immanuel (1952) *The Critique of Judgement* (1790). James Creed Meredith (trans.). Oxford: Clarendon Press.

Kennedy, Jake (2000) Review in *Record Collector* (November).

Kent, Nick (2001) 'Happy Now?' *Mojo*, 91 (June), 56–72.

King, Stephen (1983) 'Rita Hayworth and Shawshank Redemption.' *Different Seasons*. New York: Signet.

Kirk, Elise K. (1997) '"Hail to the Chief": The Origins and Legacies of an American Ceremonial Tune.' *American Music*, 15/2, 123–36.

Kittler, Friedrich (1999) *Gramophone, Film, Typewriter*. G. Winthrop-Young and M. Wutz (trans.). Stanford: Stanford University Press.

Klosterman, Chuck (2003) 'Meeting Thom is Easy.' *Spin* (June), online at http://www.spin.com/modules.php?op=modload&name=News&file=article&sid=80&mode=&order=&thold=.

Klosterman, Chuck (2003) 'No More Knives.' *Spin*, 19/7 (July), 62–70.

Kulkami, Neil and Morgan, Emma (2003) 'Alarms and Surprises.' *Bang*, 4/3 (July), 60–71.

Lamacq, Steve (1992) 'Review of *Drill* EP.' *NME* (May 16), 16.

Lévy, Pierre (1997) *Cyberculture: Rapport au Conseil de l'Europe dans le Cadre du Projet Nouvelles Technologies: Coopération Culturelle et Communication*. Paris: Odile Jacob, 169–70.

Loder, Kurt (1987) 'Stardust Memories.' *Rolling Stone* (April 23), 74ff.

Lowe, Steve (2003) 'Back to Save the Universe,' a track-by-track guide to *OK Computer*. *Q, Radiohead Special Edition* (July). Emap Metro Limited, 95.

Lowe, Steve (2003) 'What the Hell am I Doing Here?' *Q, Radiohead Special Edition* (July). Emap Metro Limited, 37.

Lyotard, Jean-François (1984) *The Postmodern Condition: A Report on Knowledge*. Geoff Bennington and Brian Massumi (trans.). Minneapolis: University of Minnesota Press.

McLean, Craig (2002) Review in *The Face* (January).

Mack, Maynard (1964) '*Gulliver's Travels*.' *Swift: A Collection of Critical Essays*. Ernest Tuveson (ed.). Englewood Cliffs, NJ: Prentice Hall, Inc., 111–14.

Manning, Toby (2003) '21st Century Fix.' *X-Ray*, 7 (August), 44–51.

Martin, Bill (2002) *Avant Rock: Experimental Music from the Beatles to Björk*. Peru, Illinois: Open Court.

Mazullo, Mark (1999) *Authenticity in Rock Music Culture* (unpublished PhD). University of Minnesota.

Meeting People is Easy (1998) Dir. Grant Gee, prod. Kudos and Parlophone (Video cassette). © EMI Records Ltd, manufactured by Capitol Records, Inc.

Menta, Richard (2000) 'Did Napster Take Radiohead's New Album to Number 1?' *MP3newswire.net* (October 28), accessed (November 21 2001) at http://mp3newswire.net/stories/2000/radiohead.html.

Meyer, Leonard B. (1989) *Style and Music*. Philadelphia: Pennsylvania University Press.

Middleton, Richard (1990) *Studying Popular Music*. Milton Keynes: Open University Press.

Miller, Mark Crispin (2002) 'What's Wrong With This Picture?' *The Nation* (January), 18ff.

Moon, Tom (2001) 'Review of *I Might Be Wrong: Live Recordings*, by Radiohead.' *Rolling Stone* (November 12), accessed (November 15 2001) at http://www.rollingstone.com/news/newsarticle.asp?nid=14922.

Moore, Alan, Sienkiewicz, Bill, Brabner, Joyce, and Yeates, Tom (1989) *Brought to Light: Thirty Years of Drug Smuggling, Arms Deals, and Covert Action*. Forestville, Calif.: Eclipse Books.

Moore, Allan F. (2001) 'Categorical Conventions in Music Discourse: Style and Genre.' *Music and Letters* 82/3.

Moore, Allan F. (2001) *Rock: The Primary Text*. Aldershot: Ashgate.

Moore, Allan F. (2002) 'Authenticity as Authentication.' *Popular Music*, 21/2.

Mulholland, Gary (2002) *This is Uncool: The 500 Greatest Singles Since Punk and Disco*. London: Cassell.

New Grove Dictionary of Music and Musicians, Vol. 10 (2000) Washington DC: Grove's Dictionaries.

O'Brien, Ed, www.greenplastic.com/articles/edsdiary/index.html.

O'Connell, Sharon (1992) 'Review of *Creep* EP.' *Melody Maker* (September 19), 33.

Oldman, James (2000) *New Musical Express* (September 30).

Oldman, James (2000) *New Musical Express* (December 23/30).

Oliveros, Pauline (2001) 'Invisible Jukebox.' *The Wire*, 209 (July).

Orwell, George (2003 [1949]) *Nineteen Eighty-Four* (centennial edn). New York: Plume.

Pagels, Elaine (1995) *The Origin of Satan*. New York: Random House.

Paphides, Peter (1993) 'P.O.P.R.I.P.?' *Melody Maker* (May 15).

Patterson, Sylvia (2001) *New Musical Express* (May 19) [no title].

Pearl Jam (1996) *No Code*. Epic/Sony.

Perkins Gilman, Charlotte (1893) *In This Our World*. Oakland: McCombs and Vaughn.

Peterson, Elmer (1971) *Tristan Tzara: Dada and Surrational Theorist*. New Brunswick, NJ: Rutgers University Press.

Pielke, Robert G. (1982) 'Are Androgyny and Sexuality Compatible?' In Vetterling-Braggin, 187–96.

Pinhas, Richard (2001) 'De Nietzsche à la Techno: Manifeste pour les machines-pensées à venir.' Cited at www.webdeleuze.com/TXT/TECHNO.html (October 29).

'Pop Will Soon be Dead!' *NME*, at http://www.nme.com/news/105175.htm.

'Radiohead Biography' (2003) at http://capitolrecords.com/radiohead/radiohead_biography.html (published May 30).

Radiohead: Live at the Astoria (1995) Dir. Brett Turnbull. Parlophone/PMI.

'Radiohead take Aimster' (2000) *BBC News* (October 2) accessed (November 23 2001) at http://news.bbc.co.uk/hi/english/entertainment/newsid_953000/953151.stm.

Randall, Mac (2000) *Exit Music: The Radiohead Story*. New York: Random House.

R.E.M. (1996) 'E-Bow The Letter.' *New Adventures in Hi-Fi*. Warner.

Reynolds, Simon (2001) 'Dissent into the Mainstream.' *The Wire*, 209 (July), 25–33.

Ricoeur, Paul (1984) *Time and Narrative*. Kathleen McLaughlin and David Pellauer (trans.), Vol. 3. Chicago: University of Chicago Press.

Rob aka Faketree (2001) 'Radiohead Tour Dates and Ticket Information: 07 August 01.' Online posting at *Follow Me Around* (September 22) at http://www.followmearound .com/tour2001/070801.html.

Robinson, John (2003) *New Musical Express* (May 10), 35 [no title].

Ross, Alex (2001) 'The Searchers: Radiohead's Unquiet Revolution.' *New Yorker* (August 20/27), 112–23.

Saneeh, Kalefa (2001) 'Rock Groups that No Longer Rock.' *New York Times on the Web* (July 1) at http://www.nytimes.com/2001/07/01/arts/01SANN.html.

Sartre, Jean-Paul (1992) *Being and Nothingness* (1943). Hazel E. Barnes (trans.). New York: Washington Square Press.

Schneiderman, Davis (2001) Chat with GooglyMinotaur (December 15), AOL Instant Messenger.

Schneiderman, Davis (2001) 'Radiohead Amnesiac iBlip.' E-mail to the author (December 24).

Scott, Sir Walter (1921) *The Lady of the Lake*. Ebenezer Charlton Black (ed.). Boston: Ginn and Company.

Skanse, Richard (2000) '"Kid A" Goes to the Head of the Class.' *Rolling Stone* (November 10) accessed (November 8 2001) at http://www.rollingstone.com/news/newsarticle.asp?nid=11974.

Stevens, Wallace (1997) *The Collected Poems of Wallace Stevens*. New York: Alfred A. Knopf.

Stiegler, Bernard (1996) *Technique et Temps: La Désorientation*. Paris: Editions Galilée.

Stone, Allucquère Rosanne (1997) 'In the Language of Vampire Speak: Overhearing our Own Voices.' *The Eight Technologies of Otherness*. Sue Golding (author/ed.). London: Routledge.

Sutcliffe, Phil (1997) Interview with Thom Yorke. *Q*, 133 (October).

Tate, Joseph (2001) 'the work of art in the age of electronic reproduction' (November 18) at http://josephtate.com/tours/.

Trilling, Lionel (1972) *Sincerity and Authenticity*. London: Oxford University Press.

Turenne, Martin (2001) 'Interview with Colin' (June 7) at www.followmearound.com/press/129html.

Tyrangiel, Josh (2003) 'How Radiohead Learned to Stop Worrying and Enjoy Being the Best Band in the World.' *Time*, 161/23 (June 9), 70–3.

Vetterling-Braggin, Mary (ed.) (1982) *'Femininity,' Masculinity,' and 'Androgyny'*. New Jersey: Littlefield, Adams.

Virilio, Paul (1994) *The Vision Machine*. Julie Rose (trans.). Bloomington and Indianapolis: Indiana University Press.

Warren, Mary Anne (1982) 'Is Androgyny the Answer to Sexual Stereotyping?' In Vetterling-Braggin, 170–86.

Watson, Ian (2001) 'The Ballad of Thom Yorke.' *Rolling Stone* (Australian edition), 589 (July), 44–50, 111.

Westenberg, Kevin (2003) 'Into the Light.' *Mojo*, 117 (August), 72–87.

Whitehill, Bruce (1992) *Games: American Boxed Games and Their Makers: 1822–1992*. Radnor, Pennsylvania: Wallace-Homestead.

Whiteley, Sheila (1997) 'Little Red Rooster v. The Honky Tonk Woman: Mick Jagger, Sexuality, Style and Image.' In Whiteley, 67–99.

Whiteley, Sheila (ed.) (1997) *Sexing the Groove: Popular Music and Gender*. London: Routledge.

Wilson, Ralph F. (2000) 'The Six Simple Principles of Viral Marketing.' *Web Marketing Today* (February 1) accessed (November 21 2001) at http://www.wilsonweb.com/wmt5/viral-principles.htm.

Winn, Marie (1996) *The Fireside Book of Children's Songs*. New York: Simon and Schuster.

Yamazaki, Yoichiro (2003) 'Thom Yorke: The New Interview.' *Q, Radiohead Special Edition* (July). Emap Metro Limited, 132–9.

Yorke, Thom (2001) 'Message from Thom' (December 11). *Follow Me Around*, accessed (December 15) at http://www.followmearound.com/news/thomxmas.html.

Yorke, Thom and Greenwood, Colin (1998) Online chat: 'Tibetan Freedom Concert' (June).

Žižek, Slavoj (2000) *The Fragile Absolute, or Why is the Christian Legacy Worth Fighting For?* London: Verso.

Žižek, Slavoj (2001) *On Belief*. London and New York: Routledge.

Track Listing

'2+2=5 (The Lukewarm.)' *Hail to the Thief (or, The Gloaming.)*. Parlophone, 2003.
'Airbag.' *OK Computer*. Parlophone, 1997.
'The Amazing Sounds of Orgy.' *Pyramid Song*. Parlophone, 2001.
'Anyone Can Play Guitar.' *Pablo Honey*. Parlophone, 1993.
'Backdrifts. (Honeymoon is Over.)' *Hail to the Thief (or, The Gloaming.)*. Parlophone, 2003.
'The Bends.' *The Bends*. Parlophone, 1995.
'Bones.' *The Bends*. Parlophone, 1995.
'Climbing Up the Walls.' *OK Computer*. Parlophone, 1997.
'Creep.' *Pablo Honey*. Parlophone, 1993.
'Cuttooth.' *Knives Out*. Parlophone, 2001.
'Dollars and Cents.' *Amnesiac*. Parlophone, 2001.
'Dollars and Cents.' *I Might Be Wrong: Live Recordings*. Parlophone, 2001.
'Electioneering.' *OK Computer*. Parlophone, 1997.
'Everything in its Right Place.' *Kid A*. Parlophone, 2000.
'Everything in its Right Place.' *I Might Be Wrong: Live Recordings*. Parlophone, 2001.
'Exit Music.' *OK Computer*. Parlophone, 1997.
'Fake Plastic Trees.' *The Bends*. Parlophone, 1995.
'Fast-track.' *Pyramid Song*. Parlophone, 2001.
'Fitter Happier.' *OK Computer*. Parlophone, 1997.
'Fog.' *Knives Out*. Parlophone, 2001.
'The Gloaming. (Softly Open our Mouths in the Cold.)' *Hail to the Thief (or, The Gloaming.)*. Parlophone, 2003.
'Go to Sleep. (Little Man being Erased.)' *Hail to the Thief (or, The Gloaming.)*. Parlophone, 2003.
'How to Disappear Completely.' *Kid A*. Parlophone, 2000.
'Hunting Bears.' *Amnesiac*. Parlophone, 2001.
'I Might Be Wrong.' *Amnesiac*. Parlophone, 2001.
'I Might Be Wrong.' *I Might Be Wrong: Live Recordings*. Parlophone, 2001.
'I Will. (No Man's Land.)' *Hail to the Thief (or, The Gloaming.)*. Parlophone, 2003.
'Idioteque.' *Kid A*. Parlophone, 2000.
'Idioteque.' *I Might be Wrong: Live Recordings*. Parlophone, 2001.
'Karma Police.' *OK Computer*. Parlophone, 1997.
'Kinetic.' *Pyramid Song*. Parlophone, 2001.
'Knives Out.' *Amnesiac*. Parlophone, 2001.
'Let Down.' *OK Computer*. Parlophone, 1997.
'Life in a Glasshouse.' *Amnesiac*. Parlophone, 2001.
'Life in a Glasshouse (slightly longer version).' *Knives Out*. Parlophone, 2001.
'Like Spinning Plates.' *Amnesiac*. Parlophone, 2001.
'Like Spinning Plates.' *I Might Be Wrong: Live Recordings*. Parlophone, 2001.

'Lucky.' *OK Computer*. Parlophone, 1997.
'Morning Bell.' *Kid A*. Parlophone, 2000.
'Morning Bell.' *I Might Be Wrong: Live Recordings*. Parlophone, 2001.
'Morning Bell/Amnesiac.' *Amnesiac*. Parlophone, 2001.
'Motion Picture Soundtrack.' *Kid A*. Parlophone, 2000.
'My Iron Lung.' *The Bends*. Parlophone, 1995.
'Myxomatosis. (Judge, Jury & Executioner.)' *Hail to the Thief (or, The Gloaming.).* Parlophone, 2003.
'The National Anthem.' *Kid A*. Parlophone, 2000.
'The National Anthem.' *I Might Be Wrong: Live Recordings*. Parlophone, 2001.
'No Surprises.' *OK Computer*. Parlophone, 1997.
'Optimistic.' *Kid A*. Parlophone, 2000.
'Packt like Sardines in a Crushd Tin Box.' *Amnesiac*. Parlophone, 2001.
'Paranoid Android.' *OK Computer*. Parlophone, 1997.
'Planet Telex.' *The Bends*. Parlophone, 1995.
'Pulk/Pull Revolving Doors.' *Amnesiac*. Parlophone, 2001.
'A Punch-up at a Wedding. (No no no no no no no no.)' *Hail to the Thief (or, The Gloaming.).* Parlophone, 2003.
'Pyramid Song.' *Amnesiac*. Parlophone, 2001.
'Sail To The Moon. (Brush the Cobwebs out of the Sky.)' *Hail to the Thief (or, The Gloaming.).* Parlophone, 2003.
'Scatterbrain. (As Dead as Leaves.)' *Hail to the Thief (or, The Gloaming.).* Parlophone, 2003.
'Sit Down. Stand Up. (Snakes & Ladders.)' *Hail to the Thief (or, The Gloaming.).* Parlophone, 2003.
'Stop Whispering.' *Pablo Honey*. Parlophone, 1993.
'Street Spirit (Fade Out).' *The Bends*. Parlophone, 1995.
'Sulk.' *The Bends*. Parlophone, 1995.
'There There. (The Boney King of Nowhere.)' *Hail to the Thief (or, The Gloaming.).* Parlophone, 2003.
'The Tourist.' *OK Computer*. Parlophone, 1997.
'Trans-atlantic Drawl.' *Pyramid Song*. Parlophone, 2001.
'Treefingers.' *Kid A*. Parlophone, 2000.
'True Love Waits.' *I Might Be Wrong: Live Recordings*. Parlophone, 2001.
'We Suck Young Blood. (Your Time is Up.)' *Hail to the Thief (or, The Gloaming.).* Parlophone, 2003.
'Where I End and You Begin. (The Sky is Falling In.)' *Hail to the Thief (or, The Gloaming.).* Parlophone, 2003.
'A Wolf at the Door. (It Girl. Rag Doll.)' *Hail to the Thief (or, The Gloaming.).* Parlophone, 2003.
'Worrywort.' *Knives Out*. Parlophone, 2001.
'You and Whose Army?' *Amnesiac*. Parlophone, 2001.

Index